Diss. ETH No. 28166

A New Perspective on Memorization in Recurrent Networks of Spiking Neurons

A thesis submitted to attain the degree of
DOCTOR OF SCIENCES of ETH ZURICH
(Dr. sc. ETH Zurich)

presented by

Patrick Murer

M.Sc. ETH
born on October 25, 1989
citizen of Beckenried (NW)

accepted on the recommendation of
Prof. Dr. Hans-Andrea Loeliger, examiner
Prof. Dr. Wulfram Gerstner, co-examiner

2022

Series in Signal and Information Processing **Vol. 35**

Editor: Hans-Andrea Loeliger

Bibliographic Information published by Die Deutsche Nationalbibliothek

Die Deutsche Nationalbibliothek lists this publication in the Deutsche Nationalbibliografie; detailed bibliographic data is available in the internet at http://dnb.dnb.de.

First Edition 2022

HARTUNG-GORRE VERLAG KONSTANZ

ISSN 1616-671X
ISBN-10: 3-86628-758-5
ISBN-13: 978-3-86628-758-7

To my family and my friends

"In order to remember any new piece of information, it must be associated to something you already know or remember in some ridiculous way."

Harry Lorayne

"One day I will find the right words, and they will be simple."

Jack Kerouac

Acknowledgments

First and foremost, I would like to express my gratitude to my supervisor, Professor Hans-Andrea Loeliger, who gave me the freedom I needed, but on the same time always challenged me with his questions, which reminded me of the bigger picture and helped me getting back on the "right" track when I was lost in some details. Thank you so much Andi for everything!

Secondly, I would like to thank Professor Wulfram Gerstner for kindly agreeing to be my co-examiner and for his valuable feedback.

Then, I would also like to thank my colleagues from the ISI lab which were part of my Ph.D. journey, namely (and in no particular order)

Sarah Neff, Nour Zalmaï, Tibor Keresztfalvi, Christian Schürch, Hampus Malmberg, Christoph Pfister, Boxiao Ma, Federico Wadehn, Elizabeth Ren, Raphael Keusch, Reto Wildhaber, Robert Graczyk, Guy Revach, Yiming Yan, and Hugo Aguettaz.

From all of you I benefited a lot. I highly appreciate the enjoyable time we spent together during either work or any social activity.

Furthermore, I thank all my friends and my family who were there whenever I needed them and who could distract me from my research if it was necessary. Special thanks go to my parents Margrit and Walter for their unconditional support, and to my siblings Petra, Fabian, and Julian.

Finally, I thank my fiancé Carolin for her ∞ love, positivity, and encouragement in every single moment of our joint journey.

Abstract

This thesis studies the capability of spiking recurrent neural network models to memorize dynamical pulse patterns (or firing signals).

In the first part, discrete-time firing signals (or firing sequences) are considered. A recurrent network model, consisting of neurons with bounded disturbance, is introduced to analyze (simple) local learning. Two modes of learning/memorization are considered: The first mode is strictly online, with a single pass through the data, while the second mode uses multiple passes through the data. In both modes, the learning is strictly local (quasi-Hebbian): At any given time step, only the weights between the neurons firing (or supposed to be firing) at the previous time step and those firing (or supposed to be firing) at the present time step are modified. The main result is an upper bound on the probability that the single-pass memorization is not perfect. It follows that the memorization capacity in this mode asymptotically scales like that of the classical Hopfield model (which, in contrast, memorizes static patterns). However, multiple-rounds memorization is shown to achieve a higher capacity with an asymptotically nonvanishing number of bits per connection/synapse. These mathematical findings may be helpful for understanding the functionality of short-term memory and long-term memory in neuroscience.

In the second part, firing signals in continuous-time are studied. It is shown how firing signals, containing firings only on a regular time grid, can be (robustly) memorized with a recurrent network model. In principle, the corresponding weights are obtained by supervised (quasi-Hebbian) multi-pass learning. The asymptotic memorization capacity is a nonvanishing number measured in bits per connection/synapse as its discrete-time analogon. Furthermore, the timing robustness of the memorized firing signals is investigated for different disturbance models. The regime of disturbances, where the relative occurrence-time of the firings is preserved over a long time span, is elaborated for the various disturbance models.

The proposed models have the potential for energy efficient self-timed neuromorphic hardware implementations.

Keywords: Spiking recurrent neural network; dynamical pulse pattern; associative memory; Hopfield model; quasi-Hebbian learning; online learning; multi-pass memorization; asymptotic memorization capacity; timing robustness.

Kurzfassung

Diese Dissertation studiert die Fähigkeit von gepulsten rückgekoppelten neuronalen Netzwerk-Modellen, dynamische Pulsmuster (oder Feuersignale) zu speichern.

Im ersten Teil werden zeitdiskrete Feuersignale (also Feuersequenzen) betrachtet. Ein rückgekoppeltes Netzwerk-Modell, bestehend aus Neuronen mit begrenzter Störung, wird eingeführt, um (einfaches) lokales Lernen zu analysieren. Zwei Lern- oder Speichermodi werden betrachtet: Der erste Modus ist strikt online mit einem einzigen Durchlauf durch die Daten, während der zweite Modus mehrere Durchläufe verwendet. In beiden Modi ist das Lernen strikt lokal (quasi-hebbisch): In jedem gegebenen Zeitschritt werden nur die Gewichte zwischen den Neuronen, welche im vorherigen Zeitschritt feuerten (oder feuern sollten) und denen, die im aktuellen Zeitschritt feuern (oder feuern sollen), geändert. Das Hauptergebnis ist eine obere Schranke für die Wahrscheinlichkeit, dass die Speicherung mittels einmaligem Durchlauf nicht perfekt ist. Es folgt, dass in diesem Modus die Speicherkapazität asymptotisch wie die des klassischen Hopfield-Modells (welches im Gegensatz statische Muster speichert) skaliert. Die Speicherung mittels mehrfachen Durchläufen erreicht hingegen nachweislich eine höhere Kapazität mit einer asymptotisch nicht verschwindenden Anzahl Bits pro Verbindung/Synapse. Diese mathematischen Erkenntnisse könnten für das neurowissenschaftliche Verständnis der Funktionsweise des Kurzzeit- und Langzeitgedächtnisses hilfreich sein.

Der zweite Teil befasst sich mit zeitkontinuierlichen Feuersignalen. Es wird gezeigt, wie Feuersignale, welche nur Feuerereignisse auf einem regelmässigen Zeitgitter aufweisen, mit einem rückgekoppelten Netzwerk-Modell (robust) gespeichert werden können. Die dazugehörigen Gewichte erhält man prinzipiell mit Hilfe von mehreren überwachten (quasi-hebbschen) Lerndurchläufen. Die asymptotische Speicherkapazität ist eine nicht verschwindende Zahl gemessen in Bits pro Verbindung/Synapse wie sein zeitdiskretes Analogon. Des Weiteren wird die zeitliche Robustheit der gespeicherten Feuersignale für unterschiedliche Störmodelle untersucht. Das Regime der Störungen, in welchem das relative zeitliche Auftreten der Feuerereignisse über eine lange Zeitspanne erhalten bleibt, wird für die verschiedenen Störmodelle ausgearbeitet.

Die vorgeschlagenen Modelle haben das Potenzial für energieeffiziente und selbstsynchronisierte Implementationen von neuromorpher Hardware.

Stichworte: Gepulstes rückgekoppeltes neuronales Netzwerk; dynamisches Pulsmuster; Assoziativspeicher; Hopfield-Modell; quasi-hebbsches Lernen; online Lernen; Speichern mittels mehrfachem Durchlauf; asymptotische Speicherkapazität; zeitliche Robustheit.

Contents

List of Figures

Chapter 1

Introduction

1.1 Background

The principles of information processing in biological neural networks are far from understood, but they obviously involve computing with electrical pulses. Thus, the interest in pulse-based, i.e., spiking (artificial) neural networks is growing, e.g., [2, 31, 42, 66, 68]. Independent interest in pulse-based representation of information comes from recent work in signal analysis [70, 71]. Thus, such networks may be studied either as models of biological neural networks, or as candidates for neuromorphic hardware, or as a mode of mathematical signal processing as in [39, 51]. In any case, memorizing long sequences of pulse (or firing) patterns must be an elementary capability of such networks. Whistling a tune after hearing it once, or no more than a few times may here remind us of the feats of memorization routinely performed in everyday activities.

The classic reference for memorization in a neural network is the Hopfield model [29], [40, Chapter 42]. Recurrent networks with higher capacities have been proposed, e.g., in [8, 13, 34, 59]. However, all these networks memorize *static* vectors (as static attractors of a dynamical network). By contrast, in this thesis, we study (in a mathematical model) how recurrent neural networks can memorize *dynamic* content, so-called firing signals (or sequences). Our approach seems to be new and is not immediately related to [21, 27, 57, 61] nor to the vast literature on (nonspiking) recurrent neural networks such as LSTM networks [28] and others [10, 17, 32, 35, 48, 56].

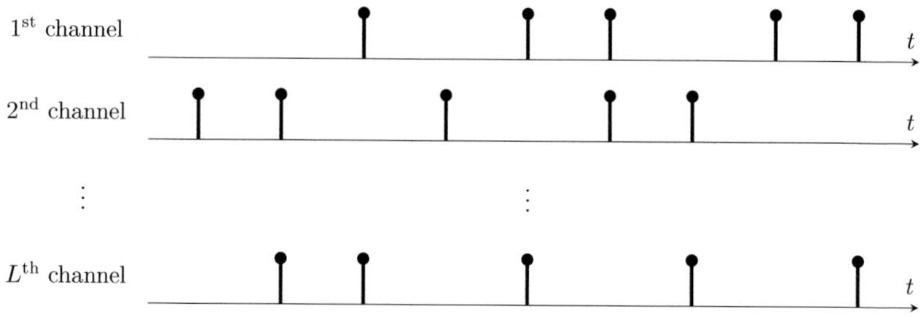

Figure 1.1: Multi-channel firing signal.

1.2 Contributions

We propose mathematical models (both in discrete-time and continuous-time) of recurrent neural networks to investigate how (dynamical) firing signals, as shown in Figure 1.1, can be memorized with such networks.

In Part I, we consider discrete-time firing signals, i.e., firing sequences. We analyze two different modes of learning/memorizing those firing sequences. The first mode is strictly online, with a single pass through the data; the second mode uses multiple passes through the data. In both modes, the learning is strictly local, or quasi Hebbian: At any given time step n, only the weights between the neurons firing (or supposed to be firing) at time step $n-1$ and those firing (or supposed to be firing) at time step n are modified. The rare phenomenon of a photographic memory could be an example for the single-pass mode, whereas a tennis player who practices his strokes every single day over a long period of time rather exemplifies the multi-pass learning mode.

The main result is an upper bound on the probability that the single-pass memorization is not perfect. From this bound, it follows that the asymptotic memorization capacity of a network consisting of L neurons, in the strict online learning mode, is at least $O\big(L/\ln(L)\big)$ bits per neuron, which vanishes (asymptotically, i.e., for $L \to \infty$) in terms of bits per connection (i.e., per synapse). By contrast, multiple-rounds memorization is easily seen to achieve a significantly higher capacity, with a nonvanishing number of bits per connection/synapse and thus exceeding the capacity of the Hopfield network. The (important) ability of single-pass online memorization thus appears to be bought at the expense of a smaller capacity, which may be of interest for understanding the functions of short-term memory and long-term memory in neuroscience [3, 4, 12, 47].

In Part II, we consider firing signals in (genuine) continuous-time. We show that a special class of continuous-time firing signals, namely signals with firings only on a regular grid, can be memorized by a fully-connected recurrent network, where each connection possesses a signal transit-time. The weights, which "memorize" such a given firing signal, can potentially be obtained by multi-pass learning, and the asymptotic memorization capacity is a nonvanishing number measured in bits per connection/synapse as its discrete-time analogon from Part I. Moreover, we also study the timing robustness (or stability) of those firing signals in continuous-time, i.e., we examine under which conditions the relative occurrence of the firings is preserved to a certain extent. This is mainly done by means of simulations, where we also take various disturbances into account. For different disturbances, the regimes where the considered firing signals can be memorized robustly, in the sense that the relative firing occurrence is preserved, are elaborated. To this end a "systematic" time correction is introduced.

1.3 Outline

This thesis is subdivided into two independent parts. However, cross references are made since both parts follow a similar structure, and the model in Part II can be seen as a generalization of the model in Part I.

Part I – Discrete-time Model

This part of the thesis is summarized in [50]. The network model and the considered firing sequences are defined in Chapter 2. There, we also give a brief comparison with the Hopfield model. Chapter 3 introduces the considered quasi-Hebbian learning rules. In Chapter 4, the main result—an upper bound on the probability of imperfect single-pass memorization—is stated in Section 4.2. In preparation, we start in Section 4.1 with a comparison of two learning rules by a simple analysis, which yields weaker results than the results obtained in Section 4.2. Chapter 4 is concluded by investigating multi-pass memorization via a least-squares approach. Then, the asymptotic memorization capacity of both learning modes is addressed in Chapter 5. Finally, in Chapter 6 some extensions of the presented model and statements are given.

Part II – Continuous-time Model

In Part II, which contains Chapters 7 to 9, we consider continuous-time firing signals. The model of the neuron and the recurrent network are defined in Chapter 7, where we also show the relation to the discrete-time model from Part I. Chapter 8 proposes first a special class of firing signals, namely signals which have firings only on a regular grid. Then, conditions which allow perfect memorization of those firing signals with the defined network model (in Chapter 7) are stated and analyzed, for the ideal case (i.e., without taking any disturbance into account). Finally, the asymptotic memorization capacity is addressed in Section 8.5.

Part II is concluded by studying the timing robustness of the considered firing signals. This is done in Chapter 9 by means of simulations for different disturbances.

Part I

Discrete-time Model

Chapter 2

The Model

2.1 Binary Neurons with Bounded Disturbance

We consider a discrete-time network model consisting of L binary neurons $\xi_1, \ldots, \xi_L$. Each neuron ξ_i is a mapping defined as

$$\xi_i \colon \mathbb{R}^L \to \{0, 1\}, \ \ \boldsymbol{y} \mapsto \xi_i(\boldsymbol{y}) := \begin{cases} 1, & \text{if } \langle \boldsymbol{y}, \boldsymbol{w}_i \rangle + \eta_i \geq \theta_i \\ 0, & \text{otherwise,} \end{cases} \tag{2.1}$$

which is characterized by a weight vector $\boldsymbol{w}_i := (w_{1,i}, \ldots, w_{L,i})^\mathsf{T} \in \mathbb{R}^L$ and a scalar threshold $\theta_i \in \mathbb{R}$, and where $\langle \boldsymbol{y}, \boldsymbol{w}_i \rangle := \boldsymbol{w}_i^\mathsf{T} \boldsymbol{y}$ denotes the standard inner product. The quantity $\eta_i \in \mathbb{R}$ is an arbitrary bounded disturbance (or error)

$$|\eta_i| < \eta, \qquad i \in \{1, \ldots, L\}, \tag{2.2}$$

for $\eta > 0$, which subsumes imprecise computations and freak firings.

The right-hand side of (2.1) can be written as

$$\xi_i(\boldsymbol{y}) = \sigma_{\theta_i}\big(\langle \boldsymbol{y}, \boldsymbol{w}_i \rangle + \eta_i\big), \tag{2.3}$$

where $\sigma_{\theta_i}(x) := \mathrm{I}[x \geq \theta_i]$, $x \in \mathbb{R}$, denotes the thresholding function. Thus, the (disturbance-free) output of a neuron is a threshold on the linear combination of its inputs, cf. Figure 2.1. Such a neuron model (without disturbance η_i) is known as the McCulloch–Pitts neuron [44].

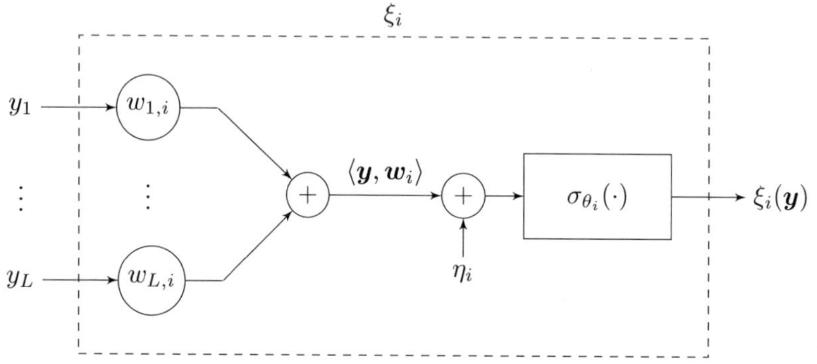

Figure 2.1: Binary neuron ξ_i with L inputs and additive disturbance η_i. The neuron is characterized by a weight vector $\boldsymbol{w}_i := (w_{1,i}, \ldots, w_{L,i})^\mathsf{T} \in \mathbb{R}^L$ and a scalar threshold $\theta_i \in \mathbb{R}$.

2.2 Fully-connected Autonomous Recurrent Network

These L binary neurons are fully connected to form an autonomous recurrent network as illustrated in Figure 2.2. All connections (synapses) possess the same fixed unit-delay (which is indicated by the filters with transfer function z^{-1} in Figure 2.2).

Initialized with some vector $\boldsymbol{y}[0] \in \mathbb{R}^L$, such a network produces the L-dimensional discrete-time signal $\boldsymbol{y}[1], \boldsymbol{y}[2], \ldots \in \{0,1\}^L$ with

$$\boldsymbol{y}[n+1] := \begin{pmatrix} \xi_1(\boldsymbol{y}[n]) \\ \vdots \\ \xi_L(\boldsymbol{y}[n]) \end{pmatrix}, \qquad n \in \mathbb{N}. \tag{2.4}$$

The signal $\boldsymbol{y}[\cdot]$ will be also referred to as firing sequence and, e.g., $y_\ell[n] = 1$ indicates a firing and $y_\ell[n] = 0$ indicates no firing in the ℓ-th channel at time step n, respectively.

As illustrated in Figure 2.3, in every time step n the network produces a binary (firing) vector $\boldsymbol{y}[n]$. In Appendix A.2, this mode of operation is demonstrated for a comprehensible example.

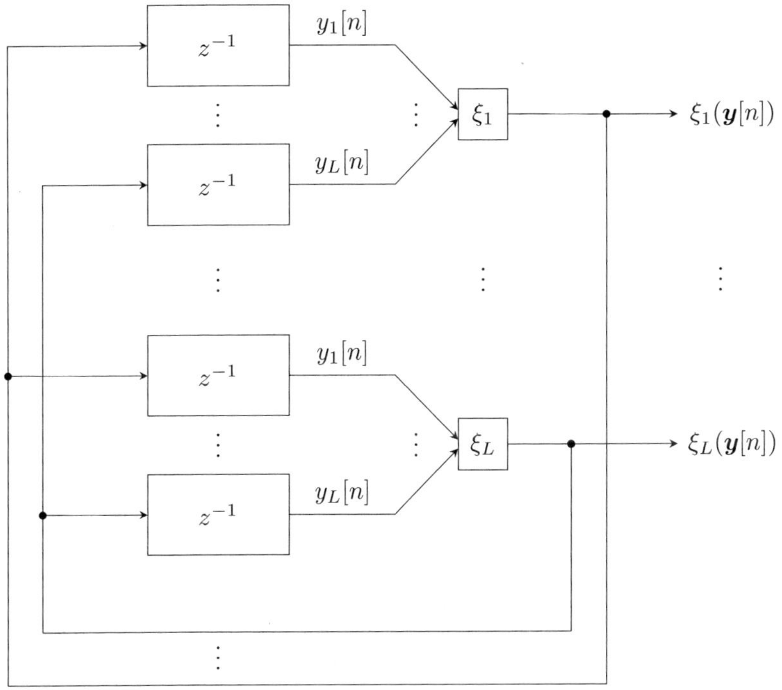

Figure 2.2: Fully-connected autonomous recurrent network consisting of L binary neurons at time step $n \in \mathbb{N}$.

2.3 Periodic Firing Sequences

Throughout this part, we want the network to memorize a given discrete-time firing signal (or firing sequence) of finite length N. More concretely, given the firing sequence

$$\bar{\boldsymbol{y}}[0], \ldots, \bar{\boldsymbol{y}}[N-1] \in \{0,1\}^L \tag{2.5}$$

we want the recursion (2.4) to yield

$$\boldsymbol{y}[n] = \bar{\boldsymbol{y}}[n \bmod N], \qquad n \in \{1, 2, \ldots\}, \tag{2.6}$$

if initialized with

$$\boldsymbol{y}[0] := \bar{\boldsymbol{y}}[0]. \tag{2.7}$$

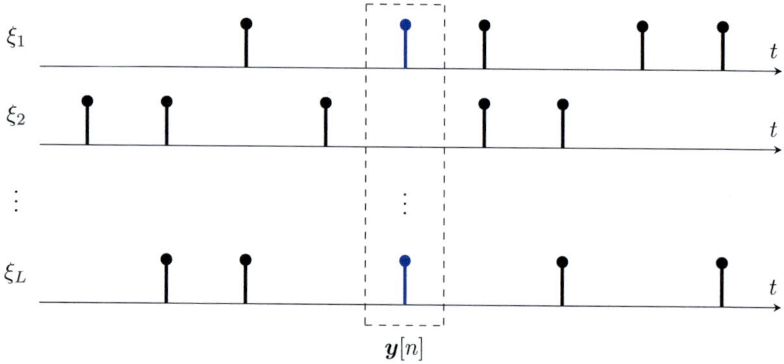

Figure 2.3: Multi-channel firing sequence as defined in (2.4).

I.e., we want the network to reproduce a periodic extension of the given firing sequence.

Note that if we initialize the network with

$$\boldsymbol{y}[0] := \bar{\boldsymbol{y}}[k], \tag{2.8}$$

for an arbitrary $k \in \{0, 1, \ldots, N-1\}$, then the network will produce the sequence

$$\boldsymbol{y}[n] = \bar{\boldsymbol{y}}[(n+k) \bmod N], \qquad n \in \{1, 2, \ldots\}. \tag{2.9}$$

Thus, such a network can be used as an associative memory.

We will usually represent the firing sequences in matrix form. E.g., for the firing sequence (2.5), we define its corresponding matrix as

$$\bar{\boldsymbol{Y}} := \big(\bar{\boldsymbol{y}}[0], \ldots, \bar{\boldsymbol{y}}[N-1]\big) \in \{0,1\}^{L \times N}, \tag{2.10}$$

i.e., $(\bar{\boldsymbol{Y}})_{\ell,n} = \bar{y}_\ell[n]$, for $(\ell, n) \in \{1, \ldots, L\} \times \{0, \ldots, N-1\}$ (notice the column index of $\bar{\boldsymbol{Y}}$ starts at zero).

2.4 Difference to the Hopfield Model

The classic reference for memorization in neural networks is the Hopfield model introduced in [29]. In Appendix A.1 a brief overview of the Hopfield model is provided. The Hopfield network is also a dynamical recurrent neural network, but it has some fundamental differences compared to the network model analyzed in this thesis.

The main difference is the "data type" of the memories in each network. The Hopfield network memorizes *static vectors* as static attractors of the dynamical system. By contrast, in this thesis, we study the memorization of *dynamical (firing) sequences*, cf. Figure 2.3. The examples in Appendix A.1 and A.2 demonstrate the two different modes of operation. The Hopfield network tries to learn its weights in order to reach an equilibrium state (as exemplified in (A.18) or (A.19)). Thus, if the Hopfield network has converged, it stops doing anything, whereas the network in Appendix A.2 keeps active all the time (as exemplified in (A.60)).

Moreover, the neurons in the Hopfield model are typically defined as in (A.1) with antipodal outputs, i.e., $\xi_i(\cdot) \in \{-1, 1\}$, whereas we consider neurons with binary outputs, i.e., $\xi_i(\cdot) \in \{0, 1\}$, cf. (2.1).

Storing Dynamic Objects in a Hopfield Network

The work in [26, 27] also considers the task of memorizing sequences but with a different approach. One of the main difference is that at least two connections (with different delays) between all the neurons are required for memorizing a given sequence $\boldsymbol{y}[0], \ldots, \boldsymbol{y}[N-1] \in \{-1, 1\}^L$ (cf. also Section 6.2). The two types of connections from neuron ξ_j to ξ_i are given by

$$\boldsymbol{w}_i^S = \frac{1}{N} \sum_{n=0}^{N-1} y_i[n] \boldsymbol{y}[n], \qquad \text{(short-time connections)} \tag{2.11}$$

$$\boldsymbol{w}_i^L = \frac{1}{N} \sum_{n=0}^{N-1} y_i[n] \boldsymbol{y}[n-1]. \qquad \text{(long-time connections)} \tag{2.12}$$

The weights $\boldsymbol{w}_i^S \in \mathbb{R}^L$ are controlling how long each state stabilizes before moving on to the next state in the sequence. On the other hand, the weights $\boldsymbol{w}_i^L \in \mathbb{R}^L$ are supposed to cause the state transitions, e.g., from $\boldsymbol{y}[k]$ to $\boldsymbol{y}[k+1]$. Note the similarity of (2.11) to (A.5), and the similarity of (2.12) to (3.3). Thus, the network does not produce a different state vector in each time step. It rather remains in a state, for a certain amount of time, before it moves on to the next state.

In this approach, all the N states $\boldsymbol{y}[0], \ldots, \boldsymbol{y}[N-1]$ are attractors of the considered dynamical system.

Furthermore, to the best of our knowledge we are not aware of any memorization-capacity consideration for a model that stores dynamic content.

Chapter 3

Quasi-Hebbian Learning

It is still a fundamental question how exactly learning takes place in a biological neural network, e.g., [6, 23, 49, 54, 58]. Thus, we will restrict ourselves to a special class of learning rules, namely learning rules which are motivated by Hebb's principle [25], [20, Chapter 19].

Hebbian learning is a local learning rule meaning that the weight (or synaptic) changes only depend on local information, i.e., only on information that is available to the synapse. Thus, weight changes are only caused by the firing activity of the pre- and postsynaptic neurons, but not on the firing activity of other neurons. The main reason of the restriction to a local learning rule is that when it comes to hardware implementation, locality is always an important property to achieve.

In summary, we will postulate a learning rule for the weights in order to memorize a given firing sequence and will analyze its performance (memorization capacity) instead of finding the optimal weights to achieve the best performance possible.

Given the firing sequence $\boldsymbol{Y} = \big(y_i[n]\big)_{(i,n)\in\{1,\ldots,L\}\times\{0,\ldots,N-1\}}$ (where $y_i[n]$ is the entry in row i and column n), cf. Section 2.3, we will consider learning rules of the following form. Starting from some initial vector $\boldsymbol{w}_i^{(0)} \in \mathbb{R}^L$ the weights are updated recursively by

$$\boldsymbol{w}_i^{(n+1)} = \boldsymbol{w}_i^{(n)} + \Delta\boldsymbol{w}_i^{(n)}, \qquad n \in \{0, 1, \ldots, N_{\text{it}}\}, \tag{3.1}$$

where the weight change $\Delta\boldsymbol{w}_i^{(n)}$ of neuron ξ_i at time step n depends only on $y_i[n]$ (the desired behaviour of this neuron at this time), and on the preceding firing vector $\boldsymbol{y}[n-1]$, and perhaps also on the previous weight vector $\boldsymbol{w}_i^{(n)}$ of this neuron, i.e.,

$$\Delta\boldsymbol{w}_i^{(n)} \text{ is a function of } y_i[n],\ \boldsymbol{y}[n-1], \text{ and perhaps } \boldsymbol{w}_i^{(n)}. \tag{3.2}$$

This type of learning may be called *quasi-Hebbian* since the restrictions (3.2) on $\Delta\boldsymbol{w}_i^{(n)}$ essentially agree with those of Hebbian learning, except that the term "Hebbian" is normally reserved for unsupervised learning. Again, the point of this restrictions is their suitability for hardware implementations, both biological and neuromorphic.

We will consider two modes of (3.1) which are described next. The first mode is strictly online with a single pass through the data (Section 3.1), while the second mode uses multiple passes through the data (Section 3.2).

3.1 Single-pass Memorization

In this mode of (3.1), we pass through the data exactly once, i.e., $N_{\text{it}} = N-1$. This mode may be viewed as a model for instantaneous (or one-shot) learning in short-term memory, e.g., [3, 47].

We will consider three different forms of $\Delta\boldsymbol{w}_i^{(n)} \in \mathbb{R}^L$:

i.) $$\Delta\boldsymbol{w}_i^{(n)} := y_i[n]\boldsymbol{y}[n-1] = \begin{cases} 0, & \text{if } y_i[n] = 0 \\ \boldsymbol{y}[n-1], & \text{if } y_i[n] = 1 \end{cases} \tag{3.3}$$

ii.) $$\Delta\boldsymbol{w}_i^{(n)} := \big(2y_i[n]-1\big)\boldsymbol{y}[n-1] = \begin{cases} -\boldsymbol{y}[n-1], & \text{if } y_i[n] = 0 \\ \boldsymbol{y}[n-1], & \text{if } y_i[n] = 1 \end{cases} \tag{3.4}$$

iii.) $$\Delta\boldsymbol{w}_i^{(n)} := y_i[n]\big(\boldsymbol{y}[n-1]-\boldsymbol{s}\big) = \begin{cases} 0, & \text{if } y_i[n] = 0 \\ \boldsymbol{y}[n-1]-\boldsymbol{s}, & \text{if } y_i[n] = 1, \end{cases} \tag{3.5}$$

with shift vector $\boldsymbol{s} \in \mathbb{R}^L$.

Note that all three forms (3.3) – (3.5) of $\Delta\boldsymbol{w}_i^{(n)}$ do not depend on the current weights $\boldsymbol{w}_i^{(n)}$. The version in (3.3) is the most elementary form of $\Delta\boldsymbol{w}_i^{(n)}$ one can think of. It simply considers all the input vectors which should cause the neuron ξ_i to fire. Note that the weight vector will only be changed if there is a desired firing. Furthermore, this form could potentially lead to a sparse weight vector, since the weight change is binary.

weights / update	sparse	not sparse
not always	(3.3)	(3.5)
always	(3.4)	–

Table 3.1: Properties of the different weight changes.

The second version (3.4) is an extension of the first form (3.3), which additionally also takes no-firings into account. The main difference is that the weight vector needs to be updated in every time step. A comparison of the learning rules (3.3) and (3.4) is done in Section 4.1. The third version (3.5) is a generalization of the first one. Instead of adding the preceding firing vector, a shifted version of it is added, resulting in non-sparse weights. It turns out that this modification is crucial to achieve a good performance, i.e., to achieve a memorization capacity that is comparable to the capacity of a Hopfield network, cf. Section 4.2. A rough classification of the properties of the learning rules (3.3) – (3.5) is given in Table 3.1.

After passing through the firing sequence exactly once, i.e., $N_{\text{it}} = N-1$, the weight vector of neuron ξ_i can be written as

$$\boldsymbol{w}_i^{(N)} = \boldsymbol{w}_i^{(N-1)} + \Delta\boldsymbol{w}_i^{(N-1)} \tag{3.6}$$

$$= \boldsymbol{w}_i^{(N-2)} + \Delta\boldsymbol{w}_i^{(N-2)} + \Delta\boldsymbol{w}_i^{(N-1)} \tag{3.7}$$

$$\vdots$$

$$= \boldsymbol{w}_i^{(0)} + \sum_{n=0}^{N-1} \Delta\boldsymbol{w}_i^{(n)}, \tag{3.8}$$

where we repeatedly applied (3.1). The expression (3.8) will be referred to as the closed form. Remember that we consider a periodic extension of $\boldsymbol{Y}$ as described in Section 2.3, which means that the time index (i.e., the column index of $\boldsymbol{Y}$) is always taken modulo N. Thus, the weight change at the beginning, e.g., for (3.3), is equal to

$$\Delta\boldsymbol{w}_i^{(0)} = y_i[0]\boldsymbol{y}[-1] \tag{3.9}$$

$$= y_i[0]\boldsymbol{y}[-1 \bmod N] \tag{3.10}$$

$$= y_i[0]\boldsymbol{y}[N-1]. \tag{3.11}$$

3.2 Multi-pass Memorization

In this mode of (3.1), we allow multiple passes through the data, i.e., $N_{\text{it}} \gg N$. This learning mode may be viewed as a model for the functionality of long-term (and/or working) memories in neuroscience, e.g., [3,4].

In Section 4.3 we present three different forms of $\Delta \boldsymbol{w}_i^{(n)} \in \mathbb{R}^L$:

i.) $$\Delta \boldsymbol{w}_i^{(n)} := \gamma^{(n)} \tilde{\boldsymbol{Y}}^\mathsf{T} \big(\tilde{\boldsymbol{y}}_i - \tilde{\boldsymbol{Y}} \boldsymbol{w}_i^{(n)}\big), \tag{3.12}$$
with $\tilde{\boldsymbol{Y}} \in \mathbb{R}^{N \times L}$ and $\tilde{\boldsymbol{y}}_i \in \mathbb{R}^N$ as defined in (4.165) and (4.166), respectively.

ii.) $$\Delta \boldsymbol{w}_i^{(n)} := \gamma^{(n)} \sum_{\tilde{n} \in \mathcal{B}_n} \Big(y_i[\tilde{n}] - \big\langle \boldsymbol{y}[\tilde{n}-1], \boldsymbol{w}_i^{(n)} \big\rangle\Big)\, \boldsymbol{y}[\tilde{n}-1] \tag{3.13}$$

iii.) $$\Delta \boldsymbol{w}_i^{(n)} := \gamma^{(n)} \Big(y_i[n] - \big\langle \boldsymbol{y}[n-1], \boldsymbol{w}_i^{(n)} \big\rangle\Big)\, \boldsymbol{y}[n-1] \tag{3.14}$$

for some step size (or learning rate) $\gamma^{(n)} > 0$.

Note that only (3.14) effectively satisfies (3.2), but the weight changes in (3.12) and (3.14) are in fact special cases of (3.13). For $\mathcal{B}_n = \{n\}$, we obtain (3.14), and for $\mathcal{B}_n = \{0, 1, \ldots, N-1\}$, (3.13) becomes (3.12) since

$$\sum_{\tilde{n}=0}^{N-1} \Big(y_i[\tilde{n}] - \big\langle \boldsymbol{y}[\tilde{n}-1], \boldsymbol{w}_i^{(n)} \big\rangle\Big)\, \boldsymbol{y}[\tilde{n}-1]$$

$$= \underbrace{\big(\boldsymbol{y}[N-1], \boldsymbol{y}[0], \ldots, \boldsymbol{y}[N-2]\big)}_{=\tilde{\boldsymbol{Y}}^\mathsf{T}} \begin{pmatrix} y_i[0] - \boldsymbol{y}[N-1]^\mathsf{T} \boldsymbol{w}_i^{(n)} \\ \vdots \\ y_i[N-1] - \boldsymbol{y}[N-2]^\mathsf{T} \boldsymbol{w}_i^{(n)} \end{pmatrix} \tag{3.15}$$

$$= \tilde{\boldsymbol{Y}}^\mathsf{T} \underbrace{\begin{pmatrix} y_i[0] \\ \vdots \\ y_i[N-1] \end{pmatrix}}_{=\tilde{\boldsymbol{y}}_i} - \tilde{\boldsymbol{Y}}^\mathsf{T} \underbrace{\begin{pmatrix} \boldsymbol{y}[N-1]^\mathsf{T} \\ \vdots \\ \boldsymbol{y}[N-2]^\mathsf{T} \end{pmatrix}}_{=\tilde{\boldsymbol{Y}}} \boldsymbol{w}_i^{(n)}. \tag{3.16}$$

Clearly, the update (3.14) is computationally much more attractive than (3.12) (especially if the signal length N is large). On the other hand, it can be shown that the recursion (3.1) with (3.12) and a constant step size, i.e., $\gamma^{(n)} = \gamma$, for all n, converges for sufficiently small $\gamma > 0$ (cf. (4.213)), whereas the recursion (3.1) with (3.14) never converges, but rather fluctuates around some fixed point. Thus, with a suitable $\mathcal{B}_n \subset \{0, 1, \ldots, N-1\}$ in (3.13) a good trade-off between computational efficiency and perfomance (convergence properties) can be obtained.

Choosing an appropriate step size $\gamma^{(n)}$ in (3.12) – (3.14) is crucial, e.g., [53,65]. If $\gamma^{(n)}$ is too small, then the recursion will take a long time to approximately converge, but if $\gamma^{(n)}$ is too large, then the recursion will be unstable.

Chapter 4

Perfect Memorization of Random Firing Sequences

For a network as in Chapter 2, we now analyze the probability of perfect memorization of a random firing sequence $\boldsymbol{Y} \in \{0,1\}^{L\times N}$ with i.i.d. entries $y_\ell[n]$ parameterized by

$$p := \Pr\big[y_\ell[n] = 1\big], \tag{4.1}$$

which we denote by $\boldsymbol{Y} \overset{\text{i.i.d.}}{\sim} \operatorname{Ber}(p)^{L\times N}$. Since we consider a periodic extension of $\boldsymbol{Y}$ (as described in Section 2.3), throughout the whole chapter all column indices of $\boldsymbol{Y}$ will be implicitly taken modulo N. Thus, the column index is an element of the set $\{0, 1, \ldots, N-1\}$.

Let $\mathcal{E}_{\boldsymbol{Y}}$ be the event that the memorization of $\boldsymbol{Y}$ is not perfect, i.e.,

$$\mathcal{E}_{\boldsymbol{Y}} := \bigcup_{(\ell,n)\in\{1,\ldots,L\}\times\{0,\ldots,N-1\}} \big\{\, \xi_\ell(\boldsymbol{y}[n-1]) \neq y_\ell[n] \,\big\}. \tag{4.2}$$

In other words, we say the firing sequence $\boldsymbol{Y}$ is perfectly memorized by the recurrent network if and only if every entry of the reproduced sequence coincides with its corresponding entry of $\boldsymbol{Y}$. Once more, at time step $n = 0$, we want to have

$$\xi_\ell(\boldsymbol{y}[N-1]) = y_\ell[0], \qquad \ell \in \{1, \ldots, L\}, \tag{4.3}$$

in order to produce a periodic extension of the given $\boldsymbol{Y}$.

In this chapter, we prove upper bounds of $\Pr[\mathcal{E}_{\boldsymbol{Y}}]$ for different learning rules. Those bounds will then yield to conditions under which perfect memorization is asymptotically possible. But the main reason to study random memorization is that it enables us to evaluate and compare the memorization capacities for the different learning rules/modes, which is done in Chapter 5.

In Section 4.1 and 4.2, we upper bound $\Pr[\mathcal{E}_{\boldsymbol{Y}}]$ for various versions of the single-pass learning mode. First, we compare two learning rules on the basis of a sufficient condition for the firing sequence $\boldsymbol{Y}$. Second, we directly examine $\Pr[\mathcal{E}_{\boldsymbol{Y}}]$ (for a slightly modified learning rule) in order to find a stronger bound implying a larger memorization capacity. Finally, in Section 4.3 we analyze multi-pass memorization via a least-squares approach.

4.1 Single-pass Memorization – Comparison of a Simple Learning Rule and Its Extension

We now analyze the two single-pass learning rules with weight changes (3.3) and (3.4) introduced in Chapter 3. Written in closed form, i.e., in the form (3.8) together with $\boldsymbol{w}_i^{(0)} := \boldsymbol{0}_L$, the weights are then, for $i \in \{1, \ldots, L\}$, given by

$$\boldsymbol{w}_i = \sum_{n \in J_i} \boldsymbol{y}[n-1], \tag{4.4}$$

$$\boldsymbol{w}_i = \sum_{n \in J_i} \boldsymbol{y}[n-1] - \sum_{n \in J_i^{\mathrm{c}}} \boldsymbol{y}[n-1], \tag{4.5}$$

for (3.3) and (3.4), respectively, and where

$$J_i := \big\{ n \in \{0, \ldots, N-1\} : y_i[n] = 1 \big\} \tag{4.6}$$

is the set of all firing positions in the i-th channel of $\boldsymbol{Y} \in \{0,1\}^{L \times N}$, and $|J_i| \in \{0, 1, \ldots, N\}$ denotes its cardinality. Let

$$J_i^{\mathrm{c}} := \{0, \ldots, N-1\} \setminus J_i \tag{4.7}$$

be the complement of J_i, i.e.,

$$J_i^{\mathrm{c}} = \big\{ n \in \{0, \ldots, N-1\} : y_i[n] = 0 \big\}. \tag{4.8}$$

First, we will state sufficient conditions for a firing sequence to be perfectly memorized by the recurrent network (introduced in Chapter 2) with weights given either in (4.4) or (4.5). Then, by using the established characterization (which is tailored to apply the Chernoff bound), we can give an upper bound on the event $\mathcal{E}_{\boldsymbol{Y}}$, i.e., that the memorization of $\boldsymbol{Y}$ is not perfect, for a random firing sequence $\boldsymbol{Y} \overset{\text{i.i.d.}}{\sim} \text{Ber}(p)^{L\times N}$. Finally, we examine under what conditions the upper bound vanishes. We will find that if

$$N < \sqrt{L}, \tag{4.9}$$

then the upper bound asymptotically vanishes (i.e., for $N \to \infty$). Thus, for a given signal length N, we need (at most) N^2 neurons in order to achieve asymptotic perfect memorization.

4.1.1 A Sufficient Characterization of the Memorizable Firing Sequences

For the recurrent network as in Chapter 2 with weight vectors

$$\boldsymbol{w}_i := \boldsymbol{w}_i^{(N)}, \tag{4.10}$$

for $i \in \{1, \ldots, L\}$, where $\boldsymbol{w}_i^{(N)}$ is defined recursively as

$$\boldsymbol{w}_i^{(n+1)} := \begin{cases} \boldsymbol{w}_i^{(n)}, & \text{if } y_i[n] = 0 \\ \boldsymbol{w}_i^{(n)} + \boldsymbol{y}[n-1], & \text{if } y_i[n] = 1, \end{cases} \tag{4.11}$$

$$\boldsymbol{w}_i^{(0)} := \boldsymbol{0}_L, \tag{4.12}$$

for $n \in \{0, \ldots, N-1\}$, we have

Proposition 4.1. *For $L, N \in \mathbb{N}$, $0 < p < 1$, let $\delta_1 := \frac{1-p-2\tilde{\eta}N}{1-p+2pN}$ with $\tilde{\eta}$ as in (4.14). If the firing sequence $\boldsymbol{Y} = \big(\boldsymbol{y}[0], \ldots, \boldsymbol{y}[N-1]\big) \in \{0,1\}^{L\times N}$ satisfies*

$$\begin{cases} (1-\delta_1)Lp^2 < \big\langle \boldsymbol{y}[n], \boldsymbol{y}[\tilde{n}] \big\rangle < (1+\delta_1)Lp^2, & \text{if } n \neq \tilde{n} \\ (1-\delta_1)Lp < \big\langle \boldsymbol{y}[n], \boldsymbol{y}[\tilde{n}] \big\rangle < (1+\delta_1)Lp, & \text{if } n = \tilde{n}, \end{cases} \tag{4.13}$$

for all $(n, \tilde{n}) \in \{0, \ldots, N-1\}^2$, then $\boldsymbol{Y}$ is perfectly memorized by the recurrent network with disturbance bound

$$\eta := \tilde{\eta} \cdot Lp, \qquad 0 < \tilde{\eta} < \frac{1-p}{2N}, \tag{4.14}$$

weight vectors (4.10), i.e.,

$$\boldsymbol{w}_i := \sum_{n \in J_i} \boldsymbol{y}[n-1], \qquad i \in \{1, \dots, L\}, \tag{4.15}$$

and thresholds

$$\theta_i := (1+\delta_1)|J_i|Lp^2 + \eta, \qquad i \in \{1, \dots, L\}, \tag{4.16}$$

i.e., $\big(\xi_1(\boldsymbol{y}[n-1]), \dots, \xi_L(\boldsymbol{y}[n-1])\big)^{\mathsf{T}} = \big(y_1[n], \dots, y_L[n]\big)^{\mathsf{T}}$ *holds for all* $n \in \{0, \dots, N-1\}$. □

Before proving this statement, we note that the condition on the right-hand side of (4.14) is necessary and ensures $\delta_1 > 0$. Otherwise, for $\delta_1 \leq 0$, the assumption (4.13) would become false for all firing sequences $\boldsymbol{Y} \in \{0,1\}^{L \times N}$. In consequence, the disturbance bound is allowed to grow with

$$\eta \propto \frac{L}{N}. \tag{4.17}$$

Proof of Proposition 4.1. Let $i \in \{1, \dots, L\}$, and let $n \in \{0, \dots, N-1\}$ be fixed but arbitrary. First, we consider the case $y_i[n] = 0$, i.e., $n \notin J_i$. Then, we have

$$\begin{aligned}
\big\langle \boldsymbol{y}[n-1], \boldsymbol{w}_i \big\rangle + \eta_i &= \sum_{\tilde{n} \in J_i} \big\langle \boldsymbol{y}[n-1], \boldsymbol{y}[\tilde{n}-1] \big\rangle + \eta_i && (4.18) \\
&< |J_i|(1+\delta_1)Lp^2 + \eta && (4.19) \\
&= \theta_i, && (4.20)
\end{aligned}$$

where in (4.18) we inserted (4.15). Inequality (4.19) follows from the assumption (4.13) (for $\tilde{n} \neq n$, because $n \notin J_i$) and (2.2). Equality (4.20) holds by definition of θ_i, cf. (4.16). Thus (4.20) implies $\xi_i(\boldsymbol{y}[n-1]) = 0 = y_i[n]$, i.e., there is no false firing.

In the case of $y_i[n] = 1$, i.e., $n \in J_i$, we have

$$|J_i| \geq 1, \tag{4.21}$$

and

$$
\begin{aligned}
\langle \boldsymbol{y}[n-1], \boldsymbol{w}_i \rangle + \eta_i &= \sum_{\tilde{n} \in J_i \setminus \{n\}} \langle \boldsymbol{y}[n-1], \boldsymbol{y}[\tilde{n}-1] \rangle \\
&\quad + \langle \boldsymbol{y}[n-1], \boldsymbol{y}[n-1] \rangle + \eta_i && (4.22)\\
&> (|J_i| - 1)(1-\delta_1)Lp^2 + (1-\delta_1)Lp - \eta && (4.23)\\
&= (1-\delta_1)|J_i|Lp \left(\frac{|J_i| - 1}{|J_i|} p + \frac{1}{|J_i|} \right) - \eta && (4.24)\\
&\geq \left((1-\delta_1)\widetilde{N}_p - \frac{\eta}{|J_i|Lp} \right) |J_i|Lp && (4.25)\\
&\geq \left((1-\delta_1)\widetilde{N}_p - \tilde{\eta} \right) |J_i|Lp && (4.26)\\
&= \left((1+\delta_1)p + \tilde{\eta} \right) |J_i|Lp && (4.27)\\
&\geq (1+\delta_1)|J_i|Lp^2 + \eta && (4.28)\\
&= \theta_i, && (4.29)
\end{aligned}
$$

where in (4.22) we inserted (4.15), and we also took out the summand for $\tilde{n} = n$ since by assumption $n \in J_i$. Inequality (4.23) follows from the assumptions (4.13) and (2.2). The step from (4.24) to (4.25) holds because the function

$$\widetilde{N}_p \colon \mathbb{R}_{>0} \to \mathbb{R}, \;\; x \mapsto \frac{x-1}{x} p + \frac{1}{x} \tag{4.30}$$

is strictly monotonic decreasing (cf. Figure 4.1), which can be seen from

$$
\begin{aligned}
\frac{d}{dx} \widetilde{N}_p(x) &= \frac{x - (x-1)}{x^2} p - \frac{1}{x^2} && (4.31)\\
&= -\frac{1}{x^2}(1-p) && (4.32)\\
&< 0, && (4.33)
\end{aligned}
$$

for all $x > 0$. Thus, we have

$$\frac{|J_i| - 1}{|J_i|} p + \frac{1}{|J_i|} \geq \widetilde{N}_p(N), \tag{4.34}$$

for $|J_i| \leq N$. In (4.25) we also used the shorthand notation $\widetilde{N}_p = \widetilde{N}_p(N)$. The inequality (4.26) follows from (4.14) and $|J_i| \geq 1$ (cf. (4.21)). In

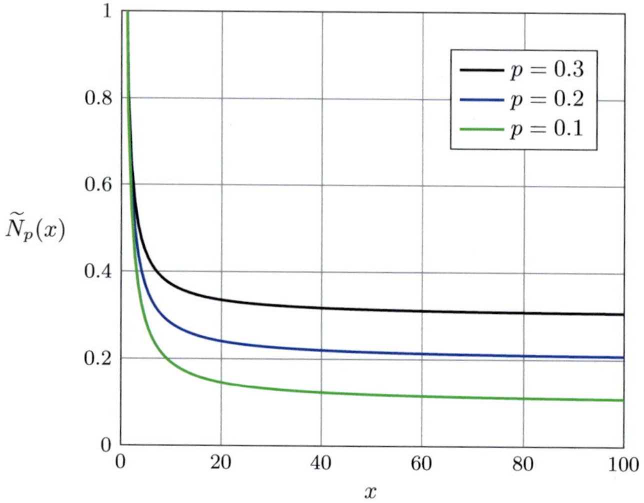

Figure 4.1: Graph of $\widetilde{N}_p(x) = \frac{x-1}{x}p + \frac{1}{x}$, for $p \in \{0.1, 0.2, 0.3\}$.

order to show (4.27), we rewrite δ_1 as

$$\delta_1 = \frac{1 - p - 2\tilde{\eta}N}{1 - p + 2pN} \tag{4.35}$$

$$= \frac{\frac{1-p}{N} - 2\tilde{\eta}}{\frac{1-p+2pN}{N}} \tag{4.36}$$

$$= \frac{\widetilde{N}_p - p - 2\tilde{\eta}}{\widetilde{N}_p + p}, \tag{4.37}$$

again with $\widetilde{N}_p = \widetilde{N}_p(N)$, and thus

$$(1-\delta_1)\widetilde{N}_p - \tilde{\eta} = \left(1 - \frac{\widetilde{N}_p - p - 2\tilde{\eta}}{\widetilde{N}_p + p}\right)\widetilde{N}_p - \tilde{\eta} \tag{4.38}$$

$$= \frac{2p\widetilde{N}_p + \tilde{\eta}\widetilde{N}_p - \tilde{\eta}p}{\widetilde{N}_p + p} \tag{4.39}$$

$$= \frac{(2\widetilde{N}_p - 2\tilde{\eta})p + \tilde{\eta}\widetilde{N}_p + \tilde{\eta}p}{\widetilde{N}_p + p} \tag{4.40}$$

$$= (1 + \delta_1)p + \tilde{\eta}. \tag{4.41}$$

Finally, (4.28) follows from (4.14) and $|J_i| \geq 1$ (cf. (4.21)), and (4.29) follows from (4.16). Thus, (4.29) implies $\xi_i(\boldsymbol{y}[n-1]) = 1 = y_i[n]$, i.e., there is no missing firing.

In total, we have $\xi_i(\boldsymbol{y}[n-1]) = y_i[n]$ which concludes the proof. ■

Now, we extend the learning rule (4.11) by also taking no-firings into account, cf. (4.43) below. This is a more realistic scenario, since only potentiation (or LTP) happens in (4.11), and therefore the weights grow with the length N. Thus, we also consider depression (or LTD), which balances the weight changes, resulting in weights that will not grow with N. Clearly, we expect a better performance of (4.43) at the expense of updating the weights in every time step, whereas in (4.11) the weights are only updated if a firing occurs.

For the recurrent network as in Chapter 2 with weight vectors

$$\boldsymbol{w}_i := \boldsymbol{w}_i^{(N)}, \tag{4.42}$$

for $i \in \{1, \ldots, L\}$, where $\boldsymbol{w}_i^{(N)}$ is defined recursively as

$$\boldsymbol{w}_i^{(n+1)} := \begin{cases} \boldsymbol{w}_i^{(n)} - \boldsymbol{y}[n-1], & \text{if } y_i[n] = 0 \\ \boldsymbol{w}_i^{(n)} + \boldsymbol{y}[n-1], & \text{if } y_i[n] = 1, \end{cases} \tag{4.43}$$

$$\boldsymbol{w}_i^{(0)} := \boldsymbol{0}_L, \tag{4.44}$$

for $n \in \{0, \ldots, N-1\}$, we have

Proposition 4.2. *For $L, N \in \mathbb{N}$, $0 < p < 1$, let $\delta_2 := \frac{1-p-2\tilde{\eta}}{1-p+2pN}$ with $\tilde{\eta}$ as in (4.46). If the firing sequence $\boldsymbol{Y} = \big(\boldsymbol{y}[0], \ldots, \boldsymbol{y}[N-1]\big) \in \{0,1\}^{L\times N}$ satisfies*

$$\begin{cases} (1-\delta_2)Lp^2 < \big\langle \boldsymbol{y}[n], \boldsymbol{y}[\tilde{n}]\big\rangle < (1+\delta_2)Lp^2, & \text{if } n \neq \tilde{n} \\ (1-\delta_2)Lp < \big\langle \boldsymbol{y}[n], \boldsymbol{y}[\tilde{n}]\big\rangle < (1+\delta_2)Lp, & \text{if } n = \tilde{n}, \end{cases} \tag{4.45}$$

for all $(n, \tilde{n}) \in \{0, \ldots, N-1\}^2$, then $\boldsymbol{Y}$ is perfectly memorized by the recurrent network with disturbance bound

$$\eta := \tilde{\eta} \cdot Lp, \qquad 0 < \tilde{\eta} < \frac{1-p}{2}, \tag{4.46}$$

weight vectors (4.42), i.e.,

$$\boldsymbol{w}_i := \sum_{n\in J_i} \boldsymbol{y}[n-1] - \sum_{n\in J_i^{\mathrm{c}}} \boldsymbol{y}[n-1], \qquad i \in \{1, \ldots, L\}, \tag{4.47}$$

and thresholds

$$\theta_i := (1+\delta_2)|J_i|Lp^2 - (1-\delta_2)|J_i^c|\widetilde{N}_p Lp + \eta, \quad i \in \{1,\dots,L\}, \tag{4.48}$$

with $\widetilde{N}_p := \widetilde{N}_p(N)$ *as in (4.30), i.e.,* $\big(\xi_1(\boldsymbol{y}[n-1]),\dots,\xi_L(\boldsymbol{y}[n-1])\big)^{\mathsf{T}} = \big(y_1[n],\dots,y_L[n]\big)^{\mathsf{T}}$ *holds for all* $n \in \{0,\dots,N-1\}$. □

As in Proposition 4.1, the condition on the right-hand side of (4.46) is necessary and ensures $\delta_2 > 0$. In consequence, the disturbance bound is allowed to grow with

$$\eta \propto L, \tag{4.49}$$

which is independent of N, and shows the improvement compared to (4.17).

The proof of Proposition 4.2 is analogous to the proof of Proposition 4.1 and is given in Appendix B.4.

4.1.2 An Upper Bound on $\Pr[\mathcal{E}_{\boldsymbol{Y}}]$

Let $\mathcal{Y}_{\text{mem}} \subseteq \{0,1\}^{L\times N}$ be the set of all memorizable firing sequences, i.e.,

$$\boldsymbol{Y} \in \mathcal{Y}_{\text{mem}} \;:\Longleftrightarrow\; \Big(\xi_i(\boldsymbol{y}[n-1]) = y_i[n], \quad \forall (i,n)\Big), \tag{4.50}$$

and for $k \in \{1,2\}$, let

$$\boldsymbol{Y} \in \mathcal{Y}_k \;:\Longleftrightarrow\; \Big(\langle \boldsymbol{y}[n], \boldsymbol{y}[\tilde{n}]\rangle \in I_{n,\tilde{n}}^{(k)}, \quad \forall (n,\tilde{n})\Big), \tag{4.51}$$

where

$$I_{n,\tilde{n}}^{(k)} := \begin{cases} \big](1-\delta_k)Lp^2, (1+\delta_k)Lp^2\big[, & \text{if } n \neq \tilde{n} \\ \big](1-\delta_k)Lp, (1+\delta_k)Lp\big[, & \text{if } n = \tilde{n}. \end{cases} \tag{4.52}$$

Note that Proposition 4.1 and 4.2 state that

$$\mathcal{Y}_k \subseteq \mathcal{Y}_{\text{mem}}, \tag{4.53}$$

for $k \in \{1,2\}$, respectively. Thus, for $\boldsymbol{Y} \overset{\text{i.i.d.}}{\sim} \text{Ber}(p)^{L\times N}$, we have

$$\begin{aligned}
\Pr[\mathcal{E}_{\boldsymbol{Y}}] &= \Pr\big[\boldsymbol{Y} \notin \mathcal{Y}_{\text{mem}}\big] &(4.54)\\
&\le \Pr\big[\boldsymbol{Y} \notin \mathcal{Y}_k\big] &(4.55)\\
&\le \sum_{n=0}^{N-1}\sum_{\tilde{n}=0}^{N-1} \Pr\Big[\big\langle \boldsymbol{y}[n], \boldsymbol{y}[\tilde{n}]\big\rangle \notin I_{n,\tilde{n}}^{(k)}\Big] &(4.56)\\
&= \sum_{n=0}^{N-1}\sum_{\tilde{n}\in\{0,\dots,N-1\}\setminus\{n\}} \Pr\Big[\big\langle \boldsymbol{y}[n], \boldsymbol{y}[\tilde{n}]\big\rangle \notin I_{n,\tilde{n}}^{(k)}\Big]\\
&\quad + \sum_{n=0}^{N-1} \Pr\Big[\big\langle \boldsymbol{y}[n], \boldsymbol{y}[n]\big\rangle \notin I_{n,n}^{(k)}\Big] &(4.57)\\
&\le 2N(N-1)e^{-\frac{1}{3}\delta_k^2 Lp^2} + 2Ne^{-\frac{1}{3}\delta_k^2 Lp} &(4.58)\\
&\le 2N^2 e^{-\frac{1}{3}\delta_k^2 Lp^2}, &(4.59)
\end{aligned}$$

where (4.55) follows from (4.53). Inequality (4.56) holds by the union bound. In (4.57) we took out the summand for $\tilde{n} = n$. Since $\boldsymbol{Y} \overset{\text{i.i.d.}}{\sim} \text{Ber}(p)^{L\times N}$, the random variables in (4.57) are binomially distributed

$$\begin{cases} \big\langle \boldsymbol{y}[n], \boldsymbol{y}[\tilde{n}]\big\rangle \sim \text{Bin}(L, p^2), & \text{if } n \ne \tilde{n}\\ \big\langle \boldsymbol{y}[n], \boldsymbol{y}[n]\big\rangle \sim \text{Bin}(L, p), & \text{if } n = \tilde{n}, \end{cases} \tag{4.60}$$

and thus applying Lemma B.7 (cf. Appendix B.2) yields (4.58). Finally, the step from (4.58) to (4.59) holds since $p^2 < p$, for $0 < p < 1$.

Size of the Set $\mathcal{Y}_{\text{mem}}$

Note that for the special case $p = 1/2$, i.e., all firing sequences are equally probable, we can lower bound $|\mathcal{Y}_{\text{mem}}|$ as follows

$$\begin{aligned}
\Pr\big[\boldsymbol{Y} \in \mathcal{Y}_{\text{mem}}\big] &= \sum_{\bar{\boldsymbol{Y}}\in\mathcal{Y}_{\text{mem}}} \Pr\big[\boldsymbol{Y} = \bar{\boldsymbol{Y}}\big] &(4.61)\\
&= \sum_{\bar{\boldsymbol{Y}}\in\mathcal{Y}_{\text{mem}}} \frac{1}{2^{LN}} &(4.62)\\
&= \frac{1}{2^{LN}}|\mathcal{Y}_{\text{mem}}|, &(4.63)
\end{aligned}$$

and thus

$$
\begin{aligned}
|\mathcal{Y}_{\text{mem}}| &= 2^{LN}\,\Pr\big[\boldsymbol{Y} \in \mathcal{Y}_{\text{mem}}\big] && (4.64)\\
&= 2^{LN}\left(1 - \Pr\big[\boldsymbol{Y} \notin \mathcal{Y}_{\text{mem}}\big]\right) && (4.65)\\
&\geq 2^{LN}\left(1 - 2N^2 e^{-\frac{1}{3}\delta_k^2 L p^2}\right), && (4.66)
\end{aligned}
$$

where (4.66) follows from (4.59).

4.1.3 Dependence of N and L

So far, we have established the upper bounds

$$
\Pr[\mathcal{E}_{\boldsymbol{Y}}] \leq 2N^2 e^{-\frac{1}{3}\delta_k^2 L p^2}, \qquad k \in \{1, 2\}, \tag{4.67}
$$

for $\boldsymbol{w}_i = \sum_{n \in J_i} \boldsymbol{y}[n-1]$ with

$$
\delta_1 = \frac{1-p-2\tilde{\eta}N}{1-p+2pN}, \qquad 0 < \tilde{\eta} < \frac{1-p}{2N}, \tag{4.68}
$$

and for $\boldsymbol{w}_i = \sum_{n \in J_i} \boldsymbol{y}[n-1] - \sum_{n \in J_i^c} \boldsymbol{y}[n-1]$ with

$$
\delta_2 = \frac{1-p-2\tilde{\eta}}{1-p+2pN}, \qquad 0 < \tilde{\eta} < \frac{1-p}{2}. \tag{4.69}
$$

Next, we state a sufficient condition such that the right-hand side of (4.67) asymptotically vanishes, i.e., for $L \to \infty$.

Proposition 4.3. *If*

$$
N < \gamma \sqrt{L} \tag{4.70}
$$

for any fixed $\gamma > 0$, *then*

$$
\lim_{L \to \infty} 2N^2 e^{-\frac{1}{3}\delta_k^2 L p^2} = 0, \qquad k \in \{1, 2\}, \tag{4.71}
$$

with δ_1 *as in (4.68), and* δ_2 *as in (4.69).* □

Proof of Proposition 4.3. The conditions on the right-hand side of (4.68) and (4.69) imply that there exist positive constants $\varepsilon_1, \varepsilon_2 > 0$ such that

$$
\delta_k > \frac{\varepsilon_k}{1-p+2pN}, \tag{4.72}
$$

for $k \in \{1, 2\}$, and thus

$$2N^2 e^{-\frac{1}{3}\delta_k^2 Lp^2} < 2N^2 e^{-\frac{1}{3}\left(\frac{\varepsilon_k}{1-p+2pN}\right)^2 Lp^2} \tag{4.73}$$

$$= 2N^2 e^{-\frac{1}{3}\frac{\varepsilon_k^2}{4p^2N^2+4p(1-p)N+(1-p)^2} Lp^2}, \tag{4.74}$$

but the right-hand side of (4.74) vanishes for $L \to \infty$ because

$$\lim_{L\to\infty} 2N^2 e^{-\frac{1}{3}\frac{\varepsilon_k^2}{4p^2N^2+4p(1-p)N+(1-p)^2} Lp^2}$$

$$= 2 \lim_{L\to\infty} \frac{N^2}{\exp\left(\frac{\varepsilon_k^2 p^2}{3}\frac{L}{4p^2N^2+4p(1-p)N+(1-p)^2}\right)} \tag{4.75}$$

$$= 2 \lim_{L\to\infty} \frac{N^2}{\exp\left(\frac{\varepsilon_k^2 p^2}{3}\frac{L/N^2}{4p^2+4p(1-p)/N+(1-p)^2/N^2}\right)} \tag{4.76}$$

$$= 2 \lim_{L\to\infty} \frac{N^2}{\exp\left(\frac{\varepsilon_k^2}{12}\frac{L}{N^2}\right)} \tag{4.77}$$

$$= 2 \lim_{L\to\infty} \frac{\gamma^2 L^\alpha}{\exp\left(\frac{\varepsilon_k^2}{12\gamma^2} L^{1-\alpha}\right)} \tag{4.78}$$

$$= 2\gamma^2 \lim_{L\to\infty} \frac{L^\alpha}{\exp\left(\frac{\varepsilon_k^2(1-\alpha)}{12\gamma^2} L\right)} \tag{4.79}$$

$$= 2\gamma^2 \lim_{x\to\infty} \frac{\ln(x)^\alpha}{x^{\frac{\varepsilon_k^2(1-\alpha)}{12\gamma^2}}} \tag{4.80}$$

$$= 2\gamma^2 \lim_{x\to\infty} \left(\frac{\ln(x)}{x^{\frac{\varepsilon_k^2(1-\alpha)}{12\gamma^2\alpha}}}\right)^\alpha \tag{4.81}$$

$$= 0, \tag{4.82}$$

for $0 < \alpha < 1$. The step from (4.76) to (4.77) holds because $N \to \infty$ as $L \to \infty$. In (4.78) we inserted the parameterization

$$N^2 = \gamma^2 L^\alpha, \qquad 0 < \alpha < 1, \tag{4.83}$$

cf. (4.70). The step from (4.79) to (4.80) follows from the variable substitution $x := e^L$. Finally, (4.82) follows from Lemma B.14 given in Appendix B.8. ■

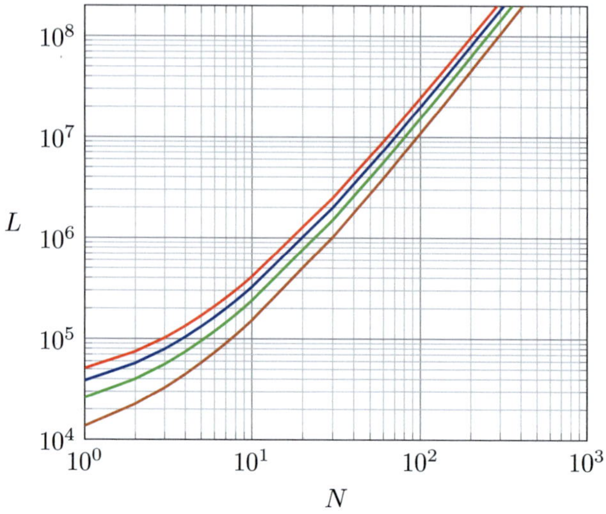

Figure 4.2: Value of L required for the right-hand side of (4.67) to equal 10^{-3}, 10^{-6}, 10^{-9}, 10^{-12} (from bottom to top) for $\delta = \frac{1}{2}(1-p)/(1-p+2pN)$, and $p = 0.1$.

In Figure 4.2, some numerical examples of the bound (4.67) are depicted. Given a fixed N, the plot shows the required value of L such that $2N^2 e^{-\frac{1}{3}\delta^2 p^2 L}$ achieves some desired level. E.g., a length of $N = 10$ requires at least $L = 3 \cdot 10^5$ neurons in order to have $\Pr[\mathcal{E}_{\boldsymbol{Y}}] \leq 10^{-9}$ (blue curve). Note that the choosen δ implies the relative disturbance bounds

$$\tilde{\eta}_1 = \frac{1-p}{4N}, \tag{4.84}$$

and

$$\tilde{\eta}_2 = \frac{1-p}{4}, \tag{4.85}$$

for the two learning rules (4.68) and (4.69), respectively.

To conclude, we summarize the results of this section. We analyzed (and compared) the two learning rules

$$\boldsymbol{w}_i = \sum_{n \in J_i} \boldsymbol{y}[n-1], \tag{4.86}$$

and

$$\boldsymbol{w}_i = \sum_{n \in J_i} \boldsymbol{y}[n-1] - \sum_{n \in J_i^c} \boldsymbol{y}[n-1]. \tag{4.87}$$

We showed that for both (4.86) and (4.87) perfect single-pass memorization is possible for firing sequences with

$$N \propto \sqrt{L}, \tag{4.88}$$

and disturbance bounds with

$$\eta_1 \propto \frac{L}{N}, \tag{4.89}$$

$$\eta_2 \propto L, \tag{4.90}$$

for (4.86) and (4.87), respectively. Thus, (4.86) allows only disturbances proportional to the ratio L/N, whereas (4.87) can deal with disturbances proportional to L (independent of N).

Finally, we want to point out that we only proved that the condition (4.88) is sufficient. With another analysis we might find better results. In the next section, we will show that a modified version of (4.86) even achieves $N \propto L/\ln(L)$.

4.2 Single-pass Memorization – Main Result

In this section, we prove an upper bound on $\Pr[\mathcal{E}_{\boldsymbol{Y}}]$ for the single-pass learning (or memorization) rule with weight changes (3.5) from Chapter 3. Written in closed form, i.e., as in (3.8) together with $\boldsymbol{w}_i^{(0)} := \mathbf{0}_L$, the expression for the weight vector becomes

$$\boldsymbol{w}_i := \sum_{n \in J_i} \big(\boldsymbol{y}[n-1] - \boldsymbol{s}\big), \qquad i \in \{1, \ldots, L\}, \tag{4.91}$$

where

$$J_i := \big\{n \in \{0, \ldots, N-1\} : y_i[n] = 1\big\} \tag{4.92}$$

is the set of all desired firing positions of neuron ξ_i, and $|J_i| \in \{0, \ldots, N\}$ denotes its cardinality. For $\boldsymbol{Y} \overset{\text{i.i.d.}}{\sim} \text{Ber}(p)^{L\times N}$, for $0 < p < 1$, the shift vector $\boldsymbol{s} \in \mathbb{R}^L$ in (4.91) is choosen such that

$$\text{E}[\boldsymbol{w}_i] = \mathbf{0}_L, \tag{4.93}$$

which implies (cf. Appendix B.5)

$$\boldsymbol{s} = p \cdot \mathbf{1}_L. \tag{4.94}$$

For $0 < p_1, p_2 < 1$, let

$$D_{KL}(p_1 \| p_2) := p_1 \ln\!\left(\frac{p_1}{p_2}\right) + (1-p_1)\ln\!\left(\frac{1-p_1}{1-p_2}\right), \tag{4.95}$$

be the Kullback–Leibler divergence (or relative entropy) between two Bernoulli distributions with success probabilities p_1 and p_2, cf., e.g., [11]. Note that in general

$$D_{KL}(p_1 \| p_2) \neq D_{KL}(p_2 \| p_1), \tag{4.96}$$

and from Lemma B.4, we have

$$D_{KL}(p_1 \| p_2) \geq 0, \tag{4.97}$$

for all $0 < p_1, p_2 < 1$, with equality if and only if $p_1 = p_2$.

4.2.1 An Upper Bound on $\Pr[\mathcal{E}_{\boldsymbol{Y}}]$

For the recurrent network as in Chapter 2 with weight vectors

$$\boldsymbol{w}_i := \boldsymbol{w}_i^{(N)}, \tag{4.98}$$

for $i \in \{1, \ldots, L\}$, where $\boldsymbol{w}_i^{(N)}$ is defined recursively as

$$\boldsymbol{w}_i^{(n+1)} := \begin{cases} \boldsymbol{w}_i^{(n)}, & \text{if } y_i[n] = 0 \\ \boldsymbol{w}_i^{(n)} + \boldsymbol{y}[n-1] - p\mathbf{1}_L, & \text{if } y_i[n] = 1, \end{cases} \tag{4.99}$$

$$\boldsymbol{w}_i^{(0)} := \mathbf{0}_L, \tag{4.100}$$

for $n \in \{0, \ldots, N-1\}$, we have

Theorem 4.1. *For all integers $L \geq 1$, and $N \geq 2$, $0 < p < 1$, $\boldsymbol{Y} \overset{\text{i.i.d.}}{\sim} \mathrm{Ber}(p)^{L \times N}$, the recurrent network with weight vectors (4.98), i.e.,*

$$\boldsymbol{w}_i := \sum_{n \in J_i} \big(\boldsymbol{y}[n-1] - p\mathbf{1}_L\big), \qquad i \in \{1, \ldots, L\}, \tag{4.101}$$

thresholds

$$\theta_i := \theta := \frac{1}{4} Lp(1-p), \qquad i \in \{1, \ldots, L\}, \tag{4.102}$$

disturbance bound

$$\eta := \tilde{\eta} \cdot \theta, \qquad 0 < \tilde{\eta} < 1, \tag{4.103}$$

and initialized with any column of $\boldsymbol{Y}$ will reproduce a periodic extension of $\boldsymbol{Y}$ with

$$\Pr[\mathcal{E}_{\boldsymbol{Y}}] < 2LNe^{-\frac{1}{8}(1-\tilde{\eta})^2 p^2 (1-p)^2 \frac{L}{N}} + LNe^{-D_{KL}\left(\frac{1+\tilde{\eta}}{2} p \| p\right) L}, \tag{4.104}$$

where $D_{KL}(p_1 \,\|\, p_2)$ denotes the Kullback–Leibler divergence (as defined in (4.95)). □

In consequence, the disturbance bound η is allowed to grow linearly with L, cf. (4.102) and (4.103), similar to (4.90) as discussed in Section 4.1.

The proof of Theorem 4.1 is given in the next section.

4.2.2 Proof of Theorem 4.1

We now prove Theorem 4.1, by using the union bound and by upper bounding the error probability of a single firing event $\{y_i[n] = a\}$, $a \in \{0, 1\}$, which amounts to bound the tails of $\langle \boldsymbol{y}[n-1], \boldsymbol{w}_i \rangle$.

The memorization of $\boldsymbol{Y}$ is perfect if and only if $\xi_i(\boldsymbol{y}[n-1]) = y_i[n]$, for all $i \in \{1, \ldots, L\}$ and for all $n \in \{0, \ldots, N-1\}$ (taken modulo N). By the union bound, we have (cf. (4.2))

$$\Pr[\mathcal{E}_{\boldsymbol{Y}}] \leq \sum_{i=1}^{L} \sum_{n=0}^{N-1} \Pr\big[\xi_i(\boldsymbol{y}[n-1]) \neq y_i[n]\big]. \tag{4.105}$$

Moreover, using the same threshold θ for all neurons and by the law of total probability, we have

$$\begin{aligned} &\Pr\big[\xi_i(\boldsymbol{y}[n-1]) \neq y_i[n]\big] \\ &\quad = (1-p)\Pr\big[\langle \boldsymbol{y}[n-1], \boldsymbol{w}_i \rangle + \eta_i \geq \theta \,\big|\, y_i[n] = 0\big] \\ &\qquad + p\Pr\big[\langle \boldsymbol{y}[n-1], \boldsymbol{w}_i \rangle + \eta_i < \theta \,\big|\, y_i[n] = 1\big]. \end{aligned} \tag{4.106}$$

Now, let $i \in \{1, \ldots, L\}$ and let $n \in \{0, \ldots, N-1\}$ be fixed but arbitrary. Then

$$\langle \boldsymbol{y}[n-1], \boldsymbol{w}_i \rangle = \left\langle \boldsymbol{y}[n-1], \sum_{\tilde{n} \in J_i} (\boldsymbol{y}[\tilde{n}-1] - p\mathbf{1}_L) \right\rangle \tag{4.107}$$

$$= \sum_{\tilde{n} \in J_i} \Big\langle \boldsymbol{y}[n-1], \underbrace{\boldsymbol{y}[\tilde{n}-1] - \mathrm{E}\big[\boldsymbol{y}[\tilde{n}-1]\big]}_{=: \tilde{\boldsymbol{y}}[\tilde{n}-1]} \Big\rangle \tag{4.108}$$

$$= \sum_{\tilde{n}=0}^{N-1} y_i[\tilde{n}] \langle \boldsymbol{y}[n-1], \tilde{\boldsymbol{y}}[\tilde{n}-1] \rangle \tag{4.109}$$

$$= y_i[n] \langle \boldsymbol{y}[n-1], \tilde{\boldsymbol{y}}[n-1] \rangle + S_{i,n}, \tag{4.110}$$

with

$$S_{i,n} := \sum_{\tilde{n} \in \{0, \ldots, N-1\} \setminus \{n\}} y_i[\tilde{n}] \langle \boldsymbol{y}[n-1], \tilde{\boldsymbol{y}}[\tilde{n}-1] \rangle, \tag{4.111}$$

where in (4.107) we inserted (4.101). The step from (4.107) to (4.108) follows from the linearity of the inner product and from

$$\mathrm{E}\big[\boldsymbol{y}[\tilde{n}-1]\big] = \mathrm{E}\Big[\big(y_1[\tilde{n}-1],\dots,y_L[\tilde{n}-1]\big)^\mathsf{T}\Big] \tag{4.112}$$

$$= \big(\mathrm{E}\big[y_1[\tilde{n}-1]\big],\dots,\mathrm{E}\big[y_L[\tilde{n}-1]\big]\big)^\mathsf{T} \tag{4.113}$$

$$= (p,\dots,p)^\mathsf{T} \tag{4.114}$$

$$= p\mathbf{1}_L, \tag{4.115}$$

for all $\tilde{n}$, since every entry of $\boldsymbol{Y}$ is Bernoulli distributed with success probability p. Equality (4.109) holds by the definition of the set $J_i \subseteq \{0,\dots,N-1\}$, cf. (4.92). Finally, in (4.110) we took out the summand for $\tilde{n} = n$ and defined the random variable (4.111). In Lemma B.2 (cf. Appendix B.1), we show that the moment generating function (MGF) of $S_{i,n}$ is upper bounded by

$$\mathrm{E}\big[e^{\lambda S_{i,n}}\big] < e^{\frac{\lambda^2}{8}LN}, \tag{4.116}$$

for all $\lambda \in \mathbb{R}$, and

$$\mathrm{E}[S_{i,n}] = 0. \tag{4.117}$$

Then, using (4.110) we can upper bound (4.106) by

$$\begin{aligned}\Pr\big[\xi_i(\boldsymbol{y}[n-1]) \neq y_i[n]\big] \\ \le \Pr\big[S_{i,n} \ge \theta - \eta_i \,\big|\, y_i[n] = 0\big] \\ + \Pr\big[\big\langle \boldsymbol{y}[n-1], \widetilde{\boldsymbol{y}}[n-1]\big\rangle + S_{i,n} < \theta - \eta_i \,\big|\, y_i[n] = 1\big].\end{aligned} \tag{4.118}$$

To get rid of the conditioning on $y_i[n]$ in (4.118), we note that an error, i.e., the event $\big\{\xi_i(\boldsymbol{y}[n-1]) \neq y_i[n]\big\}$ implies either $|S_{i,n}| \ge \theta - \eta_i$, or $|S_{i,n}| < \theta - \eta_i$ and $\big\langle \boldsymbol{y}[n-1], \widetilde{\boldsymbol{y}}[n-1]\big\rangle + S_{i,n} < \theta - \eta_i$, cf. Figure 4.3. Thus by the union bound, we obtain

$$\begin{aligned}\Pr\big[\xi_i(\boldsymbol{y}[n-1]) \neq y_i[n]\big] \\ \le \Pr\big[|S_{i,n}| \ge \theta - \eta_i\big] \\ + \Pr\big[|S_{i,n}| < \theta - \eta_i \text{ and } \big\langle \boldsymbol{y}[n-1], \widetilde{\boldsymbol{y}}[n-1]\big\rangle + S_{i,n} < \theta - \eta_i\big]\end{aligned} \tag{4.119}$$

$$\le \Pr\big[|S_{i,n}| \ge \theta - \eta_i\big] + \Pr\big[\big\langle \boldsymbol{y}[n-1], \widetilde{\boldsymbol{y}}[n-1]\big\rangle < 2(\theta - \eta_i)\big] \tag{4.120}$$

$$\le \Pr\big[|S_{i,n}| \ge \theta - \eta\big] + \Pr\big[\big\langle \boldsymbol{y}[n-1], \widetilde{\boldsymbol{y}}[n-1]\big\rangle < 2(\theta + \eta)\big] \tag{4.121}$$

$$= \Pr\big[|S_{i,n}| \ge \theta(1 - \tilde{\eta})\big] + \Pr\big[\big\langle \boldsymbol{y}[n-1], \widetilde{\boldsymbol{y}}[n-1]\big\rangle < 2\theta(1 + \tilde{\eta})\big], \tag{4.122}$$

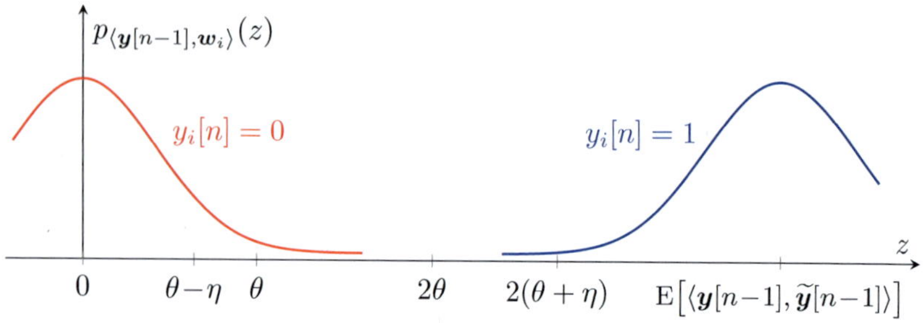

Figure 4.3: Sketch of the probability distribution of (4.110), for the realization $\langle \boldsymbol{y}[n-1], \widetilde{\boldsymbol{y}}[n-1]\rangle = \mathrm{E}\big[\langle \boldsymbol{y}[n-1], \widetilde{\boldsymbol{y}}[n-1]\rangle\big]$, in the two cases $y_i[n] = 0$ (peak on the left) and $y_i[n] = 1$ (peak on the right).

where the step from (4.119) to (4.120) follows from

$$\Big(\big\langle \boldsymbol{y}[n-1], \widetilde{\boldsymbol{y}}[n-1]\big\rangle + S_{i,n} < \theta - \eta_i \quad \text{and} \quad |S_{i,n}| < \theta - \eta_i\Big)$$
$$\Longrightarrow \quad \Big(\big\langle \boldsymbol{y}[n-1], \widetilde{\boldsymbol{y}}[n-1]\big\rangle - (\theta - \eta_i) < \theta - \eta_i\Big). \tag{4.123}$$

Inequality (4.121) holds because of (2.2), and equality (4.122) holds because of (4.103).

Now, we apply the Chernoff bound [9] to both terms on the right-hand side of (4.122). We start with

$$\Pr\big[S_{i,n} \geq \theta(1-\tilde{\eta})\big] = \Pr\Big[e^{\lambda S_{i,n}} \geq e^{\lambda\theta(1-\tilde{\eta})}\Big] \tag{4.124}$$
$$\leq \min_{\lambda>0} \frac{\mathrm{E}\big[e^{\lambda S_{i,n}}\big]}{e^{\lambda\theta(1-\tilde{\eta})}} \tag{4.125}$$
$$< \min_{\lambda>0} \frac{e^{\frac{\lambda^2}{8}LN}}{e^{\lambda\theta(1-\tilde{\eta})}} \tag{4.126}$$
$$= e^{-\frac{2\theta^2(1-\tilde{\eta})^2}{LN}} \tag{4.127}$$

Equality (4.124) holds since the function $x \mapsto e^{\lambda x}$, $\lambda > 0$, is strictly monotonic increasing. Applying Markov's inequality (Lemma B.5) yields (4.125), and (4.126) follows from (4.116). The bound on the right-hand side of (4.126) is minimized by $\lambda_{\min} := 4\theta(1-\tilde{\eta})/(LN) > 0$ which implies (4.127).

The lower tail of $S_{i,n}$, i.e., $\Pr\big[S_{i,n} \leq -\theta(1-\tilde{\eta})\big]$ can be upper bounded with the same bound (4.127) analogously, which is done in Lemma B.3 (cf. Appendix B.1). Thus by combining the bounds of both tails of $S_{i,n}$, we obtain

$$
\begin{aligned}
&\Pr\big[|S_{i,n}| \geq \theta(1-\tilde{\eta})\big] \\
&\quad = \Pr\big[S_{i,n} \geq \theta(1-\tilde{\eta})\big] + \Pr\big[S_{i,n} \leq -\theta(1-\tilde{\eta})\big] && (4.128)\\
&\quad < 2e^{-\frac{2\theta^2(1-\tilde{\eta})^2}{LN}}. && (4.129)
\end{aligned}
$$

As for the other term on the right-hand side of (4.122), we first rewrite the inner product as

$$
\begin{aligned}
\big\langle \boldsymbol{y}[n-1], \widetilde{\boldsymbol{y}}[n-1]\big\rangle &= \sum_{\ell=1}^{L} y_\ell[n-1]\,\big(y_\ell[n-1] - \mathrm{E}\big[y_\ell[n-1]\big]\big) && (4.130)\\
&= \sum_{\ell=1}^{L} \big(y_\ell[n-1] - y_\ell[n-1]\,p\big) && (4.131)\\
&= (1-p)\sum_{\ell=1}^{L} y_\ell[n-1], && (4.132)
\end{aligned}
$$

and thus

$$
\frac{1}{1-p}\big\langle \boldsymbol{y}[n-1], \widetilde{\boldsymbol{y}}[n-1]\big\rangle \sim \mathrm{Bin}(L,p). \tag{4.133}
$$

In (4.130) we inserted the definitions of $\langle\cdot\,,\cdot\rangle$ and $\widetilde{\boldsymbol{y}}[n-1]$. The step from (4.130) to (4.131) holds since $y_\ell[n-1] \sim \mathrm{Ber}(p)$, thus $y_\ell[n-1]^2 = y_\ell[n-1]$ and $\mathrm{E}\big[y_\ell[n-1]\big] = p$. Finally, (4.133) follows from (4.132) and from $y_1[n-1], \ldots, y_L[n-1] \overset{\text{i.i.d.}}{\sim} \mathrm{Ber}(p)$.

Now, we can apply the Chernoff bound to the tail of the binomial distribution and the probability on the right-hand of the right-hand side of (4.122) can be bounded by

$$
\begin{aligned}
&\Pr\big[\big\langle \boldsymbol{y}[n-1], \widetilde{\boldsymbol{y}}[n-1]\big\rangle < 2\theta(1+\tilde{\eta})\big] \\
&\quad = \Pr\left[\frac{1}{1-p}\big\langle \boldsymbol{y}[n-1], \widetilde{\boldsymbol{y}}[n-1]\big\rangle < \frac{1+\tilde{\eta}}{2}Lp\right] && (4.134)\\
&\quad \leq e^{-D_{KL}\left(\frac{1+\tilde{\eta}}{2}p\|p\right)L}, && (4.135)
\end{aligned}
$$

where in (4.134) we inserted (4.102). From (4.134) to (4.135) we applied Lemma B.6 (given in Appendix B.2) with $1-\delta = (1+\tilde{\eta})/2$, because of (4.133). Note that $0 < \tilde{\eta} < 1$ implies $0 < \delta < 1/2$.

Putting all together, we obtain

$$\begin{aligned}
&\Pr\big[\xi_i(\boldsymbol{y}[n-1]) \neq y_i[n]\big] \\
&\quad < 2e^{-\frac{2\theta^2(1-\tilde{\eta})^2}{LN}} + e^{-D_{KL}\left(\frac{1+\tilde{\eta}}{2}p\|p\right)L} && (4.136)\\
&\quad = 2e^{-\frac{1}{8}(1-\tilde{\eta})^2 p^2(1-p)^2\frac{L}{N}} + e^{-D_{KL}\left(\frac{1+\tilde{\eta}}{2}p\|p\right)L}. && (4.137)
\end{aligned}$$

Inequality (4.136) follows from (4.122) together with the two upper bounds (4.129) and (4.135). In (4.137) we inserted θ (as defined in (4.102)).

Finally, the right-hand side of (4.137) is independent on i and n, thus (4.105) yields (4.104), which concludes the proof. ■

Two remarks:

- Choosing the shift vector $\boldsymbol{s} := p\mathbf{1}_L$ is crucial in deriving the upper bound of the moment generating function (MGF) of $S_{i,n}$. The effect of the shift vector can be seen by comparing the MGFs of $X - p$ and X, for $X \sim \text{Ber}(p)$:

$$\text{E}\big[e^{\lambda X}\big] = 1 - p + pe^{\lambda} \leq e^{p(e^{\lambda}-1)}, \tag{4.138}$$

$$\text{E}\big[e^{\lambda(X-p)}\big] = (1-p)e^{-\lambda p} + pe^{\lambda(1-p)} \leq e^{\lambda^2/8}, \tag{4.139}$$

  where the inequality in (4.139) follows from Lemma B.1 in Appendix B.1 [1]. The symmetry of the bound $e^{\lambda^2/8}$ allows us to find an upper bound on the MGF of $S_{i,n}$ which yields a strong enough Chernoff bound.

- We chose the threshold such that

$$\begin{aligned}
&\frac{1}{2}\sum_{y\in\{0,1\}} \text{E}\big[\langle \boldsymbol{y}[n-1], \boldsymbol{w}_i\rangle \,\big|\, y_i[n] = y\big] \\
&\quad = \frac{1}{2}\text{E}\big[S_{i,n} \,\big|\, y_i[n] = 0\big] \\
&\qquad + \frac{1}{2}\text{E}\big[\langle \boldsymbol{y}[n-1], \tilde{\boldsymbol{y}}[n-1]\rangle + S_{i,n} \,\big|\, y_i[n] = 1\big] && (4.140)\\
&\quad = \frac{1}{2}\text{E}\big[\langle \boldsymbol{y}[n-1], \tilde{\boldsymbol{y}}[n-1]\rangle\big] && (4.141)\\
&\quad = \frac{1}{2}Lp(1-p) && (4.142)\\
&\quad = 2\theta, && (4.143)
\end{aligned}$$

i.e., 2θ is the arithmetic mean of the two expectations of the correlation $\langle \boldsymbol{y}[n-1], \boldsymbol{w}_i \rangle$, for the cases $y_i[n] = 0$ and $y_i[n] = 1$, cf. Figure 4.3.

4.2.3 Dependence of N and L

Now, we state a sufficient condition for the bound in Theorem 4.1 to asymptotically vanish.

Corollary 4.1. *If*

$$N \leq \frac{1}{8}(1-\tilde{\eta})^2 p^2 (1-p)^2 \frac{L}{2\ln(L)}, \tag{4.144}$$

then the right-hand side of (4.104), i.e.,

$$2LNe^{-\frac{1}{8}(1-\tilde{\eta})^2 p^2 (1-p)^2 \frac{L}{N}} + LNe^{-D_{KL}\left(\frac{1+\tilde{\eta}}{2}p \| p\right)L} \tag{4.145}$$

vanishes for $L \to \infty$. □

In Figure 4.4, some numerical examples of the bound (4.145) are depicted. Given a fixed N, the plot shows the required value of L such that (4.145) achieves some desired level. E.g., a length of $N = 10$ already requires at least $L = 6 \cdot 10^4$ neurons in order to have $\Pr[\mathcal{E}_{\boldsymbol{Y}}] \leq 10^{-9}$ (blue curve). Thus, the absolut numbers of required neurons are relatively large. But we want to point out that asymptotically the network is able to memorize almost square matrices $\boldsymbol{Y} \in \{0,1\}^{L \times N}$ with single-pass (one-shot) learning, because for all $\varepsilon > 0$, there exists $L_\varepsilon \in \mathbb{N}$ such that $L^2 / \ln(L) \geq L^{2-\varepsilon}$, for all $L \geq L_\varepsilon$ (cf. Lemma B.14), which implies

$$LN \geq L^{2-\varepsilon}, \tag{4.146}$$

for $N = L/\ln(L)$ and L sufficiently large.

The condition (4.144) in Corollary 4.1 is only sufficient. But it can be shown that the expression in (4.145) diverges to ∞ as $L \to \infty$ if, e.g.,

$$N > \frac{1}{8}(1-\tilde{\eta})^2 p^2 (1-p)^2 \frac{L}{2\ln(L)}, \tag{4.147}$$

or

$$N = \frac{1}{8}(1-\tilde{\eta})^2 p^2 (1-p)^2 \frac{L}{(2\ln(L))^r}, \qquad 0 < r < 1. \tag{4.148}$$

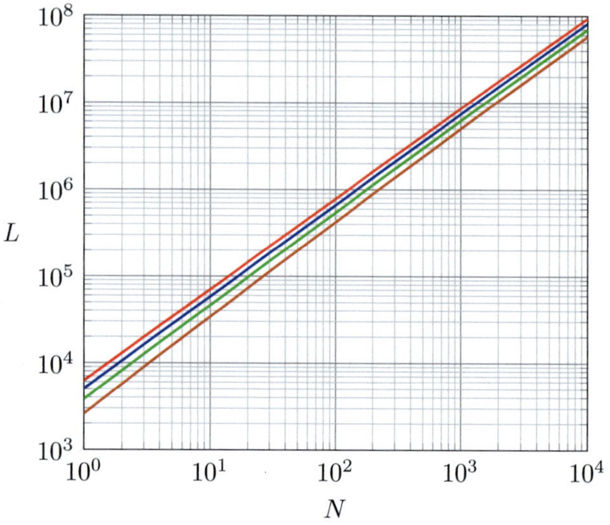

Figure 4.4: Value of L required for the bound (4.145) to equal 10^{-3}, 10^{-6}, 10^{-9}, 10^{-12} (from bottom to top) for $p = 1/2$, and $\tilde{\eta} = 1/8$.

Moreover, $L \mapsto L/\ln(L)$ grows faster than $L \mapsto L^q$, for any $0 < q < 1$, i.e.,

$$\lim_{L\to\infty} \frac{L^q}{\frac{L}{\ln(L)}} = \lim_{L\to\infty} \frac{\ln(L)}{L^{1-q}} \tag{4.149}$$

$$= 0, \tag{4.150}$$

because of Lemma B.14 in Appendix B.8. In particular, $L \mapsto L/\ln(L)$ grows faster than $L \mapsto \sqrt{L}$ as shown in Figure 4.5. Thus, given a fixed number of neurons, the learning rule analyzed in this section is able to (perfectly) memorize firing sequences with a larger length N than the two learning rules considered in Section 4.1 (and allowing a disturbance bound $\eta \propto L$).

Finally, we give a proof of Corollary 4.1:

Proof of Corollary 4.1. Let

$$\alpha := \frac{1}{8}(1-\tilde{\eta})^2 p^2 (1-p)^2, \tag{4.151}$$

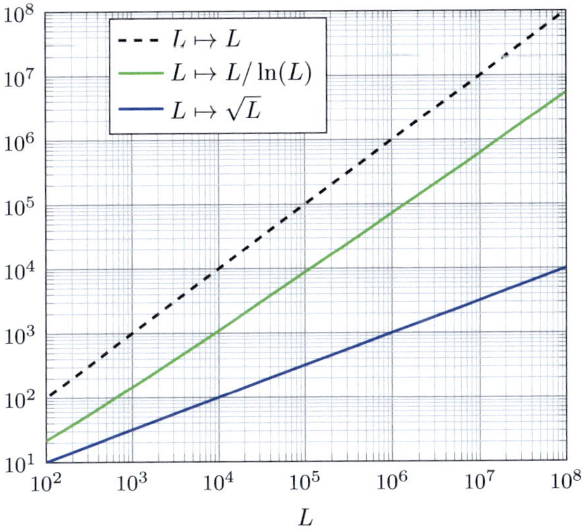

Figure 4.5: Asymptotic behaviours of $L \mapsto L/\ln(L)$ and $L \mapsto \sqrt{L}$ compared to $L \mapsto L$.

and

$$\beta := D_{KL}\left(\frac{1+\tilde{\eta}}{2}p \,\middle\|\, p\right). \tag{4.152}$$

Note that $\alpha > 0$, and $\beta > 0$, because of Lemma B.4 (given in Appendix B.2). Then, we have

$$\lim_{L\to\infty}\left(2LNe^{-\frac{1}{8}(1-\tilde{\eta})^2p^2(1-p)^2\frac{L}{N}} + LNe^{-D_{KL}\left(\frac{1+\tilde{\eta}}{2}p\|p\right)L}\right) \tag{4.153}$$

$$= \lim_{L\to\infty}\frac{2LN}{e^{\alpha\frac{L}{N}}} + \lim_{L\to\infty}\frac{LN}{e^{\beta L}} \tag{4.154}$$

$$= \lim_{L\to\infty}\frac{2\alpha\frac{L^2}{\ln(L^2)}}{e^{\ln(L^2)}} + \lim_{L\to\infty}\frac{\alpha\frac{L^2}{\ln(L^2)}}{e^{\beta L}} \tag{4.155}$$

$$= \lim_{L\to\infty}\frac{2\alpha}{\ln(L^2)} + \lim_{x\to\infty}\frac{\alpha\ln(x)^2}{2\ln(\ln(x))x^{\beta}} \tag{4.156}$$

$$= 0 + \lim_{x\to\infty}\frac{\alpha}{2\ln(\ln(x))}\left(\frac{\ln(x)}{x^{\beta/2}}\right)^2 \tag{4.157}$$

$$= 0. \tag{4.158}$$

In (4.154) we applied (4.151) and (4.152), and in (4.155) we applied the condition (4.144), i.e., $N = \alpha L/\ln(L^2)$. From (4.155) to (4.156) we did the variable substitution $x := e^L$. Finally, (4.158) follows from Lemma B.14 given in Appendix B.8. ■

4.3 Multi-pass Memorization

Perfect memorization can also be achieved via a certain least-squares problem, and solving this least-squares problem via gradient descent methods can be phrased as multi-pass learning according to (3.12) – (3.14) given in Section 3.2.

Let $i \in \{1, \dots, L\}$ be fixed but arbitrary. We recall that the network perfectly memorizes the i-th channel of $\boldsymbol{Y}$ if and only if (cf. (4.2))

$$\xi_i(\boldsymbol{y}[n-1]) = y_i[n], \qquad n \in \{0, \dots, N-1\}. \tag{4.159}$$

In this section, our approach is to choose a weight vector $\boldsymbol{w}_i \in \mathbb{R}^L$ which minimizes some cost

$$\mathrm{Cost}_i(\boldsymbol{w}_i) := \sum_{n=0}^{N-1} \kappa\big(\xi_i(\boldsymbol{y}[n-1]) - y_i[n]\big), \tag{4.160}$$

where $\kappa\colon \mathbb{R} \to \mathbb{R}_{\geq 0}$ could potentially be any nonnegative-valued function. In order to obtain a (linear) least-squares problem we use the function $\kappa(x) := |x|^2$, $x \in \mathbb{R}$, and we replace the neuron's output directly by $\big\langle \boldsymbol{y}[n-1], \boldsymbol{w}_i \big\rangle$. Then, the cost (4.160) can be written as

$$\begin{aligned}
\mathrm{Cost}_i(\boldsymbol{w}_i) &= \sum_{n=0}^{N-1} \Big(\big\langle \boldsymbol{y}[n-1], \boldsymbol{w}_i \big\rangle - y_i[n]\Big)^2 &\quad (4.161)\\
&= \sum_{n=0}^{N-1} \big(\boldsymbol{y}[n-1]^{\mathsf{T}} \boldsymbol{w}_i - y_i[n]\big)^2 &\quad (4.162)\\
&= \left\| \begin{pmatrix} \boldsymbol{y}[N-1]^{\mathsf{T}} \boldsymbol{w}_i - y_i[0] \\ \boldsymbol{y}[0]^{\mathsf{T}} \boldsymbol{w}_i - y_i[1] \\ \vdots \\ \boldsymbol{y}[N-2]^{\mathsf{T}} \boldsymbol{w}_i - y_i[N-1] \end{pmatrix} \right\|^2 &\quad (4.163)\\
&= \big\| \tilde{\boldsymbol{Y}} \boldsymbol{w}_i - \tilde{\boldsymbol{y}}_i \big\|^2, &\quad (4.164)
\end{aligned}$$

where

$$\tilde{\boldsymbol{Y}} := \begin{pmatrix} \boldsymbol{y}[N-1]^{\mathsf{T}} \\ \boldsymbol{y}[0]^{\mathsf{T}} \\ \vdots \\ \boldsymbol{y}[N-2]^{\mathsf{T}} \end{pmatrix} \in \mathbb{R}^{N \times L} \tag{4.165}$$

is the transposed matrix of $\big(\boldsymbol{y}[N-1], \boldsymbol{y}[0], \ldots, \boldsymbol{y}[N-2]\big) \in \mathbb{R}^{L\times N}$, i.e., of the one time-step cyclic-shifted version of $\boldsymbol{Y}$, and

$$\tilde{\boldsymbol{y}}_i := \begin{pmatrix} y_i[0] \\ \vdots \\ y_i[N-1] \end{pmatrix} \in \mathbb{R}^N \tag{4.166}$$

is the i-th row of $\boldsymbol{Y}$ turned into a column vector.

Proposition 4.4. *If the firing sequence* $\boldsymbol{Y} \in \{0,1\}^{L\times N}$, *for* $L, N \in \mathbb{N}$, *satisfies*

$$\operatorname{rank}(\boldsymbol{Y}) = N, \tag{4.167}$$

then $\boldsymbol{Y}$ *is perfectly memorized by the recurrent network with weight vectors minimizing the quadratic cost (4.164), thresholds*

$$\theta_i := \theta := \frac{1}{2}, \qquad i \in \{1, \ldots, L\}, \tag{4.168}$$

and disturbance bound

$$\eta := \frac{1}{2}, \tag{4.169}$$

i.e., $\big(\xi_1(\boldsymbol{y}[n-1]), \ldots, \xi_L(\boldsymbol{y}[n-1])\big)^\mathsf{T} = \big(y_1[n], \ldots, y_L[n]\big)^\mathsf{T}$ *holds for all* $n \in \{0, \ldots, N-1\}$. □

Note that condition (4.167) implies $L \geq N$.

Proof of Proposition 4.4. By definition (4.165) of $\tilde{\boldsymbol{Y}} \in \{0,1\}^{N\times L}$, we have

$$\begin{aligned} \operatorname{rank}(\tilde{\boldsymbol{Y}}) &= \operatorname{rank}(\boldsymbol{Y}^\mathsf{T}) && (4.170)\\ &= \operatorname{rank}(\boldsymbol{Y}) && (4.171)\\ &= N, && (4.172) \end{aligned}$$

where (4.170) holds because $\tilde{\boldsymbol{Y}}$ is obtained by a column-permutation of $\boldsymbol{Y}^\mathsf{T}$, which preserves the rank. From (4.170) to (4.171) we applied a standard rank property, and (4.172) holds by assumption (4.167).

Condition (4.172) implies that for any $\tilde{\boldsymbol{y}}_i \in \mathbb{R}^N$ there exists $\boldsymbol{w}_i \in \mathbb{R}^L$ such that

$$\left\|\tilde{\boldsymbol{Y}}\boldsymbol{w}_i - \tilde{\boldsymbol{y}}_i\right\|^2 = 0, \tag{4.173}$$

which implies (cf. (4.161) – (4.164))

$$\sum_{n=0}^{N-1} \Big(\langle \boldsymbol{y}[n-1], \boldsymbol{w}_i \rangle - y_i[n]\Big)^2 = 0 \tag{4.174}$$

$$\Longrightarrow \ \big\langle \boldsymbol{y}[n-1], \boldsymbol{w}_i \big\rangle = y_i[n], \qquad n \in \{0, \dots, N-1\} \tag{4.175}$$

$$\Longrightarrow \ \sigma_{1/2}\big(\langle \boldsymbol{y}[n-1], \boldsymbol{w}_i \rangle + \eta_i\big) = y_i[n], \quad n \in \{0, \dots, N-1\} \tag{4.176}$$

$$\Longrightarrow \ \xi_i(\boldsymbol{y}[n-1]) = y_i[n], \qquad n \in \{0, \dots, N-1\}, \tag{4.177}$$

for

$$-1/2 < \eta_i < 1/2. \tag{4.178}$$

The step from (4.175) to (4.176) follows because if (4.175) and (4.178) both hold, then, for $y_i[n] = 0$, we obtain

$$\sigma_{1/2}\big(\langle \boldsymbol{y}[n-1], \boldsymbol{w}_i \rangle + \eta_i\big) = \sigma_{1/2}\big(0 + \eta_i\big) \tag{4.179}$$

$$= 0, \tag{4.180}$$

and if (4.175) and (4.178) both hold, then, for $y_i[n] = 1$, we obtain

$$\sigma_{1/2}\big(\langle \boldsymbol{y}[n-1], \boldsymbol{w}_i \rangle + \eta_i\big) = \sigma_{1/2}\big(1 + \eta_i\big) \tag{4.181}$$

$$= 1. \tag{4.182}$$

Finally, (4.177) holds by definition of ξ_i, cf. (2.3) from Section 2.1. ■

Random Firing Sequences

To study the memorization capacity (in Chapter 5), we once more consider random firing sequences $\boldsymbol{Y} \overset{\text{i.i.d.}}{\sim} \text{Ber}(p)^{L\times N}$, for $0 < p \leq 1/2$. By Proposition 4.4, we have

$$\Pr[\mathcal{E}_{\boldsymbol{Y}}^{\text{c}}] \geq \Pr\big[\,\text{rank}(\boldsymbol{Y}) = N\,\big] \tag{4.183}$$

$$\geq 1 - \big(1 - p + o_N(1)\big)^N, \tag{4.184}$$

where (4.184) follows from [67], and $o_N(1)$ denotes a sequence which converges to zero, i.e., $\lim_{N\to\infty} o_N(1) = 0$, and thus

$$\Pr[\mathcal{E}_{\boldsymbol{Y}}] \leq \big(1 - p + o_N(1)\big)^N \xrightarrow{N\to\infty} 0. \tag{4.185}$$

Thus, any $\boldsymbol{Y} \overset{\text{i.i.d.}}{\sim} \text{Ber}(p)^{L\times N}$ with $L \geq N$, and in particular with

$$N = L \tag{4.186}$$

is perfectly memorizable for $N \to \infty$.

Proposition 4.4 states that the (optimal) weight vector is a minimizer of the quadratic (or least-squares) cost

$$\mathrm{Cost}_i(\boldsymbol{w}_i) = \left\|\tilde{\boldsymbol{Y}}\boldsymbol{w}_i - \tilde{\boldsymbol{y}}_i\right\|^2. \tag{4.187}$$

Now, we examine how such a weight vector can be determined (theoretically and then practically).

Analytical Closed-form Solutions

Recall that $\boldsymbol{w}_i \in \mathbb{R}^L$ minimizes (4.187) if and only if

$$\tilde{\boldsymbol{Y}}^\mathsf{T}\tilde{\boldsymbol{Y}}\boldsymbol{w}_i = \tilde{\boldsymbol{Y}}^\mathsf{T}\tilde{\boldsymbol{y}}_i. \tag{4.188}$$

Assuming that $\tilde{\boldsymbol{Y}}^\mathsf{T}\tilde{\boldsymbol{Y}} \in \mathbb{R}^{L\times L}$ is invertible (which implies $N \geq L$), then we obtain

$$\begin{align}
\boldsymbol{w}_i &= \left(\tilde{\boldsymbol{Y}}^\mathsf{T}\tilde{\boldsymbol{Y}}\right)^{-1}\tilde{\boldsymbol{Y}}^\mathsf{T}\tilde{\boldsymbol{y}}_i \tag{4.189}\\
&= \left(\tilde{\boldsymbol{Y}}^\mathsf{T}\tilde{\boldsymbol{Y}}\right)^{-1}\big(\boldsymbol{y}[N-1], \boldsymbol{y}[0], \ldots, \boldsymbol{y}[N-2]\big)\begin{pmatrix} y_i[0] \\ \vdots \\ y_i[N-1]\end{pmatrix} \tag{4.190}\\
&= \left(\tilde{\boldsymbol{Y}}^\mathsf{T}\tilde{\boldsymbol{Y}}\right)^{-1}\sum_{n=0}^{N-1} y_i[n]\boldsymbol{y}[n-1] \tag{4.191}\\
&= \sum_{n=0}^{N-1} y_i[n]\underbrace{\left(\tilde{\boldsymbol{Y}}^\mathsf{T}\tilde{\boldsymbol{Y}}\right)^{-1}\boldsymbol{y}[n-1]}_{=:\,\boldsymbol{r}[n-1]} \tag{4.192}\\
&= \sum_{n\in J_i}\boldsymbol{r}[n-1], \tag{4.193}
\end{align}$$

where

$$\begin{align}
\tilde{\boldsymbol{Y}}^\mathsf{T}\tilde{\boldsymbol{Y}} &= \big(\boldsymbol{y}[N-1], \boldsymbol{y}[0], \ldots, \boldsymbol{y}[N-2]\big)\begin{pmatrix} \boldsymbol{y}[N-1]^\mathsf{T} \\ \boldsymbol{y}[0] \\ \vdots \\ \boldsymbol{y}[N-2]^\mathsf{T}\end{pmatrix} \tag{4.194}\\
&= \sum_{n=0}^{N-1}\boldsymbol{y}[n]\boldsymbol{y}[n]^\mathsf{T}. \tag{4.195}
\end{align}$$

Note the similarity of (4.193) with (4.4) and (4.91). In Appendix B.6, we derive (4.193) via Gaussian message passing.

Moreover, $\tilde{\boldsymbol{Y}}^\mathsf{T}\tilde{\boldsymbol{Y}}$ is the Gramian matrix of $\tilde{\boldsymbol{y}}_1, \ldots, \tilde{\boldsymbol{y}}_L \in \mathbb{R}^N$, i.e., of the rows of $\boldsymbol{Y}$, because

$$\left(\tilde{\boldsymbol{Y}}^\mathsf{T}\tilde{\boldsymbol{Y}}\right)_{i,j} = \sum_{n=0}^{N-1} y_i[n] y_j[n] \tag{4.196}$$

$$= \tilde{\boldsymbol{y}}_i^\mathsf{T} \tilde{\boldsymbol{y}}_j \tag{4.197}$$

$$= \langle \tilde{\boldsymbol{y}}_i, \tilde{\boldsymbol{y}}_j \rangle. \tag{4.198}$$

Thus, $\tilde{\boldsymbol{Y}}^\mathsf{T}\tilde{\boldsymbol{Y}}$ is symmetric positive-semidefinite

$$\boldsymbol{x}^\mathsf{T}\tilde{\boldsymbol{Y}}^\mathsf{T}\tilde{\boldsymbol{Y}}\boldsymbol{x} = \boldsymbol{x}^\mathsf{T}\left(\sum_{n=0}^{N-1} \boldsymbol{y}[n]\boldsymbol{y}[n]^\mathsf{T}\right)\boldsymbol{x} \tag{4.199}$$

$$= \sum_{n=0}^{N-1} \boldsymbol{x}^\mathsf{T}\boldsymbol{y}[n]\boldsymbol{y}[n]^\mathsf{T}\boldsymbol{x} \tag{4.200}$$

$$= \sum_{n=0}^{N-1} \boldsymbol{x}^\mathsf{T}\boldsymbol{y}[n] \underbrace{\left(\boldsymbol{x}^\mathsf{T}\boldsymbol{y}[n]\right)^\mathsf{T}}_{\in \mathbb{R}} \tag{4.201}$$

$$= \sum_{n=0}^{N-1} \left(\boldsymbol{x}^\mathsf{T}\boldsymbol{y}[n]\right)^2 \tag{4.202}$$

$$\geq 0, \tag{4.203}$$

for all $\boldsymbol{x} \in \mathbb{R}^L$.

If $L > N$, then $\tilde{\boldsymbol{Y}}^\mathsf{T}\tilde{\boldsymbol{Y}} \in \mathbb{R}^{L \times L}$ is not invertible, and (4.188) has typically infinitely many solutions. E.g., if we choose $\boldsymbol{w}_i^\dagger := \tilde{\boldsymbol{Y}}^\dagger \tilde{\boldsymbol{y}}_i$ with pseudoinverse

$$\tilde{\boldsymbol{Y}}^\dagger := \lim_{\lambda \to 0} \left(\tilde{\boldsymbol{Y}}^\mathsf{T}\tilde{\boldsymbol{Y}} + \lambda^2 \boldsymbol{I}_L\right)^{-1} \tilde{\boldsymbol{Y}}^\mathsf{T}, \tag{4.204}$$

then $\boldsymbol{w}_i^\dagger$ minimizes (4.187), and in addition $\left\|\boldsymbol{w}_i^\dagger\right\| \leq \|\boldsymbol{w}_i^*\|$, for all $\boldsymbol{w}_i^*$ which also minimize (4.187).

Gradient Descent Methods

The least-squares problem could also be solved by gradient descent methods. To this end, we compute the gradient of (4.187) w.r.t. the weight vector $\boldsymbol{w} = (w_1, \ldots, w_L)^\mathsf{T} \in \mathbb{R}^L$. For $\ell \in \{1, \ldots, L\}$, we have

$$\begin{aligned}
&\frac{\partial}{\partial w_\ell} \left\| \tilde{\boldsymbol{Y}} \boldsymbol{w} - \tilde{\boldsymbol{y}}_i \right\|^2 \\
&\quad = \frac{\partial}{\partial w_\ell} \sum_{n=0}^{N-1} \left(\boldsymbol{y}[n-1]^\mathsf{T} \boldsymbol{w} - y_i[n] \right)^2 && (4.205) \\
&\quad = 2 \sum_{n=0}^{N-1} \left(\boldsymbol{y}[n-1]^\mathsf{T} \boldsymbol{w} - y_i[n] \right) y_\ell[n-1] && (4.206) \\
&\quad = 2 \underbrace{\left(y_\ell[N-1], y_\ell[0], \ldots, y_\ell[N-2] \right)}_{\ell\text{-th row of } \tilde{\boldsymbol{Y}}^\mathsf{T}} \left(\tilde{\boldsymbol{Y}} \boldsymbol{w} - \tilde{\boldsymbol{y}}_i \right), && (4.207)
\end{aligned}$$

and thus

$$\begin{aligned}
&\nabla_{\boldsymbol{w}} \left\| \tilde{\boldsymbol{Y}} \boldsymbol{w} - \tilde{\boldsymbol{y}}_i \right\|^2 \\
&\quad = \begin{pmatrix} \frac{\partial}{\partial w_1} \left\| \tilde{\boldsymbol{Y}} \boldsymbol{w} - \tilde{\boldsymbol{y}}_i \right\|^2 \\ \vdots \\ \frac{\partial}{\partial w_L} \left\| \tilde{\boldsymbol{Y}} \boldsymbol{w} - \tilde{\boldsymbol{y}}_i \right\|^2 \end{pmatrix} && (4.208) \\
&\quad = 2 \begin{pmatrix} y_1[N-1] & y_1[0] & \cdots & y_1[N-2] \\ \vdots & \vdots & & \vdots \\ y_L[N-1] & y_L[0] & \cdots & y_L[N-2] \end{pmatrix} \left(\tilde{\boldsymbol{Y}} \boldsymbol{w} - \tilde{\boldsymbol{y}}_i \right) && (4.209) \\
&\quad = 2 \tilde{\boldsymbol{Y}}^\mathsf{T} \left(\tilde{\boldsymbol{Y}} \boldsymbol{w} - \tilde{\boldsymbol{y}}_i \right). && (4.210)
\end{aligned}$$

Now, starting from some initial guess $\boldsymbol{w}_i^{(0)} \in \mathbb{R}^L$ (e.g., $\boldsymbol{w}_i^{(0)} := \boldsymbol{0}_L$) we proceed by

$$\begin{aligned}
\boldsymbol{w}_i^{(n+1)} &= \boldsymbol{w}_i^{(n)} - \tilde{\gamma}^{(n)} \nabla_{\boldsymbol{w}} \left\| \tilde{\boldsymbol{Y}} \boldsymbol{w} - \tilde{\boldsymbol{y}}_i \right\|^2 \Big|_{\boldsymbol{w} = \boldsymbol{w}_i^{(n)}} && (4.211) \\
&= \boldsymbol{w}_i^{(n)} + \gamma^{(n)} \tilde{\boldsymbol{Y}}^\mathsf{T} \left(\tilde{\boldsymbol{y}}_i - \tilde{\boldsymbol{Y}} \boldsymbol{w}_i^{(n)} \right), && (4.212)
\end{aligned}$$

for $n \in \{0, 1, \ldots, N_\text{it}\}$, $N_\text{it} \in \mathbb{N}$, and with step size (or learning rate) $\gamma^{(n)} > 0$. The recursion (4.212) with constant step size $\gamma^{(n)} := \gamma$, for all n, converges to a minimizer of $\left\| \tilde{\boldsymbol{Y}} \boldsymbol{w}_i - \tilde{\boldsymbol{y}}_i \right\|^2$ if

$$0 < \gamma < \frac{2}{\lambda_\text{max}(\tilde{\boldsymbol{Y}}^\mathsf{T} \tilde{\boldsymbol{Y}})}, \qquad (4.213)$$

where $\lambda_{\max}(\tilde{\boldsymbol{Y}}^\mathsf{T}\tilde{\boldsymbol{Y}}) > 0$ denotes the largest eigenvalue of $\tilde{\boldsymbol{Y}}^\mathsf{T}\tilde{\boldsymbol{Y}}$.

Replacing gradient descent as in (4.212) by stochastic gradient descent yields

$$\boldsymbol{w}_i^{(n+1)} = \boldsymbol{w}_i^{(n)} + \gamma^{(n)} \left(y_i[n] - \langle \boldsymbol{y}[n-1], \boldsymbol{w}_i^{(n)} \rangle \right) \boldsymbol{y}[n-1], \tag{4.214}$$

which is (3.14). (Recall, the time indices of $y_i[\cdot]$ and $\boldsymbol{y}[\cdot]$ in (4.214) are taken modulo N.) From (4.212) to (4.214) we approximated each component of the gradient by a single summand in (4.206), instead of taking the whole sum on the right-hand side of (4.206). Better performance can be achieved by approximating the sum on the right-hand side of (4.206) not only with a single term but with multiple terms, which results in

$$\boldsymbol{w}_i^{(n+1)} = \boldsymbol{w}_i^{(n)} + \gamma^{(n)} \sum_{\tilde{n} \in \mathcal{B}_n} \left(y_i[\tilde{n}] - \langle \boldsymbol{y}[\tilde{n}-1], \boldsymbol{w}_i^{(n)} \rangle \right) \boldsymbol{y}[\tilde{n}-1], \tag{4.215}$$

for some subset (usually called batch) $\mathcal{B}_n \subset \{0, 1, \ldots, N-1\}$ at every iteration step $n \in \{0, 1, \ldots, N_{\text{it}}\}$, $N_{\text{it}} \gg N$.

It is shown in [64] that if at every iteration step the time indices of $y_i[\cdot]$ and $\boldsymbol{y}[\cdot]$ in (4.214) are chosen randomly, then (4.214) converges exponentially in expectation to a minimizer of $\left\| \tilde{\boldsymbol{Y}} \boldsymbol{w}_i - \tilde{\boldsymbol{y}}_i \right\|^2$.

A comparison of the recursions (4.212), (4.214), and (4.215) is given in Section 3.2.

4.3.1 Auxiliary Channels

For a given firing sequence $\boldsymbol{Y} \in \{0,1\}^{L \times N}$, let

$$\boldsymbol{Y}_{\text{aux}} := \begin{pmatrix} \boldsymbol{Y} \\ \boldsymbol{I}_N \end{pmatrix} \in \{0,1\}^{(L+N) \times N}, \tag{4.216}$$

where $\boldsymbol{I}_N \in \{0,1\}^{N \times N}$ denotes the $N \times N$ identity matrix. Clearly, $\text{rank}(\boldsymbol{Y}_{\text{aux}}) = N$, and thus by Proposition 4.4 $\boldsymbol{Y}_{\text{aux}}$ is perfectly memorizable. Since $\boldsymbol{Y}$ is uniquely identifiable from $\boldsymbol{Y}_{\text{aux}}$, every L-channel firing sequence of length N is memorizable with multi-pass learning by a recurrent network consisting of $L + N$ neurons.

Weights

Let $\boldsymbol{e}_k \in \{0,1\}^K$, $K \in \mathbb{N}$, be the unit column-vector (of any dimension $K \geq k$) with a single one at index $k \in \{1, \ldots, K\}$ and zeros elsewhere.

As above, for $i \in \{1, \dots, L+N\}$, the i-th weight vector $\boldsymbol{w}_i \in \mathbb{R}^{L+N}$ can be determined by applying gradient descent methods to the quadratic cost

$$\left\| \tilde{\boldsymbol{Y}}_{\text{aux}} \boldsymbol{w}_i - \tilde{\boldsymbol{y}}_{\text{aux},i} \right\|^2, \tag{4.217}$$

where

$$\tilde{\boldsymbol{Y}}_{\text{aux}} := \begin{pmatrix} \boldsymbol{y}[N-1]^\mathsf{T} & \boldsymbol{e}_N^\mathsf{T} \\ \boldsymbol{y}[0]^\mathsf{T} & \boldsymbol{e}_1^\mathsf{T} \\ \vdots & \vdots \\ \boldsymbol{y}[N-2]^\mathsf{T} & \boldsymbol{e}_{N-1}^\mathsf{T} \end{pmatrix} = \begin{pmatrix} \tilde{\boldsymbol{Y}} & \tilde{\boldsymbol{I}}_N \end{pmatrix} \in \{0,1\}^{N \times (L+N)} \tag{4.218}$$

with $\tilde{\boldsymbol{Y}} \in \{0,1\}^{N \times L}$ as in (4.165), and

$$\tilde{\boldsymbol{I}}_N := \begin{pmatrix} \boldsymbol{0}_{N-1}^\mathsf{T} & 1 \\ \boldsymbol{I}_{N-1} & \boldsymbol{0}_{N-1} \end{pmatrix} \in \{0,1\}^{N \times N}, \tag{4.219}$$

and

$$\tilde{\boldsymbol{y}}_{\text{aux},i} := \begin{cases} \tilde{\boldsymbol{y}}_i, & \text{if } i \in \{1, \dots, L\} \\ \boldsymbol{e}_{i-L}, & \text{if } i \in \{L+1, \dots, L+N\} \end{cases} \tag{4.220}$$

with $\tilde{\boldsymbol{y}}_i \in \{0,1\}^N$ as in (4.166).

Memorization Capacity

The memorization capacity is introduced in Chapter 5. Since the network with N auxiliary channels is able to memorize any firing sequence $\boldsymbol{Y} \in \{0,1\}^{L \times N}$, the total number of bits which can be memorized by the network is equal to the number of all firing sequences contained in $\{0,1\}^{L \times N}$. Thus, we have

$$C_{\text{tot}} = LN \qquad [\,\text{bits}\,], \tag{4.221}$$

$$C_{\text{neuron}} = \frac{LN}{L+N} \qquad [\,\text{bits per neuron}\,], \tag{4.222}$$

$$C_{\text{synapse}} = \frac{LN}{(L+N)^2} \qquad [\,\text{bits per connection}\,]. \tag{4.223}$$

Note that the recurrent network is fully connected and consists of $L+N$ neurons.

Because the network with auxiliary channels is able to memorize firing sequences of any length, we want to choose N such that C_{synapse} is asymptotically, i.e., for $L \to \infty$, as large as possible. Note that (4.223) vanishes as $L \to \infty$ if $N \geq L^2$, or if $N = N_0$, for any constant $N_0 \in \mathbb{N}$. For $N = cL$, $c > 0$, we obtain

$$C_{\text{synapse}} = \frac{cL^2}{(L + cL)^2} \tag{4.224}$$

$$= \frac{c}{(1 + c)^2}, \tag{4.225}$$

which is maximized for $c = 1$ and yields

$$C_{\text{synapse}} = \frac{1}{4} \text{ [bits per connection]}. \tag{4.226}$$

Thus, choosing $N = L$ results in a nonvanishing capacity measured in bits per connection comparable to (5.15).

Chapter 5

Memorization Capacity

We define the memorization capacity of a network (as introduced in Chapter 2) to be the number of all firing sequences which can be perfectly memorized. Clearly, if a learning rule is able to perfectly memorize all $\boldsymbol{Y} \in \{0,1\}^{L \times N}$, then the (total) capacity would be $C_{\text{tot}} = LN$ bits.

In Chapter 4, we state under which conditions random firing sequences $\boldsymbol{Y} \overset{\text{i.i.d.}}{\sim} \text{Ber}(p)^{L \times N}$ are asymptotically memorizable with single-pass (one-shot) or multi-pass learning. Thus, at least the set of all firing sequences that are typical to $\boldsymbol{Y} \overset{\text{i.i.d.}}{\sim} \text{Ber}(p)^{L \times N}$, which we denote by $\mathcal{Y}_{\text{typical}}^{(L,N)}(p)$, can be memorized by the two learning rules (4.99) (single-pass) and (4.212) (multi-pass). A rigorous definition of $\mathcal{Y}_{\text{typical}}^{(L,N)}(p)$ is given in Appendix B.3, where we also prove the most fundamental properties of the typical set $\mathcal{Y}_{\text{typical}}^{(L,N)}(p)$. Lemma B.10 (for $\varepsilon \to 0$) on page 163 states that the size of $\mathcal{Y}_{\text{typical}}^{(L,N)}(p)$ is

$$\left|\mathcal{Y}_{\text{typical}}^{(L,N)}(p)\right| \approx 2^{LNH_b(p)}, \tag{5.1}$$

for L sufficiently large, and

$$\lim_{L\to\infty} \frac{1}{L} \log_2\!\left(\left|\mathcal{Y}_{\text{typical}}^{(L,N)}(p)\right|\right) = NH_b(p), \tag{5.2}$$

where

$$H_b(p) := -p\log_2(p) - (1-p)\log_2(1-p), \tag{5.3}$$

for $0 < p < 1$, is the binary entropy function, i.e., the entropy [11] of

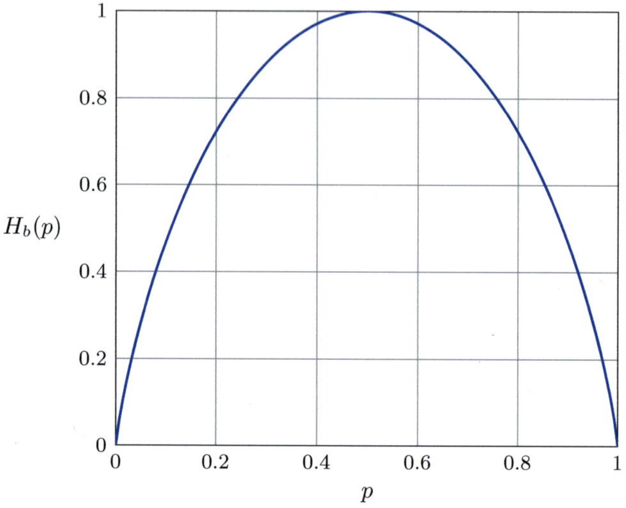

Figure 5.1: Graph of the binary entropy function.

$X \sim \text{Ber}(p)$. Note that

$$0 < H_b(p) \leq 1, \qquad 0 < p < 1, \tag{5.4}$$

where the upper bound holds with equality if and only if $p = 1/2$, cf. Figure 5.1.

Thus, from (5.1) we obtain the lower bound

$$C_{\text{tot}} \geq \log_2\left(\left|\mathcal{Y}^{(L,N)}_{\text{typical}}(p)\right|\right) \tag{5.5}$$

$$\approx LNH_b(p) \ \ [\,\text{bits}\,] \tag{5.6}$$

on the total memorization capacity. Next, we compare the capacities of the two learning modes (single-pass vs. multi-pass) by applying the asymptotically achievable lengths N from Chapter 4, and by normalizing the capacity with the number of neurons (Section 5.1) or with the number of connections (Section 5.2).

5.1 Capacity per Neuron

Recall, the network we are considering consists of L neurons. Thus, from (5.5) and (5.2) it follows that the asymptotic memorization capacity measured in bits per neuron is lower bounded by

$$\begin{aligned} C_{\text{neuron}} &= \frac{1}{L} C_{\text{tot}} && (5.7) \\ &\geq \frac{1}{L} \log_2\left(\left|\mathcal{Y}_{\text{typical}}^{(L,N)}(p)\right|\right) && (5.8) \\ &= H_b(p) N \;\; [\text{bits per neuron}], && (5.9) \end{aligned}$$

for $L \to \infty$.

For the single-pass learning rule (4.99), Corollary 4.1 states that the length $N = C_{p,\tilde{\eta}}\, L/\ln(L)$ is asymptotically achievable. Thus, from (5.9) we obtain

$$C_{\text{single-pass}} \geq H_b(p) C_{p,\tilde{\eta}} \frac{L}{\ln(L)} \;\; [\text{bits per neuron}] \tag{5.10}$$

with constant

$$C_{p,\tilde{\eta}} := \frac{1}{16}(1-\tilde{\eta})^2 p^2 (1-p)^2 > 0, \tag{5.11}$$

for $0 < p, \tilde{\eta} < 1$.

For the multi-pass learning rule (4.212), the length $N = L$ is asymptotically achievable, cf. (4.186). Thus, from (5.9) we obtain

$$C_{\text{multi-pass}} \geq H_b(p) L \;\; [\text{bits per neuron}]. \tag{5.12}$$

Both memorization capacities $C_{\text{single-pass}}$ and $C_{\text{multi-pass}}$ (in bits per neuron) are unbounded in L.

5.2 Capacity per Connection

The capacity per connection (i.e., per nonzero weight) is

$$C_{\text{synapse}} = \frac{1}{L} C_{\text{neuron}} \quad [\,\text{bits per connection}\,], \tag{5.13}$$

because in both learning modes the network is fully connected. Then, from (5.10) and (5.12) we obtain

$$C_{\text{single-pass}} \geq H_b(p) C_{p,\tilde{\eta}} \frac{1}{\ln(L)} \quad [\,\text{bits per connection}\,], \tag{5.14}$$

$$C_{\text{multi-pass}} \geq H_b(p) \quad [\,\text{bits per connection}\,]. \tag{5.15}$$

Thus, in bits per connection the capacity $C_{\text{single-pass}}$ seems to vanish, whereas $C_{\text{multi-pass}}$ does not vanish for $L \to \infty$.

5.3 Comparison with the Hopfield Network

The capacity of the Hopfield model consisting of L neurons is $L/(2\ln(L))$ vectors with the Hebbian learning rule [45], and $L/\sqrt{2\ln(L)}$ vectors with the Storkey learning rule [63]. However, for a fair comparison with the results presented in this thesis, it should be noted that each vector consists of L random bits, resulting in a capacity of $L/(2\ln(L))$ bits per neuron and $L/\sqrt{2\ln(L)}$ bits per neuron, respectively.

It follows that the capacity (5.10) of single-pass memorization is (at least) of the same order as the capacity of the Hopfield model with Hebbian learning while the capacity (5.12) of multi-pass learning exceeds the capacity of the Hopfield model.

Table 5.1 summarizes all the asymptotic memorization capacities. The last row in this table points out that the capacity of the Hopfield model is on the same order as the single-pass capacity, which both vanish in terms of bits per connection (i.e., per synapse). By contrast, multiple-rounds memorization achieves a significantly higher capacity, with a nonvanishing number of bits per connection/synapse and exceeding the capacity of the Hopfield network. The (important) ability of single-pass online memorization thus appears to be bought at the expense of a smaller capacity. These mathematical findings may be of interest for understanding the functionality of short-term memory and long-term memory in neuroscience [3, 4, 12, 47].

Asymptotic capacity in	Hopfield	Single-pass	Multi-pass
bits	$\frac{1}{2}\frac{L^2}{\ln(L)}$	$C_{p,\tilde{\eta}}H_b(p)\frac{L^2}{\ln(L)}$	$H_b(p)L^2$
bits per neuron	$\frac{1}{2}\frac{L}{\ln(L)}$	$C_{p,\tilde{\eta}}H_b(p)\frac{L}{\ln(L)}$	$H_b(p)L$
bits per connection	$\frac{1}{2}\frac{1}{\ln(L)}$	$C_{p,\tilde{\eta}}H_b(p)\frac{1}{\ln(L)}$	$H_b(p)$

Table 5.1: Asymptotic memorization capacities.

Chapter 6

Some Extensions

We finish this part by addressing some practical aspects. This hopefully contributes to make the proposed model more attractive towards practical applications. The analyses given in this chapter are not rigorous, they rather sketch out some further ideas.

In Section 6.1, we again point out (by generalizing the initialization) that the discussed recurrent network implements the functionality of an (auto)associative memory. Sections 6.2 and 6.3 propose extensions of the analyzed network. We consider the network as in Chapter 2 but with multiple connections between the neurons. We roughly sketch in which order this extension improves the performance of the network, and additionally we show that this extension can be seen as a correlation over a window of multiple input vectors instead of only a single input vector. Then, we also provide a more sophisticated recalling process, where only desired sections of the memorized firing sequence can be recalled. Finally, in Section 6.4 we present a way to memorize *any* firing sequence with online/instantaneous (single-pass) learning as described in Section 4.2. The whole network consists of two separate networks (from Chapter 2) running in parallel as shown in Figure 6.4. The XOR operation turns the whole network into a biologically implausible system. Nonetheless, the obtained network may be interesting as such, or as a system for processing pulsed/spiking signals in general.

6.1 Associative Recall & Error-correcting Capability

The main property of an associative (or content-addressable) memory is the capability to recall a memorized pattern from an incomplete information content of that pattern. In our case, the recurrent network clearly has that property, since it reproduces (or recalls) a memorized firing sequence from the initialization of a single column of that firing sequence.

Moreover, associative memories enable also error-correcting in the sense that the memorized pattern can be recalled even from an *erroneous* incomplete information content of that memorized pattern, e.g., [60]. To demonstrate this capability, let us assume that the network perfectly memorizes the firing sequence $\bar{\boldsymbol{Y}} = (\bar{\boldsymbol{y}}[0], \bar{\boldsymbol{y}}[1], \dots, \bar{\boldsymbol{y}}[N{-}1]) \in \{0,1\}^{L\times N}$. Then, as long as we initialize the network with

$$\boldsymbol{y}[0] := \bar{\boldsymbol{y}}[0] + \boldsymbol{e}, \tag{6.1}$$

where the error $\boldsymbol{e} \in \mathbb{R}^L$ satisfies

$$\|\boldsymbol{e}\| < \frac{\eta}{\max_{i\in\{1,\dots,L\}} \|\boldsymbol{w}_i\|}, \tag{6.2}$$

the network perfectly reproduces $\bar{\boldsymbol{Y}}$.

Now, we justify why in this case the network still reproduces $\bar{\boldsymbol{Y}}$. Since $\bar{\boldsymbol{Y}}$ is perfectly memorized, we only need to establish $\xi_i(\boldsymbol{y}[0]) = \bar{y}_i[1]$, for all i, since $\xi_i(\bar{\boldsymbol{y}}[n-1]) = \bar{y}_i[n]$, for $n \geq 2$, holds by assumption for all i. For the sake of convenience, we assume that the only disturbance (at the beginning) comes from an erroneous initialization as in (6.1). Thus, we obtain

$$\begin{aligned}
\xi_i(\boldsymbol{y}[0]) &= \sigma_{\theta_i}\big(\langle \boldsymbol{y}[0], \boldsymbol{w}_i\rangle\big) && (6.3)\\
&= \sigma_{\theta_i}\big(\langle \bar{\boldsymbol{y}}[0], \boldsymbol{w}_i\rangle + \langle \boldsymbol{e}, \boldsymbol{w}_i\rangle\big) && (6.4)\\
&= \sigma_{\theta_i}\big(\langle \bar{\boldsymbol{y}}[0], \boldsymbol{w}_i\rangle + \eta_i\big) && (6.5)\\
&= \bar{y}_i[1] && (6.6)
\end{aligned}$$

From (6.3) to (6.4) we inserted (6.1). In (6.5) we defined the disturbance to be $\eta_i := \langle \boldsymbol{e}, \boldsymbol{w}_i \rangle \in \mathbb{R}$, which is bounded because

$$
\begin{aligned}
|\eta_i| &= |\langle \boldsymbol{e}, \boldsymbol{w}_i \rangle| && (6.7)\\
&\leq \|\boldsymbol{e}\| \cdot \|\boldsymbol{w}_i\| && (6.8)\\
&\leq \|\boldsymbol{e}\| \cdot \max_{i \in \{1,\ldots,L\}} \|\boldsymbol{w}_i\| && (6.9)\\
&< \eta. && (6.10)
\end{aligned}
$$

The inequality in (6.8) follows from the Cauchy–Schwarz inequality, and (6.10) follows from (6.2).

Finally, the step from (6.5) to (6.6) holds because $\bar{\boldsymbol{Y}}$ is perfectly memorized, and because the disturbance is bounded as in (6.10).

Example

Let $\boldsymbol{w}_i$ be defined as in (4.101), and η as in (4.103) from Theorem 4.1. Then,

$$
\begin{aligned}
\|\boldsymbol{w}_i\| &\leq \sum_{n \in J_i} \big\|\boldsymbol{y}[n-1] - p\mathbf{1}_L\big\| && (6.11)\\
&\leq N\|\mathbf{1}_L\| && (6.12)\\
&= N\sqrt{L}, && (6.13)
\end{aligned}
$$

and $\eta = \alpha L$, for $0 < \alpha < 1/16$. Thus, by (6.2) the norm of the initialization error is allowed to grow with (at least) $\sqrt{L}/N$, i.e.,

$$
\|\boldsymbol{e}\| \propto \frac{\sqrt{L}}{N}. \qquad (6.14)
$$

6.2 Multiple Connections – Correlation Over a Window

In this section we consider a generalized neuron model. We assume that each neuron ξ_i consists of $M \geq 2$ weight vectors $\boldsymbol{w}_i^{[1]}, \ldots, \boldsymbol{w}_i^{[M]} \in \mathbb{R}^L$, and

$$\xi_i(\boldsymbol{y}^{[1]}, \ldots, \boldsymbol{y}^{[M]}) := \sigma_{\theta_i}\left(\sum_{m=1}^{M} \langle \boldsymbol{y}^{[m]}, \boldsymbol{w}_i^{[m]} \rangle + \eta_i \right), \tag{6.15}$$

for input vectors $\boldsymbol{y}^{[1]}, \ldots, \boldsymbol{y}^{[M]} \in \mathbb{R}^L$, scalar threshold $\theta_i \in \mathbb{R}$, and bounded disturbance $|\eta_i| < \eta$. Clearly, for the special case $M = 1$, (6.15) reduces to (2.3). Note that the neuron's output is still binary, i.e., $\xi_i(\boldsymbol{y}^{[1]}, \ldots, \boldsymbol{y}^{[M]}) \in \{0, 1\}$.

Furthermore, we assume that the neurons $\xi_1, \ldots, \xi_L$ form a recurrent network which produces the firing sequence $\boldsymbol{y}[M], \boldsymbol{y}[M+1], \ldots \in \{0,1\}^L$ with

$$\boldsymbol{y}[n] := \begin{pmatrix} \xi_1\big(\boldsymbol{y}[n-1], \ldots, \boldsymbol{y}[n-M]\big) \\ \vdots \\ \xi_L\big(\boldsymbol{y}[n-1], \ldots, \boldsymbol{y}[n-M]\big) \end{pmatrix}, \quad n \in \{M, M+1, \ldots\}, \tag{6.16}$$

if initialized with some vectors $\boldsymbol{y}[0], \ldots, \boldsymbol{y}[M-1] \in \mathbb{R}^L$ (cf. Section 2.2). An illustration of (6.16) is given in Figure 6.1. Then, as in Section 2.3 we want to periodically reproduce a given firing sequence $\boldsymbol{Y} \in \{0,1\}^{L\times N}$.

For a random firing sequence $\boldsymbol{Y} \overset{\text{i.i.d.}}{\sim} \text{Ber}(p)^{L\times N}$, $0 < p < 1$, we fix the weight vectors to be

$$\boldsymbol{w}_i^{[m]} := \sum_{n\in J_i} \big(\boldsymbol{y}[n-m] - p\mathbf{1}_L\big), \qquad m \in \{1, \ldots, M\}, \tag{6.17}$$

where

$$J_i := \big\{n \in \{0, \ldots, N-1\} : y_i[n] = 1\big\}, \tag{6.18}$$

for $i \in \{1, \ldots, L\}$, similar to (4.101) on page 33. Then, we rewrite the output of neuron ξ_i at time step n as

$$\xi_i\big(\boldsymbol{y}[n-1], \ldots, \boldsymbol{y}[n-M]\big) = \sigma_{\theta_i}\left(\sum_{m=1}^{M} \langle \boldsymbol{y}[n-m], \boldsymbol{w}_i^{[m]} \rangle + \eta_i \right) \tag{6.19}$$

$$= \sigma_{\theta_i}\big(\langle \breve{\boldsymbol{y}}[n-1], \breve{\boldsymbol{w}}_i \rangle + \eta_i\big), \tag{6.20}$$

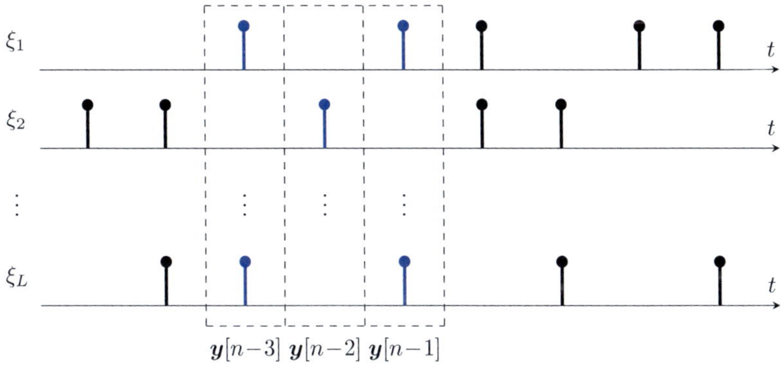

Figure 6.1: Multi-channel firing sequence as in (6.16), for $M = 3$.

where

$$\breve{\boldsymbol{y}}[n-1] := \begin{pmatrix} \boldsymbol{y}[n-1] \\ \vdots \\ \boldsymbol{y}[n-M] \end{pmatrix} \in \mathbb{R}^{ML}, \tag{6.21}$$

and

$$\breve{\boldsymbol{w}}_i := \begin{pmatrix} \boldsymbol{w}_i^{[1]} \\ \vdots \\ \boldsymbol{w}_i^{[M]} \end{pmatrix} \in \mathbb{R}^{ML}. \tag{6.22}$$

Note that the inner product in (6.19) is in $\mathbb{R}^L$, whereas the inner product in (6.20) is in $\mathbb{R}^{ML}$.

Inserting (6.17) into (6.22) yields

$$\breve{\boldsymbol{w}}_i = \begin{pmatrix} \sum_{\tilde{n}\in J_i} \left(\boldsymbol{y}[\tilde{n}-1] - p\mathbf{1}_L\right) \\ \vdots \\ \sum_{\tilde{n}\in J_i} \left(\boldsymbol{y}[\tilde{n}-M] - p\mathbf{1}_L\right) \end{pmatrix} \tag{6.23}$$

$$= \sum_{\tilde{n}\in J_i} \begin{pmatrix} \boldsymbol{y}[\tilde{n}-1] - p\mathbf{1}_L \\ \vdots \\ \boldsymbol{y}[\tilde{n}-M] - p\mathbf{1}_L \end{pmatrix} \tag{6.24}$$

$$= \sum_{\tilde{n}\in J_i} \big(\breve{\boldsymbol{y}}[\tilde{n}-1] - p\mathbf{1}_{ML}\big), \tag{6.25}$$

and thus, we obtain

$$\begin{aligned}
&\big\langle \breve{\boldsymbol{y}}[n-1], \breve{\boldsymbol{w}}_i \big\rangle \\
&\quad = \sum_{\tilde{n}\in J_i} \big\langle \breve{\boldsymbol{y}}[n-1], \breve{\boldsymbol{y}}[\tilde{n}-1] - p\mathbf{1}_{ML} \big\rangle && (6.26)\\
&\quad = \sum_{\tilde{n}=n-(M-1)}^{n+M-1} y_i[\tilde{n}] \big\langle \breve{\boldsymbol{y}}[n-1], \breve{\boldsymbol{y}}[\tilde{n}-1] - p\mathbf{1}_{ML} \big\rangle + S_{i,n}^{[M]} && (6.27)\\
&\quad = y_i[n] \big\langle \breve{\boldsymbol{y}}[n-1], \breve{\boldsymbol{y}}[n-1] - p\mathbf{1}_{ML} \big\rangle \\
&\qquad + \sum_{\tilde{n}\in\mathcal{M}_n\setminus\{n\}} y_i[\tilde{n}] \big\langle \breve{\boldsymbol{y}}[n-1], \breve{\boldsymbol{y}}[\tilde{n}-1] - p\mathbf{1}_{ML} \big\rangle + S_{i,n}^{[M]}, && (6.28)
\end{aligned}$$

where

$$\mathcal{M}_n := \big\{ n-(M-1), \ldots, n+M-1 \big\}, \tag{6.29}$$

and

$$S_{i,n}^{[M]} := \sum_{\tilde{n}\in J_i\setminus\mathcal{M}_n} y_i[\tilde{n}] \big\langle \breve{\boldsymbol{y}}[n-1], \breve{\boldsymbol{y}}[\tilde{n}-1] - p\mathbf{1}_{ML} \big\rangle. \tag{6.30}$$

For $M = 1$, (6.27) reduces to (4.110) as expected. Note that for $\boldsymbol{Y} \overset{\text{i.i.d.}}{\sim} \text{Ber}(p)^{L\times N}$, we have $\breve{\boldsymbol{y}}[n] \overset{\text{i.i.d.}}{\sim} \text{Ber}(p)^{ML}$, for all $n \in \{0, 1, \ldots, N-1\}$. Moreover, if $\tilde{n} \notin \{n-(M-1), \ldots, n+M-1\}$, then $\breve{\boldsymbol{y}}[n-1]$ and $\breve{\boldsymbol{y}}[\tilde{n}-1]$ are independent, and we can apply Lemma B.2 which yields

$$\mathrm{E}\big[S_{i,n}^{[M]}\big] = 0, \tag{6.31}$$

and

$$\mathrm{E}\Big[e^{\lambda S_{i,n}^{[M]}}\Big] < e^{\frac{\lambda^2}{8}MLN}. \tag{6.32}$$

For the sake of clarity, we only consider the case

$$y_i[\tilde{n}] = 0, \qquad \tilde{n} \in \mathcal{M}_n \setminus \{n\}, \tag{6.33}$$

for which (6.28) becomes

$$\big\langle \breve{\boldsymbol{y}}[n-1], \breve{\boldsymbol{w}}_i \big\rangle = y_i[n] \big\langle \breve{\boldsymbol{y}}[n-1], \breve{\boldsymbol{y}}[n-1] - p\mathbf{1}_{ML} \big\rangle + S_{i,n}^{[M]} \tag{6.34}$$

with

$$\frac{1}{1-p}\langle \breve{\boldsymbol{y}}[n-1], \breve{\boldsymbol{y}}[n-1] - p\mathbf{1}_{ML}\rangle \sim \mathrm{Bin}(ML, p), \tag{6.35}$$

cf. (4.133). Thus, for (6.33), the inner product (6.34) has exactly the same form/statistics as (4.110) with L replaced by ML.

It seems that in the single-pass learning mode the generalization to M weight vectors achieves a performance comparable to the performance of an ordinary network (as defined in Chapter 2) with ML neurons. However, the networks are not completely equivalent. In the generalized version, for a rigorous analysis we would also need to consider the case where condition (6.33) is not satisfied. This distinction of cases is not necessary for ordinary networks (i.e., for $M = 1$).

In addition, by the identity (cf. the step from (6.19) to (6.20))

$$\sum_{m=1}^{M} \langle \boldsymbol{y}[n-m], \boldsymbol{w}_i^{[m]}\rangle = \langle \breve{\boldsymbol{y}}[n-1], \breve{\boldsymbol{w}}_i\rangle \tag{6.36}$$

with $\breve{\boldsymbol{y}}[n-1], \breve{\boldsymbol{w}}_i \in \mathbb{R}^{ML}$ as in (6.21) and (6.22), respectively, a similar result can be expected for the multi-pass mode.

Interpretation

The correlation over a window of size M as defined in (6.16), and illustrated in Figure 6.1, is equivalent to a fully-connected recurrent network with M-fold connections, i.e., every neuron has M connections to every other neuron (and itself) in the network. An example of such a network is depicted in Figure 6.2, for $M = 2$. Note that the connections (synapses) possess different delays: The m-th connection from ξ_ℓ back to ξ_i has a delay which is m-times of some fixed unit-delay (indicated by the filters with transfer function z^{-m} in Figure 6.2, i.e., $y_\ell^{[m]}[n] = y_\ell[n-m]$).

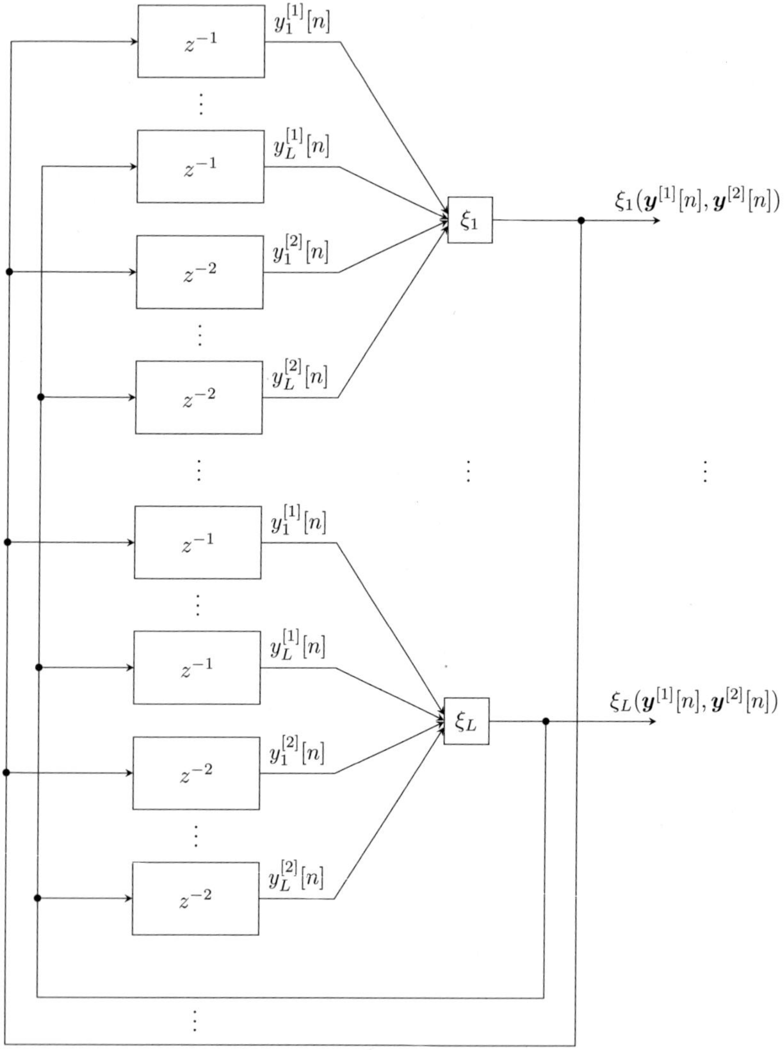

Figure 6.2: Fully-connected autonomous recurrent network consisting of L neurons as in (6.16), for $M = 2$.

6.3 Use Case: Multiple Recalling Cycles

In this section we have (memorized) firing sequences $\boldsymbol{Y} \in \{0,1\}^{L\times N}$ with N large, i.e., $N \gg 1$ in mind. In this case the recalling process might take a long time, which can be unpractical especially if we are only interested in a specific section of $\boldsymbol{Y}$. E.g., for some reason we only want to recall the beginning of $\boldsymbol{Y}$ instead of the whole sequence. To this end, we partition $\boldsymbol{Y}$ into two separate recalling cycles $\mathcal{C}_1$ and $\mathcal{C}_2$ as follows.

Let $N_1 \in \{1,\ldots,N-2\}$. Then, we want to have:

- If the network is initialized with $\boldsymbol{y}[n]$, for $n \in \{0,\ldots,N_1-1\}$, then it produces the (firing) sequence

$$\boldsymbol{y}\big[(n+k) \bmod N_1\big], \qquad k \in \{1,2,\ldots\}. \tag{6.37}$$

  This mode is referred to as the recalling cycle $\mathcal{C}_1$.

- If the network is initialized with $\boldsymbol{y}[n]$, for $n \in \{N_1,\ldots,N-1\}$, then it produces the (firing) sequence

$$\boldsymbol{y}\big[\big((n+k) \bmod (N-N_1)\big)+N_1\big], \qquad k \in \{1,2,\ldots\}. \tag{6.38}$$

  This mode is referred to as the recalling cycle $\mathcal{C}_2$.

An illustration of the partition of $\boldsymbol{Y}$ into the two recalling cylces $\mathcal{C}_1$ and $\mathcal{C}_2$ as in (6.37) and (6.38) is shown in Figure 6.3. We note that the argument of $\boldsymbol{y}[\cdot]$ in (6.37) and (6.38) clearly satisfies

$$(n+k) \bmod N_1 \in \{0,\ldots,N_1-1\}, \tag{6.39}$$

and

$$\big((n+k) \bmod (N-N_1)\big)+N_1 \in \{N_1,\ldots,N-1\}, \tag{6.40}$$

for all $(n,k) \in \mathbb{N}^2$, respectively.

The described method can be easily generalized to multiple recalling cycles $\mathcal{C}_1,\mathcal{C}_2,\mathcal{C}_3,\ldots$

Example

In the multi-pass learning mode, as discussed in Section 4.3, the implementation of recalling cycles can be achieved by adapting $\tilde{\boldsymbol{Y}} \in \mathbb{R}^{N\times L}$ and $\tilde{\boldsymbol{y}}_i \in \mathbb{R}^N$ in (4.164) on page 43 accordingly.

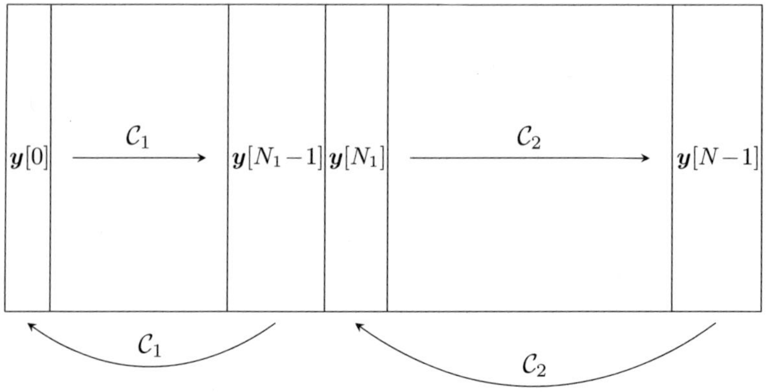

Figure 6.3: Firing sequence partitioned into two separate recalling cylces $\mathcal{C}_1$ and $\mathcal{C}_2$.

Assuming that $\boldsymbol{Y} \in \{0,1\}^{L\times N}$ can be perfectly memorized by multipass learning (as in Section 4.3), i.e., $\operatorname{rank}(\boldsymbol{Y}) = N$, then the learning rule (4.212) with

$$\tilde{\boldsymbol{Y}} := \begin{pmatrix} \boldsymbol{y}[0]^\mathsf{T} \\ \vdots \\ \boldsymbol{y}[N_1-2]^\mathsf{T} \\ \boldsymbol{y}[N_1-1]^\mathsf{T} \\ \boldsymbol{y}[N_1]^\mathsf{T} \\ \vdots \\ \boldsymbol{y}[N-2]^\mathsf{T} \\ \boldsymbol{y}[N-1]^\mathsf{T} \end{pmatrix} \in \mathbb{R}^{N\times L}, \qquad \tilde{\boldsymbol{y}}_i := \begin{pmatrix} y_i[1] \\ \vdots \\ y_i[N_1-1] \\ y_i[0] \\ y_i[N_1+1] \\ \vdots \\ y_i[N-1] \\ y_i[N_1] \end{pmatrix} \in \mathbb{R}^N \tag{6.41}$$

perfectly memorizes $\boldsymbol{Y}$ and additionally induces the recalling cycles $\mathcal{C}_1$ and $\mathcal{C}_2$ as depicted in Figure 6.3. This can be seen by noting that $\operatorname{rank}(\boldsymbol{Y}) = N$ and (4.212) imply $\tilde{\boldsymbol{Y}}\boldsymbol{w}_i = \tilde{\boldsymbol{y}}_i$. Then, e.g., the last equality reads as $\langle \boldsymbol{y}[N-1], \boldsymbol{w}_i\rangle = y_i[N_1]$, cf. (6.41), which implies $\xi_i(\boldsymbol{y}[N-1]) = y_i[N_1]$. Similarly, we have $\xi_i(\boldsymbol{y}[N_1-1]) = y_i[0]$.

Both $\tilde{\boldsymbol{Y}}$ and $\tilde{\boldsymbol{y}}_i$ in (6.41) are permutations of $\tilde{\boldsymbol{Y}}$ and $\tilde{\boldsymbol{y}}_i$ as in (4.164), respectively.

6.4 Online Memorization of Adversarial Firing Sequences by Means of Two Parallel RNNs

Now, we propose a procedure which is able to asymptotically memorize any (might be adversarial) given firing sequence by instantaneous/online learning as in Section 4.2.

Given an arbitrary firing sequence $\boldsymbol{Y} \in \{0,1\}^{L \times N}$, where $y_\ell[n]$ denotes the entry at row ℓ and column n of $\boldsymbol{Y}$. Then, we sample two firing sequences $\boldsymbol{Y}^{(1)}, \boldsymbol{Y}^{(2)} \in \{0,1\}^{L \times N}$ as follows. If $y_\ell[n] = 0$, then

$$\begin{pmatrix} y_\ell^{(1)}[n] \\ y_\ell^{(2)}[n] \end{pmatrix} \sim \mathcal{U}\left(\left\{\begin{pmatrix} 0 \\ 0 \end{pmatrix}, \begin{pmatrix} 1 \\ 1 \end{pmatrix}\right\}\right), \tag{6.42}$$

and if $y_\ell[n] = 1$, then

$$\begin{pmatrix} y_\ell^{(1)}[n] \\ y_\ell^{(2)}[n] \end{pmatrix} \sim \mathcal{U}\left(\left\{\begin{pmatrix} 0 \\ 1 \end{pmatrix}, \begin{pmatrix} 1 \\ 0 \end{pmatrix}\right\}\right), \tag{6.43}$$

independently for all $(\ell, n) \in \{1, \ldots, L\} \times \{0, \ldots, N-1\}$, where $y_\ell^{(\nu)}[n]$ is the entry of $\boldsymbol{Y}^{(\nu)}$, $\nu \in \{1,2\}$, in row ℓ and column n, respectively, and $\mathcal{U}(\mathcal{A})$ denotes the uniform distribution over the set $\mathcal{A}$.

Thus, the sampled $\boldsymbol{Y}^{(1)}$ and $\boldsymbol{Y}^{(2)}$ clearly satisfy

$$\boldsymbol{Y} = \left(\boldsymbol{Y}^{(1)} + \boldsymbol{Y}^{(2)}\right) \bmod 2. \tag{6.44}$$

Moreover, by the law of total probability and from (6.42) – (6.43), we have

$$\begin{aligned}
\Pr\big[y_\ell^{(\nu)}[n] = 1\big] &= \big(1 - \Pr\big[y_\ell[n] = 1\big]\big) \Pr\big[y_\ell^{(\nu)}[n] = 1 \,\big|\, y_\ell[n] = 0\big] \\
&\qquad + \Pr\big[y_\ell[n] = 1\big] \Pr\big[y_\ell^{(\nu)}[n] = 1 \,\big|\, y_\ell[n] = 1\big] && (6.45) \\
&= \big(1 - \Pr\big[y_\ell[n] = 1\big]\big) \frac{1}{2} + \Pr\big[y_\ell[n] = 1\big] \frac{1}{2} && (6.46) \\
&= \frac{1}{2}, && (6.47)
\end{aligned}$$

for all $(\ell, n, \nu) \in \{1, \ldots, L\} \times \{0, \ldots, N-1\} \times \{1, 2\}$. Since all entries of $\boldsymbol{Y}^{(\nu)}$ are drawn independently by construction, we obtain

$$\boldsymbol{Y}^{(\nu)} \overset{\text{i.i.d.}}{\sim} \operatorname{Ber}(1/2)^{L \times N}, \tag{6.48}$$

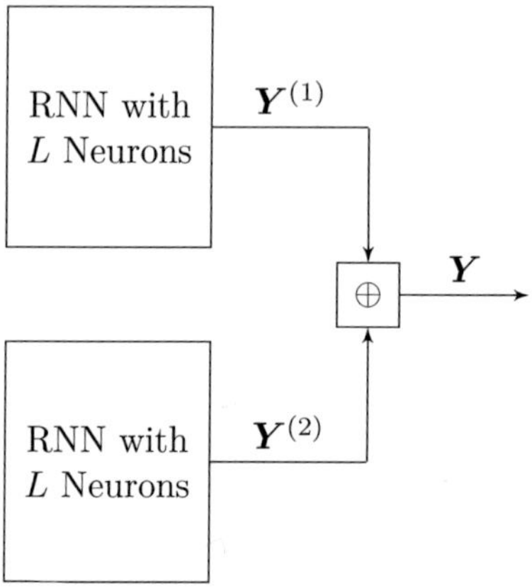

Figure 6.4: Two parallel RNNs which asymptotically memorize an adversarial $\boldsymbol{Y} \in \{0,1\}^{L \times N}$, that satisfies (6.51), with online learning.
The node on the right illustrates the component-wise XOR operation, i.e., addition modulo 2 as in (6.44).

for $\nu \in \{1,2\}$, but $\boldsymbol{Y}^{(1)}$ and $\boldsymbol{Y}^{(2)}$ are *not* independent. For $\nu \in \{1,2\}$, let $\mathcal{E}_{\boldsymbol{Y}^{(\nu)}}$ be the event that the memorization of $\boldsymbol{Y}^{(\nu)}$ is *not* perfect. Then, by the union bound and by the bound (4.104) in Theorem 4.1 (with $p = 1/2$, cf. (6.48)) we obtain

$$\Pr\big[\mathcal{E}_{\boldsymbol{Y}}\big] \leq \Pr\big[\mathcal{E}_{\boldsymbol{Y}^{(1)}}\big] + \Pr\big[\mathcal{E}_{\boldsymbol{Y}^{(2)}}\big] \tag{6.49}$$

$$< 4LNe^{-\frac{1}{128}(1-\tilde{\eta})^2 \frac{L}{N}} + 2LNe^{-D_{KL}\left(\frac{1+\tilde{\eta}}{4} \| \frac{1}{2}\right)L}, \tag{6.50}$$

and from Corollary 4.1 we know that as long as

$$N \leq \frac{1}{128}(1-\tilde{\eta})^2 \frac{L}{2\ln(L)}, \tag{6.51}$$

the right-hand side of (6.50) vanishes as $L \to \infty$.

This demonstrates that any given (adversarial) firing sequence $\boldsymbol{Y} \in \{0,1\}^{L \times N}$ satisfying (6.51) can be asymptotically memorized with online learning by means of two recurrent networks, each consisting of L neurons, running in parallel as shown in Figure 6.4.

Procedure for Online Memorizing $\boldsymbol{Y}$

1.) From $\boldsymbol{Y} \in \{0,1\}^{L\times N}$, we construct (sample) $\boldsymbol{Y}^{(1)}$ and $\boldsymbol{Y}^{(2)}$ according to (6.42) and (6.43).

2.) Each $\boldsymbol{Y}^{(\nu)}$, $\nu \in \{1,2\}$, is memorized by a recurrent network with thresholds

$$\theta_\ell^{(\nu)} := \frac{1}{16}L, \tag{6.52}$$

and weight vectors

$$\boldsymbol{w}_\ell^{(\nu)} := \sum_{n=0}^{N-1} y_\ell^{(\nu)}[n]\Big(\boldsymbol{y}^{(\nu)}[n-1] - \frac{1}{2}\mathbf{1}_L\Big), \tag{6.53}$$

for $(\ell,\nu) \in \{1,\ldots,L\} \times \{1,2\}$, where $\theta_\ell^{(\nu)} \in \mathbb{R}$ and $\boldsymbol{w}_\ell^{(\nu)} \in \mathbb{R}^L$ are the thresholds and weight vectors, respectively, of the network corresponding to $\boldsymbol{Y}^{(\nu)}$.

3.) Recalling $\boldsymbol{Y}$ via the relation

$$\boldsymbol{Y} = \big(\boldsymbol{Y}^{(1)} + \boldsymbol{Y}^{(2)}\big) \bmod 2. \tag{6.54}$$

Asymptotic Memorization Capacity

With the described method all firing sequences $\boldsymbol{Y} \in \{0,1\}^{L\times N}$ are asymptotically memorizable, thus

$$C_{\text{tot}} = LN \ \ [\text{bits}], \tag{6.55}$$

but $2L$ neurons are required instead of L neurons (cf. Figure 6.4) yielding

$$C_{\text{neuron}} = \frac{N}{2} \ \ [\text{bits per neuron}] \tag{6.56}$$

with N as in (6.51). For $p = 1/2$, the capacity in (5.9) becomes

$$C_{\text{neuron}} = N \ \ [\text{bits per neuron}] \tag{6.57}$$

with N as in (6.51). Thus, this procedure halves the asymptotic memorization capacity with respect to the single-pass memorization capacity of a single network (cf. Chapter 5).

Part II

Continuous-time Model

Chapter 7

The Model

7.1 The Neuron Model

We consider a continuous-time neuron model as follows. Given an L-dimensional input signal $\boldsymbol{y}(t) := \big(y_1(t), \ldots, y_L(t)\big)^{\mathsf{T}} \in \mathbb{R}^L$, $t \in \mathbb{R}$, a neuron ξ_i produces a score signal[1]

$$z_i(t) := \sum_{\ell=1}^{L} w_{\ell,i} \, \big(h * y_\ell\big)(t) + \eta_i(t), \qquad t \in \mathbb{R}, \tag{7.1}$$

with weights $\boldsymbol{w}_i := (w_{1,i}, \ldots, w_{L,i})^{\mathsf{T}} \in \mathbb{R}^L$ and additive disturbance $\eta_i(\cdot)$ explained in Section 7.1.2, and where

$$\big(h * y_\ell\big)(t) := \int_{\mathbb{R}} h(s) \, y_\ell(t-s) \, ds \tag{7.2}$$

denotes the convolution of $y_\ell(\cdot)$ with the neuron's impulse response $h(\cdot)$, cf. Figure 7.1. The neuron ξ_i outputs (or fires) an unit pulse at the time instant where the score signal $z_i(\cdot)$ exceeds a threshold $\theta_i \in \mathbb{R}$ and at least T_{r} time units (seconds) have passed by since the previous firing. The quantity $T_{\mathrm{r}} > 0$ will be referred to as *refractory period.* Thus, the output signal of ξ_i is a pulse train

$$\xi_i(\boldsymbol{y}(t)) = \sum_j \delta\big(t - t_j^{(i)}\big), \qquad t \in \mathbb{R}, \tag{7.3}$$

[1] May be viewed as membrane potential or postsynaptic potential.

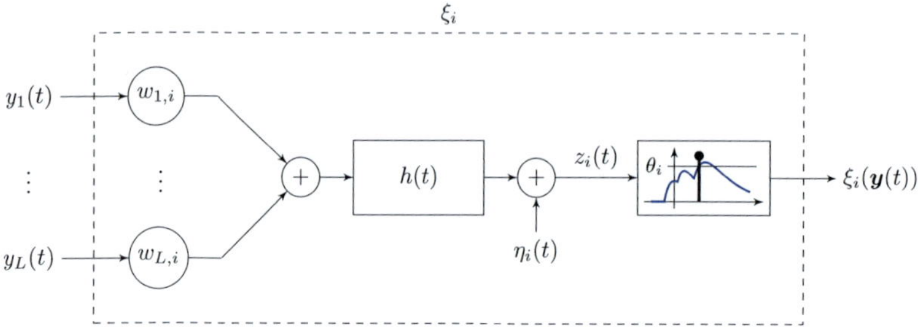

Figure 7.1: Continuous-time model of a neuron ξ_i with L inputs, impulse response $h(\cdot)$, and additive disturbance $\eta_i(\cdot)$. The neuron is characterized by a weight vector $\boldsymbol{w}_i := (w_{1,i}, \dots, w_{L,i})^\mathsf{T} \in \mathbb{R}^L$ and a scalar threshold $\theta_i \in \mathbb{R}$.

with *firing times* $t_1^{(i)} < t_2^{(i)} < \cdots$ such that

$$t_{j+1}^{(i)} - t_j^{(i)} \geq T_\mathrm{r}, \qquad j \in \mathbb{N}, \tag{7.4}$$

where $\delta(\cdot)$ is the Dirac delta having property

$$\int_{[a,b]} f(t)\,\delta(t-\tau)\,dt = \int_{[a,b]} f(t)\,\delta(\tau-t)\,dt \tag{7.5}$$

$$= \begin{cases} f(\tau), & \text{if } a \leq \tau \leq b \\ 0, & \text{otherwise,} \end{cases} \tag{7.6}$$

for $a, b, \tau \in \mathbb{R}$, $a < b$, and $f(\cdot)$ continuous at $t = \tau$. We also use the shorthand notation

$$\delta_\tau(t) := \delta(t-\tau), \qquad t \in \mathbb{R}, \tag{7.7}$$

for the Dirac delta at fixed time-instant $\tau \in \mathbb{R}$. The terms Dirac delta and pulse will be used interchangeably.

The introduced neuron model might be seen as a special case of the "zero order" Spike Response Model (SRM_0) [18], [19, Chapter 4]. Other related models can be found, e.g., in [7, 30, 51, 62, 66].

7.1.1 Neuron Impulse Response

We consider the following three impulse responses:

$$\text{i.)}\quad h_{\text{rect}}(t) := \mathrm{I}\big[0 \le t < T_{\text{r}}\big] = \begin{cases} 1, & \text{if } 0 \le t < T_{\text{r}} \\ 0, & \text{otherwise,} \end{cases} \tag{7.8}$$

$$\text{ii.)}\quad h_{\text{rect},\alpha}(t) := \begin{cases} \frac{1}{\alpha}(t/T_{\text{r}}), & \text{if } 0 \le t < \alpha T_{\text{r}} \\ 1, & \text{if } \alpha T_{\text{r}} \le t < (1-\alpha) T_{\text{r}} \\ \frac{1}{\alpha}(1 - t/T_{\text{r}}), & \text{if } (1-\alpha) T_{\text{r}} \le t < T_{\text{r}} \\ 0, & \text{otherwise,} \end{cases} \tag{7.9}$$

$$\text{iii.)}\quad h_{\text{bio},\beta}(t) := \frac{t}{\beta} e^{1-t/\beta}\, \mathrm{I}\big[t \ge 0\big] = \begin{cases} \frac{t}{\beta} e^{1-t/\beta}, & \text{if } t \ge 0 \\ 0, & \text{otherwise,} \end{cases} \tag{7.10}$$

for all $t \in \mathbb{R}$, and $0 < \alpha < 1/2$, $\beta > 0$. The different pulse shapes are depicted in Figure 7.2.

Thus, we consider causal impulse responses, i.e., $h(t) = 0$, for $t < 0$. In addition, both $h_{\text{rect}}(\cdot)$ and $h_{\text{rect},\alpha}(\cdot)$ are of finite duration since

$$h_{\text{rect}}(t) = h_{\text{rect},\alpha}(t) = 0, \qquad t \notin [0, T_{\text{r}}[, \tag{7.11}$$

for all $0 < \alpha < 1/2$.

The "rectangular" impulse response $h_{\text{rect}}(\cdot)$ is physically not realizable. But it serves as a starting point for which rigorous statements can be formulated. By simulations we then try to verify the statements with $h_{\text{rect},\alpha}(\cdot)$ which has finite raising and falling slopes, and primary with $h_{\text{bio},\beta}(\cdot)$ which seems a biologically plausible choice. E.g., the pulse shape of $h_{\text{bio},\beta}(\cdot)$ is used in [19, 22, 41] as EPSP.

Some Properties of $h_{\text{bio},\beta}(\cdot)$

First, we show that

$$\max_{t \in \mathbb{R}} h_{\text{bio},\beta}(t) = h_{\text{bio},\beta}(\beta) = 1. \tag{7.12}$$

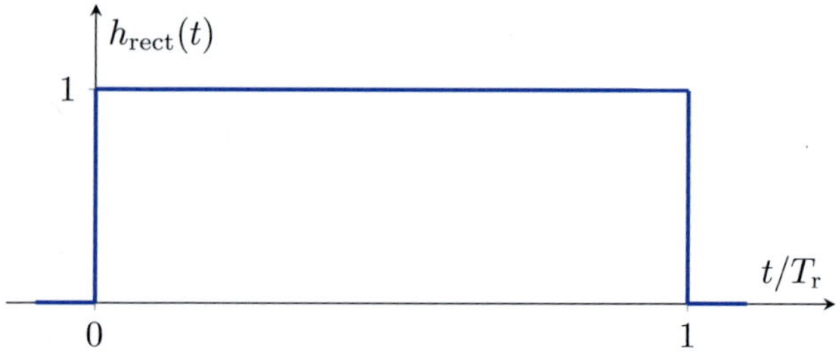

(a) Pulse shape of $h_{\text{rect}}(\cdot)$.

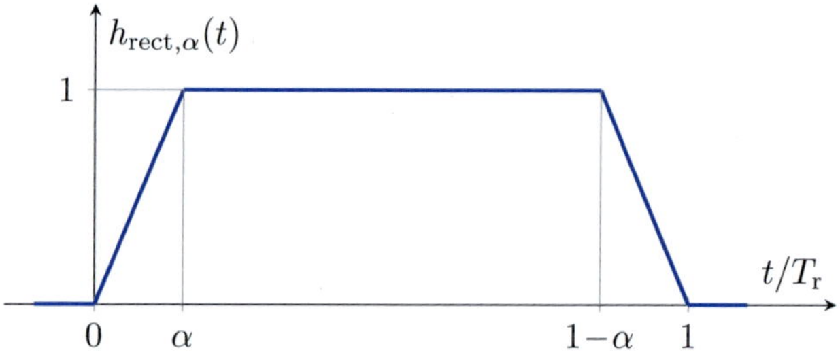

(b) Pulse shape of $h_{\text{rect},\alpha}(\cdot)$, for $0 < \alpha < 1/2$.

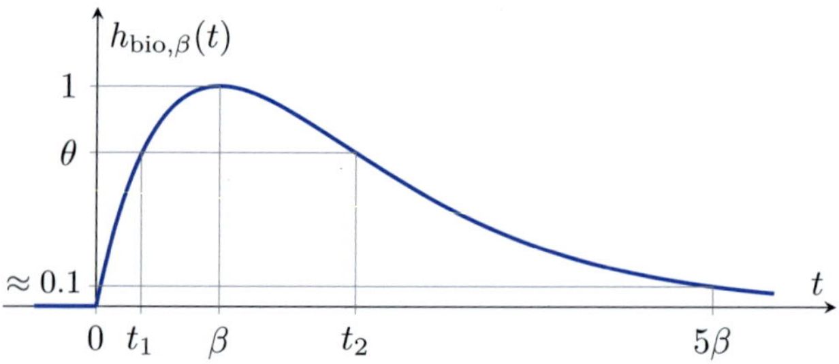

(c) Pulse shape of $h_{\text{bio},\beta}(\cdot)$, for $\beta > 0$.

Figure 7.2: Pulse shapes of $h_{\text{rect}}(\cdot)$, $h_{\text{rect},\alpha}(\cdot)$, and $h_{\text{bio},\beta}(\cdot)$.

Thus, $h_{\text{bio},\beta}(\cdot)$ attains its maximum at $t = \beta$, because

$$\frac{d}{dt} h_{\text{bio},\beta}(t) = \frac{1}{\beta}\left(e^{1-t/\beta} - \frac{t}{\beta} e^{1-t/\beta}\right) \tag{7.13}$$

$$= \frac{1}{\beta}\left(1 - \frac{t}{\beta}\right) e^{1-t/\beta}, \tag{7.14}$$

and setting (7.14) equal to zero yields $t = \beta$.

For t large, $h_{\text{bio},\beta}(t)$ vanishes, because

$$\lim_{t\to\infty} h_{\text{bio},\beta}(t) = \frac{e}{\beta} \lim_{t\to\infty} \frac{t}{e^{t/\beta}} \tag{7.15}$$

$$= \frac{e}{\beta} \lim_{x\to\infty} \frac{\ln(x)}{x^{1/\beta}} \tag{7.16}$$

$$= 0, \tag{7.17}$$

where we introduced the variable substitution $x := e^t$, and applied Lemma B.14.

For $0 < \theta < 1$, we have

$$\Big(h_{\text{bio},\beta}(t) = \theta\Big) \implies \Big(t \in \{t_1, t_2\}\Big), \tag{7.18}$$

with

$$t_1 := -\beta\, W_0\left(-\frac{\theta}{e}\right), \tag{7.19}$$

$$t_2 := -\beta\, W_{-1}\left(-\frac{\theta}{e}\right), \tag{7.20}$$

where $W_0(\cdot)$ and $W_{-1}(\cdot)$ are two branches of the Lambert $W(\cdot)$ function, cf. Figure 7.2c. We are mainly interested in the time instant t_1 where $h_{\text{bio},\beta}(\cdot)$ reaches θ from below. Note that $0 < t_1 < \beta$ and $t_2 > \beta$.

Finally, we show that $h_{\text{bio},\beta}(\cdot)$ can be obtained by the concatenation of two first order low-pass filters both with impulse response $g(t) := g_0 e^{-t/\beta}\, \mathrm{I}\big[t \geq 0\big]$, $t \in \mathbb{R}$, because

$$(g * g)(t) = \int_{-\infty}^{\infty} g(s) g(t - s)\, ds \tag{7.21}$$

$$= g_0^2 \int_0^t e^{-s/\beta} e^{-(t-s)/\beta}\, ds \tag{7.22}$$

$$= g_0^2 e^{-t/\beta} \int_0^t 1\, ds \tag{7.23}$$

$$= g_0^2 t e^{-t/\beta}, \tag{7.24}$$

for $t > 0$, and by choosing $g_0 := \sqrt{e/\beta}$ we obtain $(g * g)(t) = h_{\text{bio},\beta}(t)$, for all $t \in \mathbb{R}$.

7.1.2 Disturbance Model

The additive disturbance $\eta_i(\cdot)$ subsumes any form of imperfection, e.g., finite computational precision, noisy neurons, delay mismatch/jitter, threshold noise, etc.

Any imperfection essentially results in

- a shifted firing
- a false firing
- a missing firing

which can be modelled by a corresponding disturbance. In Chapter 8, we start with the ideal case, i.e., no disturbances are taken into account. We specify a class of firing signals which can be perfectly memorized by the continuous-time recurrent network (as defined next). Then, in Chapter 9 we examine the timing robustness of those memorizable firing signals in continuous-time by allowing various disturbances such as delay mismatch, firing-time jitter, or additive noise on the score signals.

7.2 Fully-connected Autonomous Recurrent Network with Connection Delays

Now, we consider L neurons $\xi_1, \ldots, \xi_L$ which are fully connected to form an autonomous recurrent network as in Figure 7.3. Every connection (synapse) from ξ_ℓ to ξ_i is characterized by a delay (transit time) $\tau_{\ell,i} > 0$, and for each neuron ξ_i, we define its delay vector as

$$\boldsymbol{\tau}_i := (\tau_{1,i}, \ldots, \tau_{L,i})^{\mathsf{T}} \in \mathbb{R}^L, \qquad i \in \{1, \ldots, L\}. \tag{7.25}$$

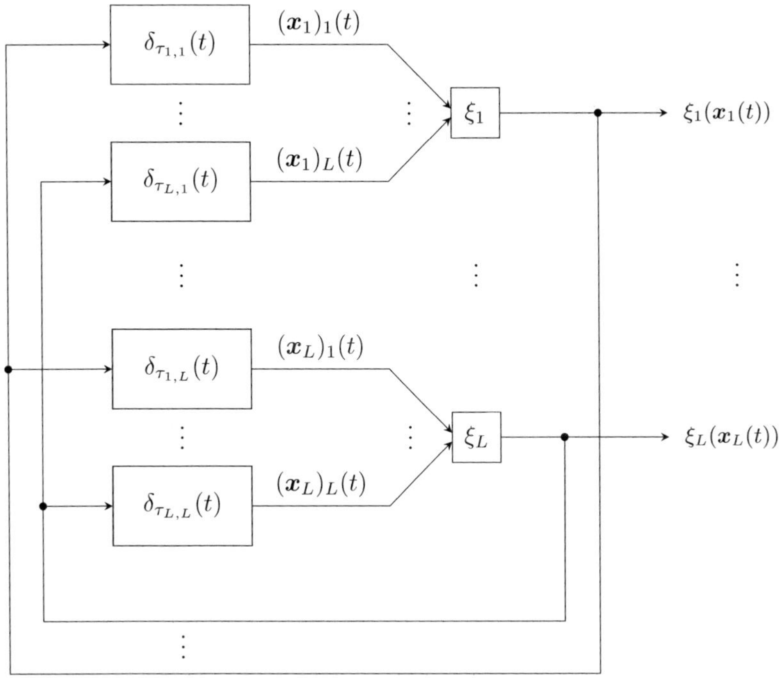

Figure 7.3: Fully-connected continuous-time autonomous recurrent network with connection delays consisting of L neurons.

If initialized appropriately, such a network produces an L-dimensional firing signal $\boldsymbol{y}(\cdot) := \big(y_1(\cdot), \dots, y_L(\cdot)\big)^{\mathsf{T}}$ satisfying

$$\boldsymbol{y}(t) = \big(\xi_1(\boldsymbol{x}_1(t)), \dots, \xi_L(\boldsymbol{x}_L(t))\big)^{\mathsf{T}} \in \mathbb{R}^L, \qquad t \in \mathbb{R}, \tag{7.26}$$

with input signals

$$\begin{aligned} \boldsymbol{x}_i(t) &:= \big((\boldsymbol{x}_i)_1(t), \dots, (\boldsymbol{x}_i)_L(t)\big)^{\mathsf{T}} && (7.27)\\ &= \big((y_1 * \delta_{\tau_{1,i}})(t), \dots, (y_L * \delta_{\tau_{L,i}})(t)\big)^{\mathsf{T}} && (7.28)\\ &= \big(y_1(t-\tau_{1,i}), \dots, y_L(t-\tau_{L,i})\big)^{\mathsf{T}} \in \mathbb{R}^L, && (7.29) \end{aligned}$$

for $i \in \{1, \dots, L\}$. The step from (7.28) to (7.29) follows from

$$\big(y_\ell * \delta_{\tau_{\ell,i}}\big)(t) = \int_{\mathbb{R}} y_\ell(s)\, \delta(t - s - \tau_{\ell,i})\, ds \tag{7.30}$$

$$= y_\ell(t - \tau_{\ell,i}), \qquad t \in \mathbb{R}, \tag{7.31}$$

where we applied (7.6).

Because of (7.3), all the signals $y_\ell(\cdot)$, for $\ell \in \{1, \ldots, L\}$, consist of Dirac deltas, and thus all signals in the network of Figure 7.3 are pulse trains.

It would also be interesting to study networks with multiple connections. For example, we could assume that from ξ_ℓ to ξ_i there exist two connections with different delays $\tau_{\ell,i}^{[1]}$ and $\tau_{\ell,i}^{[2]}$ (cf. Section 6.2).

Finally, it is important to remark that such a network runs in continuous-time without any clock or synchronization signal, and thus is suitable for implementation in clockless analog circuits.

7.2.1 Relation to the Discrete-time Model

For the special case

$$h(t) := h_{\text{rect}}(t), \qquad t \in \mathbb{R}, \tag{7.32}$$

and

$$\tau_{\ell,i} := T_{\text{r}}, \qquad (\ell, i) \in \{1, \ldots, L\}^2, \tag{7.33}$$

the recurrent network in Figure 7.3 can be reduced to the discrete-time model from Part I as follows.

For (7.33), the input vectors (7.29) are given by

$$\boldsymbol{x}_i(t) = \big(y_1(t - T_{\text{r}}), \ldots, y_L(t - T_{\text{r}})\big)^{\mathsf{T}} \tag{7.34}$$

$$= \boldsymbol{y}(t - T_{\text{r}}), \qquad t \in \mathbb{R}, \tag{7.35}$$

for $i \in \{1, \ldots, L\}$, (which is independent of i) and thus (7.26) becomes

$$\boldsymbol{y}(t) = \big(\xi_1(\boldsymbol{y}(t - T_{\text{r}})), \ldots, \xi_L(\boldsymbol{y}(t - T_{\text{r}}))\big)^{\mathsf{T}}, \qquad t \in \mathbb{R}. \tag{7.36}$$

Then, assuming that the network is initialized such that

$$y_\ell(t) = \sum_{\tilde{n}=0}^{n-1} y_\ell[\tilde{n}]\, \delta(t - \tilde{n}T_{\text{r}}), \qquad 0 \le t < nT_{\text{r}}, \tag{7.37}$$

for $\ell \in \{1, \ldots, L\}$, $n \in \mathbb{N}$, where $y_\ell[\tilde{n}] \in \{0, 1\}$ indicates the firings at $t = \tilde{n}T_{\text{r}}$, i.e., we assume that in $t \in [0, nT_{\text{r}}[$ all firings occur only at multiples of T_r. The score signal of ξ_i is then given by

$$z_i(t) = \sum_{\ell=1}^{L} w_{\ell,i} \big(h_\mathrm{rect} * \delta_{\tau_{\ell,i}} * y_\ell\big)(t) + \eta_i(t) \tag{7.38}$$

$$= \sum_{\ell=1}^{L} w_{\ell,i} \sum_{\tilde{n}=0}^{n-1} y_\ell[\tilde{n}] \big(h_\mathrm{rect} * \delta_{T_\mathrm{r}} * \delta_{\tilde{n}T_\mathrm{r}}\big)(t) + \eta_i(t) \tag{7.39}$$

$$= \sum_{\tilde{n}=0}^{n-1} \sum_{\ell=1}^{L} y_\ell[\tilde{n}]\, w_{\ell,i}\, h_\mathrm{rect}\big(t - (\tilde{n}+1)T_\mathrm{r}\big) + \eta_i(t) \tag{7.40}$$

$$= \sum_{\tilde{n}=0}^{n-1} \big\langle \boldsymbol{y}[\tilde{n}], \boldsymbol{w}_i \big\rangle\, \mathrm{I}\big[(\tilde{n}+1)T_\mathrm{r} \le t < (\tilde{n}+2)T_\mathrm{r}\big] + \eta_i(t), \tag{7.41}$$

for $0 \le t < (n+1)T_\mathrm{r}$, with

$$\boldsymbol{y}[\tilde{n}] := \big(y_1[\tilde{n}], \ldots, y_L[\tilde{n}]\big)^\mathsf{T} \in \{0,1\}^L, \tag{7.42}$$

$$\boldsymbol{w}_i := (w_{1,i}, \ldots, w_{L,i})^\mathsf{T} \in \mathbb{R}^L. \tag{7.43}$$

From (7.39) to (7.40) we repeatedly applied $\big(f * \delta_\tau\big)(t) = f(t-\tau)$, $t \in \mathbb{R}$, cf. (7.6). Thus, $z_i(\cdot)$ is a piecewise constant function which jumps only at $t = \tilde{n}T_\mathrm{r}$, for $\tilde{n} \in \{1, \ldots, n\}$, implying that in $t \in [0, (n+1)T_\mathrm{r}[$ all firings occur only at multiples of T_r, and we can write

$$y_\ell(t) = \sum_{\tilde{n}=0}^{n} y_\ell[\tilde{n}]\, \delta(t - \tilde{n}T_\mathrm{r}), \qquad 0 \le t < (n+1)T_\mathrm{r}. \tag{7.44}$$

We have showed that the assumption (7.37) implies (7.44), for all $n \in \mathbb{N}$. Thus, by induction all firings occur only at multiples of T_r, for all $t \ge 0$, and the score signal of ξ_i can be written as

$$z_i(t) = \sum_{\tilde{n}\in\mathbb{N}} \big\langle \boldsymbol{y}[\tilde{n}], \boldsymbol{w}_i \big\rangle\, \mathrm{I}\big[(\tilde{n}+1)T_\mathrm{r} \le t < (\tilde{n}+2)T_\mathrm{r}\big] + \eta_i(t), \tag{7.45}$$

for $t \ge 0$, with $\boldsymbol{y}[\tilde{n}]$ as in (7.42), where $y_\ell[\tilde{n}] \in \{0,1\}$ indicates whether there is a firing or not at $t = \tilde{n}T_\mathrm{r}$ in the ℓ-th channel.

Since all firings occur only at multiples of T_r, i.e.,

$$t_j^{(\ell)} \in \big\{kT_\mathrm{r} : k \in \mathbb{N}\big\}, \qquad (\ell, j) \in \{1, \ldots, L\} \times \mathbb{N}, \tag{7.46}$$

we only need to evaluate the score signals at $t = nT_\mathrm{r}$, $n \in \mathbb{N}$. (Note that (7.4) is clearly satisfied.) Thus, we can replace (7.36) by the recursion

$$\boldsymbol{y}[n] = \begin{pmatrix} \sigma_{\theta_1}\big(z_1(nT_\mathrm{r})\big) \\ \vdots \\ \sigma_{\theta_L}\big(z_L(nT_\mathrm{r})\big) \end{pmatrix} \tag{7.47}$$

$$= \begin{pmatrix} \sigma_{\theta_1}\big(\langle \boldsymbol{y}[n-1], \boldsymbol{w}_1 \rangle + \eta_1(nT_\mathrm{r})\big) \\ \vdots \\ \sigma_{\theta_L}\big(\langle \boldsymbol{y}[n-1], \boldsymbol{w}_L \rangle + \eta_L(nT_\mathrm{r})\big) \end{pmatrix}, \tag{7.48}$$

for $n \in \mathbb{N}$, $n \geq 1$, and

$$\boldsymbol{y}(t) = \sum_{n \in \mathbb{N}} \boldsymbol{y}[n]\, \delta(t - nT_\mathrm{r}), \qquad t \geq 0, \tag{7.49}$$

which is fully determined by the sequence $(\boldsymbol{y}[n])_{n \in \mathbb{N}}$ defined as in (7.48). The step from (7.47) to (7.48) follows from (7.45).

The recursion (7.48), which fully determines the produced continuous-time firing signal $\boldsymbol{y}(\cdot)$, is equivalent to (2.4) from Chapter 2.

Chapter 8

Perfect Memorization in the Ideal Case

As a starting point we consider the case where $\eta_i(t) = 0$, for all $t \geq 0$, $i \in \{1, \ldots, L\}$, i.e., we assume no imperfections at all. Furthermore, for the sake of analysis we consider a special class of firing signals, namely firing signals which have firings only on a regular grid. Those firing signals are defined next.

8.1 Firing Signals with Firings Only on a Regular Grid

For $K \in \mathbb{N}$, $K \geq 2$, let

$$\mu_{T_\mathrm{r}} := \frac{T_\mathrm{r}}{K}, \tag{8.1}$$

be the *grid size*. Recall, T_r is the neuron's refractory period introduced in Section 7.1.

Now, we are given a firing signal

$$\boldsymbol{y}\colon \mathbb{R} \to \mathbb{R}^L,\ \ t \mapsto \boldsymbol{y}(t) := \big(y_1(t), \ldots, y_L(t)\big)^\mathsf{T}, \tag{8.2}$$

where the signal in the ℓ-th channel contains only finitely many firings

$$y_\ell(t) = \sum_{j=1}^{J_\ell} \delta\big(t - t_j^{(\ell)}\big), \qquad t \in \mathbb{R}, \tag{8.3}$$

with firing times $0 < t_1^{(\ell)} < \cdots < t_{J_\ell}^{(\ell)} < \infty$ satisfying (7.4), i.e.,

$$t_{j+1}^{(\ell)} - t_j^{(\ell)} \geq T_\mathrm{r}, \qquad j \in \{1, \ldots, J_\ell - 1\}, \tag{8.4}$$

and

$$t_j^{(\ell)} \in \{n\mu_{T_\mathrm{r}} : n \in \mathbb{N}\}, \qquad j \in \{1, \ldots, J_\ell\}, \tag{8.5}$$

where $J_\ell \in \mathbb{N}$ denotes the number of firings in the ℓ-th channel. Thus, we assume that all firings occur only at multiples of μ_{T_r}.

In this case, every such firing signal $\boldsymbol{y}(\cdot)$ of signal duration (or length) equal to NT_r, for $N \in \mathbb{N}$, is uniquely specified by the matrix

$$\boldsymbol{Y}_N^{(K)} := \big(\boldsymbol{y}[0], \boldsymbol{y}[1], \ldots, \boldsymbol{y}[NK]\big) \tag{8.6}$$

$$= \begin{pmatrix} y_1[0] & y_1[1] & \cdots & y_1[NK] \\ y_2[0] & y_2[1] & \cdots & y_2[NK] \\ \vdots & \vdots & \ddots & \vdots \\ y_L[0] & y_L[1] & \cdots & y_L[NK] \end{pmatrix} \in \{0,1\}^{L \times (NK+1)}, \tag{8.7}$$

where the binary entries $y_\ell[n]$, $(\ell, n) \in \{1, \ldots, L\} \times \{0, 1, \ldots, NK\}$ of $\boldsymbol{Y}_N^{(K)}$ indicate if there is a firing ($y_\ell[n] = 1$) or not ($y_\ell[n] = 0$) at $t = n\mu_{T_\mathrm{r}}$ in the ℓ-th channel, and

$$\boldsymbol{y}[n] := \big(y_1[n], \ldots, y_L[n]\big)^\mathsf{T} \in \{0,1\}^L. \tag{8.8}$$

Note that the column index of $\boldsymbol{Y}_N^{(K)}$ is taken modulo $NK + 1$ similar as in Part I. Thus, (8.3) can be rewritten as

$$y_\ell(t) = \sum_{n=0}^{NK} y_\ell[n]\, \delta(t - n\mu_{T_\mathrm{r}}), \qquad t \in \mathbb{R}. \tag{8.9}$$

Moreover, let

$$\tilde{\boldsymbol{y}}_\ell := \big(y_\ell[0], y_\ell[1], \ldots, y_\ell[NK]\big)^\mathsf{T} \in \{0,1\}^{NK+1} \tag{8.10}$$

be the ℓ-th row of $\boldsymbol{Y}_N^{(K)}$ turned into a column vector. Then, condition (8.4) can be written as

$$\tilde{\boldsymbol{y}}_\ell \in \mathcal{Y}_N^{(K)}, \qquad \ell \in \{1, \ldots, L\}, \tag{8.11}$$

where

$$\mathcal{Y}_N^{(K)} := \Bigg\{ \big(y[0], \ldots, y[NK]\big)^{\mathsf{T}} \in \{0,1\}^{NK+1} : \\ \sum_{k=0}^{K-1} y\big[n + k \bmod (NK+1)\big] \in \{0,1\},\ n \in \{0, \ldots, NK\} \Bigg\} \quad (8.12)$$

is the set of all binary vectors (of dimension $NK + 1$) which have in every circular window of length K at most one firing, or equivalently, after a firing at least $K - 1$ zeros have to follow. The cardinality of $\mathcal{Y}_N^{(K)} \subset \{0,1\}^{NK+1}$ is addressed in Appendix B.7.

8.2 Delays & Weights

All delays are fixed and given (or known) such that

$$\tau_{\min} \leq \tau_{\ell,i} \leq \mu_{T_\mathrm{r}} - \tau_{\min}, \qquad (\ell, i) \in \{1, \ldots, L\}^2, \quad (8.13)$$

with parameter $0 < \tau_{\min} < \mu_{T_\mathrm{r}}/2$. The quantity μ_{T_r} denotes the firing signal grid size as defined in Section 8.1. In all experiments we choose the delays beforehand randomly according to

$$\tau_{\ell,i} \overset{\text{i.i.d.}}{\sim} \mathcal{U}\big([\tau_{\min}, \mu_{T_\mathrm{r}} - \tau_{\min}]\big), \qquad (\ell, i) \in \{1, \ldots, L\}^2. \quad (8.14)$$

Given a firing signal $\boldsymbol{Y}_N^{(K)} = \big(y_i[n]\big) \in \{0,1\}^{L \times (NK+1)}$ (where $y_i[n]$ is the binary entry in row i and column n) as defined in Section 8.1. Then, for $i \in \{1, \ldots, L\}$, and a fixed threshold $\theta_i > 0$, the weight vector of the i-th neuron $\boldsymbol{w}_i := (w_{1,i}, \ldots, w_{L,i})^{\mathsf{T}} \in \mathbb{R}^L$ is defined as

$$\boldsymbol{w}_i := \underset{\tilde{\boldsymbol{w}}_i \in \mathbb{R}^L}{\operatorname{argmin}} \Big\| \Delta \boldsymbol{W}_i \, \tilde{\boldsymbol{w}}_i - \theta_i \, \tilde{\boldsymbol{y}}_i \Big\|^2, \quad (8.15)$$

where $\tilde{\boldsymbol{y}}_i \in \{0,1\}^{NK+1}$ is the column vector consisting of all the samples (on the grid) of the i-th channel as defined in (8.10), and

$$\Delta \boldsymbol{W}_i := \begin{pmatrix} \big(\Delta \boldsymbol{w}_i^{(0)}\big)^{\mathsf{T}} \\ \vdots \\ \big(\Delta \boldsymbol{w}_i^{(NK)}\big)^{\mathsf{T}} \end{pmatrix} \in \mathbb{R}^{(NK+1) \times L} \quad (8.16)$$

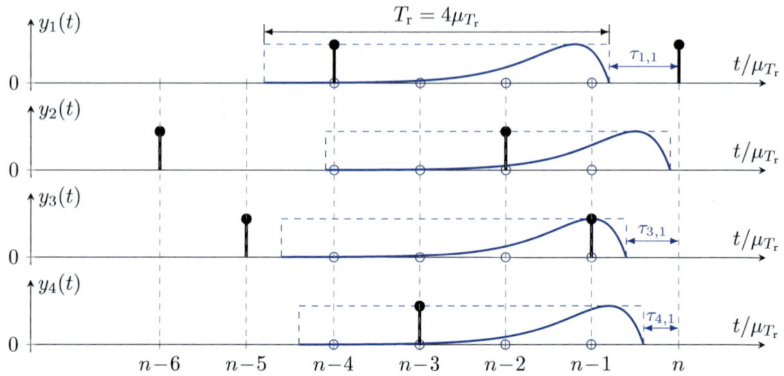

Figure 8.1: An example for a 4-channel local receptive field of neuron ξ_1 with impulse response $h_{\text{bio},\beta}(\cdot)$, $\beta = 0.4\mu_{T_r}$, at firing time $t_j^{(1)} = n\mu_{T_r}$, $n \in \mathbb{N}$, for $K = 4$ and $\boldsymbol{\tau}_1 = \frac{1}{10}(8,1,6,4)^{\mathsf{T}}\mu_{T_r}$.

with entries

$$(\Delta \boldsymbol{W}_i)_{n,\ell} = \left(\Delta \boldsymbol{w}_i^{(n)}\right)_\ell := \sum_{k=1}^{K} h(k\mu_{T_r} - \tau_{\ell,i})\, y_\ell[n-k], \tag{8.17}$$

for $(n,\ell) \in \{0,\dots,NK\} \times \{1,\dots,L\}$, where the indices $\tilde{n} := n-k$ of $y_\ell[\tilde{n}]$ in (8.17) are taken modulo $NK+1$, i.e.,

$$y_\ell[n-k] := y_\ell\big[(n-k) \bmod (NK+1)\big]. \tag{8.18}$$

The n-th row of $\Delta \boldsymbol{W}_i$, i.e., the vector $\Delta \boldsymbol{w}_i^{(n)} \in \mathbb{R}^L$ indicates the weight change of ξ_i at time $t = n\mu_{T_r}$. In Figure 8.1, the computation of $\Delta \boldsymbol{w}_1^{(n)}$ is illustrated for a 4-channel toy example, where the blue curves represent the corresponding time-reversed and delayed impulse responses, cf. (8.17).

8.3 Score Signals Sampled on the Grid

In this section we show that the score signals of the recurrent network sampled at $t = n\mu_{T_r}$ can be expressed as an inner product in $\mathbb{R}^L$, namely

$$z_i(n\mu_{T_r}) = \langle \Delta \boldsymbol{w}_i^{(n)}, \boldsymbol{w}_i \rangle, \qquad n \in \mathbb{N}, \tag{8.19}$$

for firing signals and delays as introduced in Section 8.1 and 8.2, respectively. This result motivates (8.15), and we can state a sufficient condition (Proposition 8.1) on the weight-change matrix $\Delta \boldsymbol{W}_i$ such that perfect memorization is potentially possible as discussed in the next section.

Proposition 8.1. *For any $L, N, K \in \mathbb{N}$, $K \geq 2$, firing signal $\mathbf{Y}_N^{(K)} := (\tilde{\boldsymbol{y}}_1, \ldots, \tilde{\boldsymbol{y}}_L)^\mathsf{T} \in \{0,1\}^{L \times (NK+1)}$ with channel signals*

$$\tilde{\boldsymbol{y}}_i \in \mathcal{Y}_N^{(K)}, \qquad i \in \{1, \ldots, L\}, \tag{8.20}$$

as in Section 8.1, delays as in (8.13), causal neuron impulse response $h(\cdot)$ such that

$$h(t) = 0, \qquad t \geq T_r, \tag{8.21}$$

and if

$$\operatorname{rank}(\Delta \boldsymbol{W}_i) = NK + 1, \qquad i \in \{1, \ldots, L\}, \tag{8.22}$$

with $\Delta \boldsymbol{W}_i \in \mathbb{R}^{(NK+1) \times L}$ as defined in (8.17), then the score signals of the recurrent network with weight vectors (8.15) and thresholds

$$\theta_i > 0, \qquad i \in \{1, \ldots, L\}, \tag{8.23}$$

satisfy

$$z_i(n\mu_{T_r}) = \theta_i \, y_i[n], \qquad n \in \{0, 1, \ldots, NK\}, \tag{8.24}$$

for all $i \in \{1, \ldots, L\}$. □

Note that the condition $\operatorname{rank}(\Delta \boldsymbol{W}_i) = NK + 1$ implies $L \geq NK + 1$, i.e., the number of neurons required has to be at least as large as the number of samples (in a channel).

Proof of Proposition 8.1. Let $i \in \{1, \ldots, L\}$ be fixed but arbitrary. In the disturbance-free case, i.e., $\eta_i(t) = 0$, for all $t \in \mathbb{R}$, the score signal of the i-th neuron in the RNN evaluated at $t = n\mu_{T_\mathrm{r}}$, $n \in \mathbb{N}$, is given by

$$z_i(n\mu_{T_\mathrm{r}}) = \sum_{\ell=1}^{L} w_{\ell,i} \big(h * (\boldsymbol{x}_i)_\ell\big)(n\mu_{T_\mathrm{r}}), \tag{8.25}$$

where $(\boldsymbol{x}_i)_\ell(\cdot)$ denotes the ℓ-th component of $\boldsymbol{x}_i(\cdot)$ as in (7.28), i.e.,

$$(\boldsymbol{x}_i)_\ell(t) = \big(y_\ell * \delta_{\tau_{\ell,i}}\big)(t), \tag{8.26}$$

for $t \in \mathbb{R}$. Equation (8.25) follows from (7.1) and (7.26), cf. Chapter 7.

Now, we rewrite the convolution in (8.25) as

$$\begin{aligned}
&\big(h * (\boldsymbol{x}_i)_\ell\big)(n\mu_{T_\mathrm{r}}) \\
&\quad= \big(h * \delta_{\tau_{\ell,i}} * y_\ell\big)(n\mu_{T_\mathrm{r}}) && (8.27)\\
&\quad= \int_{\mathbb{R}} \big(h * \delta_{\tau_{\ell,i}}\big)(s)\, y_\ell(n\mu_{T_\mathrm{r}} - s)\, ds && (8.28)\\
&\quad= \int_{\mathbb{R}} h(s-\tau_{\ell,i})\, y_\ell(n\mu_{T_\mathrm{r}} - s)\, ds && (8.29)\\
&\quad= \int_{[\tau_{\ell,i},\, \tau_{\ell,i}+T_\mathrm{r}[} h(s-\tau_{\ell,i})\, y_\ell(n\mu_{T_\mathrm{r}} - s)\, ds && (8.30)\\
&\quad= \int_{[\tau_{\ell,i},\, \tau_{\ell,i}+T_\mathrm{r}[} h(s-\tau_{\ell,i}) \sum_{k=0}^{NK} y_\ell[k]\, \delta(n\mu_{T_\mathrm{r}} - s - k\mu_{T_\mathrm{r}})\, ds && (8.31)\\
&\quad= \sum_{k=0}^{NK} y_\ell[k] \int_{[\tau_{\ell,i},\, \tau_{\ell,i}+T_\mathrm{r}[} h(s-\tau_{\ell,i})\, \delta\big((n-k)\mu_{T_\mathrm{r}} - s\big)\, ds && (8.32)\\
&\quad= \sum_{k=0}^{NK} y_\ell[k]\, h\big((n-k)\mu_{T_\mathrm{r}} - \tau_{\ell,i}\big) \\
&\qquad\qquad \cdot \mathrm{I}\big[\tau_{\ell,i} \le (n-k)\mu_{T_\mathrm{r}} < \tau_{\ell,i} + K\mu_{T_\mathrm{r}}\big] && (8.33)\\
&\quad= \sum_{k'=1}^{K} y_\ell[n-k']\, h(k'\mu_{T_\mathrm{r}} - \tau_{\ell,i}) && (8.34)\\
&\quad= \big(\Delta \boldsymbol{w}_i^{(n)}\big)_\ell && (8.35)
\end{aligned}$$

where (8.27) follows from (8.26). In (8.28) we applied the definition of the (continuous-time) convolution, cf. (7.2), and in (8.29) we applied

$\big(h * \delta_{\tau_{\ell,i}}\big)(s) = h(s - \tau_{\ell,i})$, for $s \in \mathbb{R}$. The step from (8.29) to (8.30) follows from the assumption that $h(\cdot)$ is causal, i.e., $h(t) = 0$, for $t < 0$, and from (8.21). In (8.31) we inserted the representation (8.9), cf. Section 8.1. Equation (8.32) holds because of the linearity of integration. From (8.32) to (8.33) we used the defining property of the Dirac delta, cf. (7.6), and $T_\mathrm{r} = K\mu_{T_\mathrm{r}}$. Equation (8.34) follows from the substitution $k' := n - k$ and (8.13). Finally, (8.35) holds because of the definition (8.17).

Thus, we can write $z_i(n\mu_{T_\mathrm{r}})$ as standard inner product in $\mathbb{R}^L$

$$z_i(n\mu_{T_\mathrm{r}}) = \sum_{\ell=1}^{L} w_{\ell,i}\,\big(h * (\boldsymbol{x}_i)_\ell\big)(n\mu_{T_\mathrm{r}}) \tag{8.36}$$

$$= \sum_{\ell=1}^{L} w_{\ell,i}\,\big(\Delta\boldsymbol{w}_i^{(n)}\big)_\ell \tag{8.37}$$

$$= \big\langle \Delta\boldsymbol{w}_i^{(n)}, \boldsymbol{w}_i \big\rangle, \tag{8.38}$$

where $\big(\Delta\boldsymbol{w}_i^{(n)}\big)_\ell$ denotes the ℓ-th component of the vector $\Delta\boldsymbol{w}_i^{(n)} \in \mathbb{R}^L$, and

$$\langle \boldsymbol{a}, \boldsymbol{b} \rangle := \boldsymbol{a}^\mathsf{T}\boldsymbol{b} = \boldsymbol{b}^\mathsf{T}\boldsymbol{a} = \sum_{\ell=1}^{L} a_\ell b_\ell, \tag{8.39}$$

for vectors $\boldsymbol{a}, \boldsymbol{b} \in \mathbb{R}^L$. The weight vector (8.15) thus minimizes the quadratic cost

$$\big\|\Delta\boldsymbol{W}_i\,\boldsymbol{w}_i - \theta_i\,\tilde{\boldsymbol{y}}_i\big\|^2 = \left\|\begin{pmatrix} \big(\Delta\boldsymbol{w}_i^{(0)}\big)^\mathsf{T}\boldsymbol{w}_i - \theta_i\,y_i[0] \\ \big(\Delta\boldsymbol{w}_i^{(1)}\big)^\mathsf{T}\boldsymbol{w}_i - \theta_i\,y_i[1] \\ \vdots \\ \big(\Delta\boldsymbol{w}_i^{(NK)}\big)^\mathsf{T}\boldsymbol{w}_i - \theta_i\,y_i[NK] \end{pmatrix}\right\|^2 \tag{8.40}$$

$$= \sum_{n=0}^{NK} \Big|\big(\Delta\boldsymbol{w}_i^{(n)}\big)^\mathsf{T}\boldsymbol{w}_i - \theta_i\,y_i[n]\Big|^2 \tag{8.41}$$

$$= \sum_{n=0}^{NK} \big|z_i(n\mu_{T_\mathrm{r}}) - \theta_i\,y_i[n]\big|^2, \tag{8.42}$$

where in (8.40) we inserted the definitions of $\tilde{\boldsymbol{y}}_i$ and $\Delta\boldsymbol{W}_i$ as in (8.10) and (8.16), respectively. The step from (8.40) to (8.41) follows from the definition of the L_2-norm, i.e., $\|\boldsymbol{a}\|^2 := \sum_{n=1}^{N} |a_n|^2$, for $\boldsymbol{a} \in \mathbb{R}^N$, and finally (8.42) follows from (8.38).

Then, condition (8.22), i.e., $\operatorname{rank}(\Delta\boldsymbol{W}_i) = NK + 1$ implies that $\theta_i\,\tilde{\boldsymbol{y}}_i \in \mathbb{R}^{NK+1}$ is an element of the vector space spanned by the columns of $\Delta\boldsymbol{W}_i$. Thus, there exists $\boldsymbol{w}_i \in \mathbb{R}^L$ such that

$$\left\|\Delta\boldsymbol{W}_i\,\boldsymbol{w}_i - \theta_i\,\tilde{\boldsymbol{y}}_i\right\|^2 = 0, \tag{8.43}$$

for any $\tilde{\boldsymbol{y}}_i \in \{0,1\}^{NK+1}$, $\theta_i \in \mathbb{R}$, and thus by (8.42) we have

$$\sum_{n=0}^{NK} \left|z_i(n\mu_{T_\mathrm{r}}) - \theta_i\,y_i[n]\right|^2 = 0, \tag{8.44}$$

which again implies $z_i(n\mu_{T_\mathrm{r}}) = \theta_i\,y_i[n]$, for $n \in \{0,1,\ldots,NK\}$. ■

8.4 Remarks

Proposition 8.1 is a theoretical result and not directly applicable in many (practical) cases. However, we illustrate that by properly choosing the parameters the stated result holds "sufficiently well" also for $h_{\mathrm{bio},\beta}(\cdot)$ even though it violates condition (8.21).

We study under what conditions equation (8.24) results in perfect memorization. To this end the delays need to be modified when using $h_{\mathrm{rect}}(\cdot)$ as impulse response.

Moreover, we examine the condition number of $\Delta\boldsymbol{W}_i$, we briefly discuss how the weights in Proposition 8.1 can be determined, and we also give an extension which potentially improves the robustness of the presented network.

8.4.1 Open Loop Score Signals for $h_{\mathrm{rect}}(\cdot)$ and $h_{\mathrm{bio},\beta}(\cdot)$

We now elaborate under which conditions (8.24), i.e.,

$$z_i(n\mu_{T_\mathrm{r}}) = \theta_i\,y_i[n], \tag{8.45}$$

for all $n \in \mathbb{N}$, actually results in perfect memorization.

Given a firing signal $\boldsymbol{Y}_N^{(K)}$ (and a threshold $\theta_i > 0$), we compute the i-th weight vector $\boldsymbol{w}_i \in \mathbb{R}^L$ according to (8.15), for $h_{\mathrm{rect}}(\cdot)$ and $h_{\mathrm{bio},\beta}(\cdot)$. The corresponding open loop score signals of the i-th neuron are shown

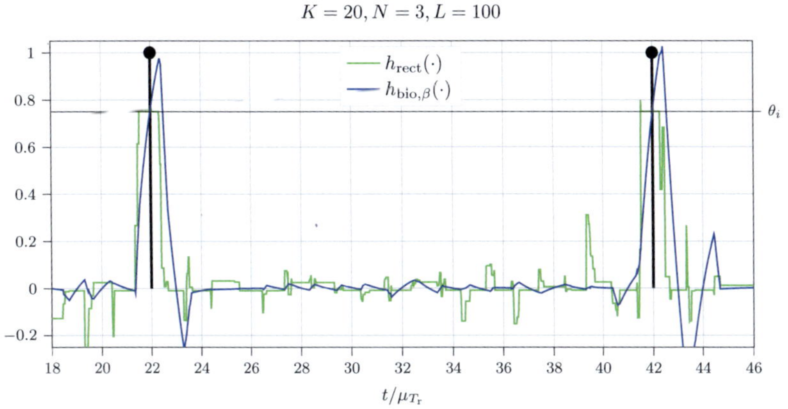

Figure 8.2: Open loop score signal of ξ_i with learnt weights as in (8.15) using $h_{\text{rect}}(\cdot)$ (green) or $h_{\text{bio},\beta}(\cdot)$ (blue), $\beta = T_r/8$, and $\tau_{\min} = 0.3\mu_{T_r}$.

in Figure 8.2, for an example of $\boldsymbol{Y}_3^{(20)}$ with $L = 100$. The *open loop* score signals are obtained by directly feed in the given firing signal $\boldsymbol{Y}_N^{(K)}$, i.e.,

$$z_i(t) = \sum_{\ell=1}^{L} w_{\ell,i} \left(h * \delta_{\tau_{\ell,i}} * y_\ell\right)(t), \qquad t \in \mathbb{R}, \tag{8.46}$$

for

$$y_\ell(t) = \sum_{n=0}^{NK} y_\ell[n]\, \delta(t - n\mu_{T_r}), \qquad t \in \mathbb{R}, \tag{8.47}$$

where $y_\ell[n]$ is the entry in row ℓ and column n of $\boldsymbol{Y}_N^{(K)}$. This method allows us to study the connection of the least-squares solution of (8.15) and its corresponding score signal in the recurrent network. It is usually enough to analyze a single neuron (or channel) in order to understand the relationship between the learnt weights and its (potential) score signal, and thus we only need to determine one single weight vector.

In the example of Figure 8.2, we have $\text{rank}(\Delta\boldsymbol{W}_i) = 61$ (i.e., full rank) for $h_{\text{bio},\beta}(\cdot)$, and $\text{rank}(\Delta\boldsymbol{W}_i) = 54$ for $h_{\text{rect}}(\cdot)$. Experiments indicated that for this particular example we need $L \approx 250$ neurons such that $\Delta\boldsymbol{W}_i$ has full rank in the case of $h_{\text{rect}}(\cdot)$. Note that (8.45) typically does not hold at the beginning (even in the full-rank case) for the open loop score signal as illustrated in Figure 8.2. Since we initialize all score signals to be equal to zero, the periodic/circular extension is not properly taken into account and ends up violating (8.45) in the starting time.

By properly choosing β, e.g., $\beta = T_\mathrm{r}/8$ as in Figure 8.2 such that (8.21) is "almost" fulfilled (can be seen as an imperfection, cf. Chapter 9) perfect memorization seems to be possible, since the score signal crosses the threshold from below (almost) exactly at the desired time instances. In contrast, even if (8.45) holds, the rectangular impulse response has the problem of typically reaching the threshold level too early and additionally it does not cross, but rather remains at the threshold level. Nonetheless, by adapting the delays appropriately, perfect memorization becomes possible also for $h(\cdot) = h_{\mathrm{rect}}(\cdot)$, which is elaborated next.

Delays on the Grid for $h_{\mathrm{rect}}(\cdot)$

If we assume

$$\tau_{\ell,i} \in \big\{\mu_{T_\mathrm{r}}, 2\mu_{T_\mathrm{r}}, \ldots, K\mu_{T_\mathrm{r}}\big\}, \qquad (\ell, i) \in \{1, \ldots, L\}^2, \tag{8.48}$$

i.e., there exists $k_{\ell,i} \in \{1, \ldots, K\}$ such that $\tau_{\ell,i} = k_{\ell,i}\,\mu_{T_\mathrm{r}}$, then (8.46), for $h(\cdot) = h_{\mathrm{rect}}(\cdot)$, becomes

$$
\begin{aligned}
&z_i(t)\\
&= \sum_{\ell=1}^{L} w_{\ell,i} \big(h_{\mathrm{rect}} * \delta_{\tau_{\ell,i}} * y_\ell\big)(t) && (8.49)\\
&= \sum_{\ell=1}^{L} w_{\ell,i} \int_{\mathbb{R}} h_{\mathrm{rect}}(s - \tau_{\ell,i})\, y_\ell(t-s)\, ds && (8.50)\\
&= \sum_{\ell=1}^{L} w_{\ell,i} \int_{[\tau_{\ell,i},\, \tau_{\ell,i}+T_\mathrm{r}[} y_\ell(t-s)\, ds && (8.51)\\
&= \sum_{\ell=1}^{L} w_{\ell,i} \sum_{k=0}^{NK} y_\ell[k] \int_{[\tau_{\ell,i},\, \tau_{\ell,i}+T_\mathrm{r}[} \delta(t - s - k\mu_{T_\mathrm{r}})\, ds && (8.52)\\
&= \sum_{\ell=1}^{L} w_{\ell,i} \sum_{k=0}^{NK} y_\ell[k]\, \mathrm{I}\big[\tau_{\ell,i} \le t - k\mu_{T_\mathrm{r}} < \tau_{\ell,i} + T_\mathrm{r}\big] && (8.53)\\
&= \sum_{\ell=1}^{L} w_{\ell,i} \sum_{k=0}^{NK} y_\ell[k]\, \mathrm{I}\big[(k + k_{\ell,i})\mu_{T_\mathrm{r}} \le t < (k + k_{\ell,i} + K)\mu_{T_\mathrm{r}}\big], && (8.54)
\end{aligned}
$$

for $t \in \mathbb{R}$, i.e., the score signal is a piecewise constant function which jumps only at multiples of μ_{T_r}. Thus, we can write

$$z_i(t) = \sum_{n\in\mathbb{N}} z_i(n\mu_{T_\mathrm{r}})\,\mathrm{I}\big[n\mu_{T_\mathrm{r}} \le t < (n+K)\mu_{T_\mathrm{r}}\big], \qquad t \in \mathbb{R}, \tag{8.55}$$

with (evaluating (8.54) at $t = n\mu_{T_\mathrm{r}}$)

$$\begin{aligned}
z_i(n\mu_{T_\mathrm{r}}) &= \sum_{\ell=1}^{L} w_{\ell,i} \sum_{k=0}^{NK} y_\ell[k]\,\mathrm{I}\big[k + k_{\ell,i} \le n < k + k_{\ell,i} + K\big] && (8.56)\\
&= \sum_{\ell=1}^{L} w_{\ell,i} \sum_{k=0}^{NK} y_\ell[k]\,\mathrm{I}\big[n - k_{\ell,i} - K < k \le n - k_{\ell,i}\big] && (8.57)\\
&= \sum_{\ell=1}^{L} w_{\ell,i} \sum_{k\in\{n-k_{\ell,i}-K+1,\dots,n-k_{\ell,i}\}} y_\ell[k] && (8.58)\\
&= \sum_{\ell=1}^{L} w_{\ell,i} \left(\Delta\boldsymbol{w}_i^{(n)}\right)_\ell && (8.59)\\
&= \left\langle \Delta\boldsymbol{w}_i^{(n)}, \boldsymbol{w}_i \right\rangle, && (8.60)
\end{aligned}$$

where

$$\begin{aligned}
\left(\Delta\boldsymbol{w}_i^{(n)}\right)_\ell &:= \sum_{k\in\{n-k_{\ell,i}-K+1,\dots,n-k_{\ell,i}\}} y_\ell[k] && (8.61)\\
&= \sum_{k\in\{n-k_{\ell,i}-k' :\; k'\in\{0,\dots,K-1\}\}} y_\ell[k] && (8.62)\\
&= \sum_{k'=0}^{K-1} y_\ell[n - k_{\ell,i} - k'], && (8.63)
\end{aligned}$$

which coincides with (8.17) because

$$\begin{aligned}
\left(\Delta\boldsymbol{w}_i^{(n)}\right)_\ell &= \sum_{k=1}^{K} h_{\mathrm{rect}}(k\mu_{T_\mathrm{r}} - \tau_{\ell,i})\, y_\ell[n-k] && (8.64)\\
&= \sum_{k=1}^{K} \mathrm{I}\big[0 \le \underbrace{(k - k_{\ell,i})}_{=:\,k'} \mu_{T_\mathrm{r}} < K\mu_{T_\mathrm{r}}\big]\, y_\ell[n-k] && (8.65)\\
&= \sum_{k'=0}^{K-1} y_\ell[n - (k_{\ell,i} + k')]. && (8.66)
\end{aligned}$$

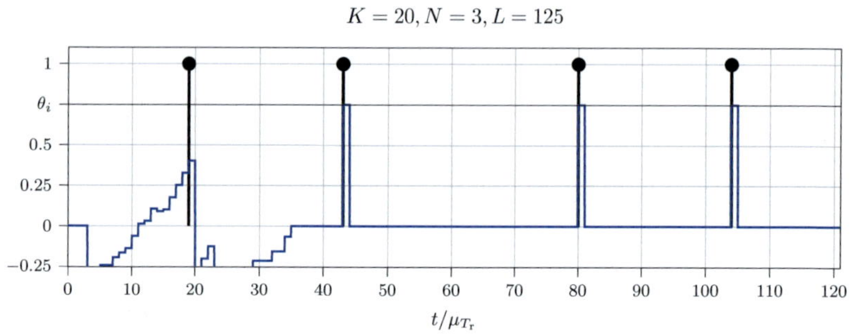

(a) Example with $\mathrm{rank}(\Delta \boldsymbol{W}_i) = 61$ (full rank).

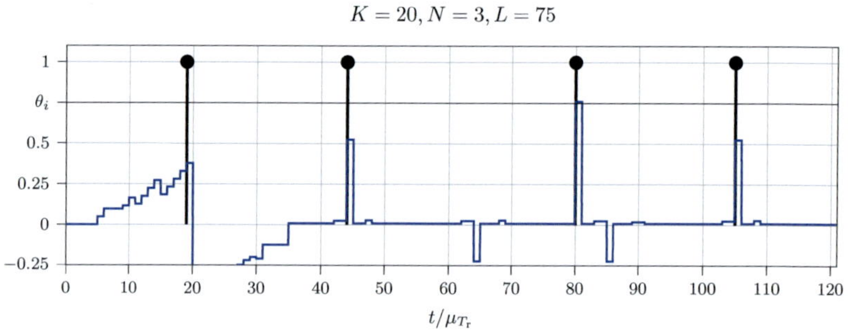

(b) Example with $\mathrm{rank}(\Delta \boldsymbol{W}_i) = 56$.

Figure 8.3: Open loop score signal of ξ_i with learnt weights as in (8.15) using $h_{\text{rect}}(\cdot)$ and delays drawn at random i.i.d. uniformly from $\{\mu_{T_r}, \ldots, K\mu_{T_r}\}$.

Two different examples of (8.55) are shown in Figure 8.3. Figure 8.3a depicts an example where (8.45) holds (except at the beginning as explained above), whereas Figure 8.3b depicts a situation where (8.45) does not hold. However, in both cases perfect memorization of $\boldsymbol{Y}_N^{(K)}$ can be achieved by using an effective threshold (smaller than θ_i in (8.15)), e.g., $\bar{\theta}_i = 0.5$. These examples illustrate that using $h_{\text{rect}}(\cdot)$ with delays on the grid as in (8.48) enables potential perfect memorization of firing signals introduced in Section 8.1. In Appendix A.3, a small example for the case of a rectangular impulse response with delays on the grid is developed.

8.4.2 Learning of the Weights

If $L > NK+1$ and $\Delta \boldsymbol{W}_i \in \mathbb{R}^{(NK+1)\times L}$ has full rank (as in (8.22)), then the least-squares (cf. (8.15))

$$\min_{\tilde{\boldsymbol{w}}_i \in \mathbb{R}^L} \left\| \Delta \boldsymbol{W}_i \, \tilde{\boldsymbol{w}}_i - \theta_i \, \tilde{\boldsymbol{y}}_i \right\|^2 \tag{8.67}$$

has infinitely many solutions. In this case $\theta_i \, \tilde{\boldsymbol{y}}_i \in \mathbb{R}^{NK+1}$ is in the span of the columns of $\Delta \boldsymbol{W}_i$ and thus any minimizer $\boldsymbol{w}_i \in \mathbb{R}^L$ of (8.67) satisfies

$$\Delta \boldsymbol{W}_i \, \boldsymbol{w}_i = \theta_i \, \tilde{\boldsymbol{y}}_i, \tag{8.68}$$

i.e., the minimized quadratic cost is equal to zero.

In all simulations we choose (unless stated otherwise) the pseudoinverse solution

$$\boldsymbol{w}_i^\dagger := \Delta \boldsymbol{W}_i^\dagger \, \tilde{\boldsymbol{y}}_i, \tag{8.69}$$

where

$$\Delta \boldsymbol{W}_i^\dagger := \lim_{\lambda \to 0} \left((\Delta \boldsymbol{W}_i)^\mathsf{T} \Delta \boldsymbol{W}_i + \lambda^2 \boldsymbol{I}_L \right)^{-1} (\Delta \boldsymbol{W}_i)^\mathsf{T} \tag{8.70}$$

is the (Moore–Penrose) pseudoinverse of $\Delta \boldsymbol{W}_i$ similar as in Part I (Section 4.3). The solution/minimizer (8.69) is special, namely it has the smallest L_2-norm among all minimizers of (8.67), i.e., $\|\boldsymbol{w}_i\| \geq \left\|\boldsymbol{w}_i^\dagger\right\|$, for all $\boldsymbol{w}_i$ satisfying (8.68), with equality if and only if $\boldsymbol{w}_i = \boldsymbol{w}_i^\dagger$.

In Figure 8.4 the components of the weight vector (8.69) are plotted for the examples in Figure 8.3. Interestingly, in both cases the arithmetic mean is approximately equal to zero, i.e.,

$$\frac{1}{L} \sum_{\ell=1}^{L} w_{\ell,i}^\dagger \approx 0. \tag{8.71}$$

The extreme values of the full rank case (blue) are smaller than in the case where $\Delta \boldsymbol{W}_i$ has not full rank (green). This might be since in the former case L (dimension of $\boldsymbol{w}_i$) is larger than in the latter case, which potentially reduces the influence of a single input/connection.

Bounding the extreme values $\max_\ell |w_{\ell,i}|$ of the solutions of (8.68) by some bound $w_\mathrm{b} > 0$ is thus desirable. One way to achieve this is to replace the least-squares (8.67) with

$$\min_{\tilde{\boldsymbol{w}}_i \in \mathbb{R}^L} \left(\left\| \Delta \boldsymbol{W}_i \, \tilde{\boldsymbol{w}}_i - \theta_i \, \tilde{\boldsymbol{y}}_i \right\|^2 + \rho(\tilde{\boldsymbol{w}}_i) \right) \tag{8.72}$$

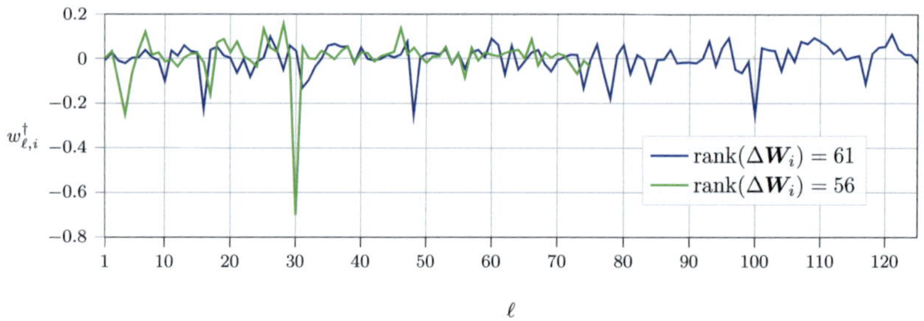

Figure 8.4: Distribution of the weights (8.69) for the examples in Figure 8.3.

and choosing the regularizer $\rho(\cdot)$ appropriately as shown in [33]. Then (8.72) selects a solution of (8.68) which in addition fulfills

$$|w_{\ell,i}| \leq w_{\mathrm{b}}, \qquad \ell \in \{1, \ldots, L\}. \tag{8.73}$$

This property is helpful especially for the jitter analysis in Chapter 9.

The underdetermined linear system of equations (8.68) can be solved iteratively by applying gradient descent methods to (8.67) (as described in Section 4.3). Starting from some initial guess $\boldsymbol{w}_i^{(0)} \in \mathbb{R}^L$ we proceed by

$$\boldsymbol{w}_i^{(n+1)} = \boldsymbol{w}_i^{(n)} + \gamma^{(n)} (\Delta \boldsymbol{W}_i)^{\mathsf{T}} \Big(\theta_i \, \tilde{\boldsymbol{y}}_i - \Delta \boldsymbol{W}_i \, \boldsymbol{w}_i^{(n)} \Big), \tag{8.74}$$

for $n \in \{0, 1, \ldots, N_{\mathrm{it}}\}$, $N_{\mathrm{it}} \in \mathbb{N}$, with step size (or learning rate)

$$0 < \gamma^{(n)} < \frac{2}{\lambda_{\max}\big((\Delta \boldsymbol{W}_i)^{\mathsf{T}} \Delta \boldsymbol{W}_i\big)}, \tag{8.75}$$

where $\lambda_{\max}\big((\Delta \boldsymbol{W}_i)^{\mathsf{T}} \Delta \boldsymbol{W}_i\big) > 0$ is the largest e-value of $(\Delta \boldsymbol{W}_i)^{\mathsf{T}} \Delta \boldsymbol{W}_i \in \mathbb{R}^{L \times L}$. Or more practically, we replace (8.74) by stochastic gradient descent

$$\boldsymbol{w}_i^{(n+1)} = \boldsymbol{w}_i^{(n)} + \gamma^{(n)} \Big(\theta_i \, y_i[n] - \big\langle \Delta \boldsymbol{w}_i^{(n)}, \boldsymbol{w}_i^{(n)} \big\rangle \Big) \, \Delta \boldsymbol{w}_i^{(n)}. \tag{8.76}$$

Recall, the time indices n of $y_i[n]$ and $\Delta \boldsymbol{w}_i^{(n)}$ in (8.76) are taken modulo $NK + 1$, cf. (8.18). The batch version of (8.76) is analogous to (4.215) on page 49.

The learning rule in (8.76) satisfies the condition of quasi-Hebbian learning defined in Chapter 3, and thus can be seen as a form of spike-timing-dependent plasticity (STDP) [19, Chapter 10]. Since Hebbian learning is unsupervised, we also refer to [14–16, 43], and a comparison of STDP in supervised versus unsupervised and reinforcement learning can be found in [52].

8.4.3 The Condition Number of $\Delta \boldsymbol{W}_i$

Table 8.1 shows some numerical examples of the condition number of $\Delta \boldsymbol{W}_i$ (as defined in (8.17)), i.e.,

$$\kappa(\Delta \boldsymbol{W}_i) := \frac{\sigma_{\max}(\Delta \boldsymbol{W}_i)}{\sigma_{\min}(\Delta \boldsymbol{W}_i)}, \tag{8.77}$$

where $\sigma_{\max}(\Delta \boldsymbol{W}_i)$ and $\sigma_{\min}(\Delta \boldsymbol{W}_i)$ denote the largest and the smallest singular value of $\Delta \boldsymbol{W}_i \in \mathbb{R}^{(NK+1)\times L}$, respectively. In the experiments for $\Delta \boldsymbol{W}_i^{(m)}$, $m \in \{1,2,3,4\}$, the delays $\boldsymbol{\tau}_i^{(m)}$ where drawn according to (8.14) with parameter $\tau_{\min} = 0.3\mu_{T_\mathrm{r}}$, and the firing signal $\boldsymbol{Y}^{(m)} := \left(\tilde{\boldsymbol{y}}_1^{(m)}, \ldots, \tilde{\boldsymbol{y}}_L^{(m)}\right)^\mathsf{T}$ was drawn according to $\tilde{\boldsymbol{y}}_1^{(m)}, \ldots, \tilde{\boldsymbol{y}}_L^{(m)} \overset{\text{i.i.d.}}{\sim} \mathcal{U}(\mathcal{Y}_N^{(K)})$, cf. (8.11). All experiments were executed with impulse response $h_{\mathrm{bio},\beta}(\cdot)$, for $\beta = T_\mathrm{r}/8$.

These examples illustrate that the condition number of $\Delta \boldsymbol{W}_i$ is comparable to the condition number of a matrix with the same dimensions and random i.i.d. entries drawn from $\mathcal{U}([0,1])$. Note that $0 \leq h_{\mathrm{bio},\beta}(t) \leq 1$, for all t, and $\sum_{k=1}^{K} y_\ell[n-k] \in \{0,1\}$, for all (ℓ, n), thus we have (cf. (8.17))

$$0 \leq \left(\Delta \boldsymbol{w}_i^{(n)}\right)_\ell \leq 1. \tag{8.78}$$

The results from Table 8.1 give the impression that $\Delta \boldsymbol{W}_i$ likely has full rank already in the square case, i.e., for $L = NK + 1$. But in order to have a well-conditioned (i.e., $\kappa(\Delta \boldsymbol{W}_i)$ as small as possible) least-squares problem in (8.15), the experiments indicate that choosing $L = (NK+1) + L_\mathrm{m}$ with some margin $L_\mathrm{m} \in \mathbb{N}$ helps. Moreover, for a well-conditioned $\Delta \boldsymbol{W}_i$, we expect some robustness against disturbances as addressed in Chapter 9.

L	$\kappa(\Delta\boldsymbol{W}_i^{(1)})$	$\kappa(\Delta\boldsymbol{W}_i^{(2)})$	$\kappa(\Delta\boldsymbol{W}_i^{(3)})$	$\kappa(\Delta\boldsymbol{W}_i^{(4)})$	$\kappa(\boldsymbol{U}^{(1)})$	$\kappa(\boldsymbol{U}^{(2)})$	$\kappa(\boldsymbol{U}^{(3)})$	$\kappa(\boldsymbol{U}^{(4)})$
101	2027.83	5354.82	1695.83	3283.58	1497.71	2718.52	6847.25	1351.28
111	367.68	436.45	577.26	397.62	364.76	286.01	290.42	423.59
151	126.12	144.74	124.64	133.18	89.59	96.51	79.18	80.36
201	98.36	109.89	82.33	94.81	60.24	55.37	56.09	57.22
501	61.27	58.17	53.76	60.20	31.11	30.63	30.12	30.74
1 001	51.18	46.58	50.34	47.88	25.02	25.16	25.08	25.11

(a) $N = 10$, i.e., $NK + 1 = 101$

L	$\kappa(\Delta\boldsymbol{W}_i^{(1)})$	$\kappa(\Delta\boldsymbol{W}_i^{(2)})$	$\kappa(\Delta\boldsymbol{W}_i^{(3)})$	$\kappa(\Delta\boldsymbol{W}_i^{(4)})$	$\kappa(\boldsymbol{U}^{(1)})$	$\kappa(\boldsymbol{U}^{(2)})$	$\kappa(\boldsymbol{U}^{(3)})$	$\kappa(\boldsymbol{U}^{(4)})$
1 001	31 272.53	21 125.73	92 111.96	89 326.44	58 455.47	95 812.92	75 996.94	98 048.40
1 011	5346.52	3616.28	5032.51	4433.03	7945.63	8557.55	12 610.30	10 873.68
1 051	1158.21	1186.30	1207.48	1370.77	2096.38	2018.66	2028.07	1878.27
1 101	653.69	662.35	758.81	649.06	1179.62	1074.95	1092.70	1071.13
1 501	182.51	191.39	190.45	189.25	294.94	301.26	298.96	295.07
2 001	126.27	128.08	123.61	125.76	185.72	185.08	188.26	184.81

(b) $N = 100$, i.e., $NK + 1 = 1\,001$

Table 8.1: The condition number κ (i.e., the ratio $\sigma_{\max}/\sigma_{\min}$) of $\Delta\boldsymbol{W}_i \in \mathbb{R}^{(NK+1)\times L}$ as given in (8.17) and of a matrix $\boldsymbol{U} \in \mathbb{R}^{(NK+1)\times L}$ with i.i.d. entries drawn from $\mathcal{U}([0,1])$, for $K = 10$.

8.4.4 Using the Neuron's Refractory Period

Let us consider again the open loop score signal (8.46) using $h_{\text{bio},\beta}(\cdot)$ as impulse response. We assume that (8.45) holds, which implies that after a firing at $t = n_f \mu_{T_r}$, $n_f \in \mathbb{N}$, the (open loop) score signal has to return back to zero within the time span of μ_{T_r}, i.e.,

$$z_i\big((n_f + n)\mu_{T_r}\big) = 0, \qquad n \in \{1, 2, \ldots\}. \tag{8.79}$$

We now relax condition (8.79) as follows. After a firing at $t = n_f \mu_{T_r}$ we do not require (8.79), we only require

$$z_i\big((n_f + n)\mu_{T_r}\big) = 0, \qquad n \in \big\{\lfloor K/2 \rfloor + 1, \lfloor K/2 \rfloor + 2, \ldots\big\}, \tag{8.80}$$

instead. This can be required, since (by assumption) after a firing at least $K - 1$ zeros have to follow, i.e., $y_i[n_f + n] = 0$, for $n \in \{1, \ldots, K-1\}$, cf. (8.11). Thus, the (open loop) score signal in (8.80) has more time to return back to zero after a firing, namely it has to be back at zero after $T_r/2$ seconds.

The relaxation from (8.79) to (8.80) can be obtained by setting the corresponding rows of $\Delta \boldsymbol{W}_i$ equal to zero

$$\Delta \boldsymbol{w}_i^{(n_f+n)} := \boldsymbol{0}_L, \qquad n \in \big\{1, \ldots, \lfloor K/2 \rfloor\big\}, \tag{8.81}$$

for all $n_f \in \{n \in \{0, \ldots, NK\} : y_i[n] = 1\}$.

The effect of (8.81) on the score signal is illustrated in Figure 8.5. The blue curve is exactly the same score signal as in Figure 8.2, i.e., without (8.81), and the green curve shows the score signal obtained when applying (8.81).

Note that (8.81) reduces the rank of $\Delta \boldsymbol{W}_i$ (if $L \geq NK + 1$), thus indeed less neurons are required. Moreover, the score signal obtained with (8.81) typically has a larger slope than the score signal obtained by directly using $\Delta \boldsymbol{W}_i$ at the time point where they cross the threshold level (from below). Thus, (8.81) helps improving the robustness against timing jitter in the network.

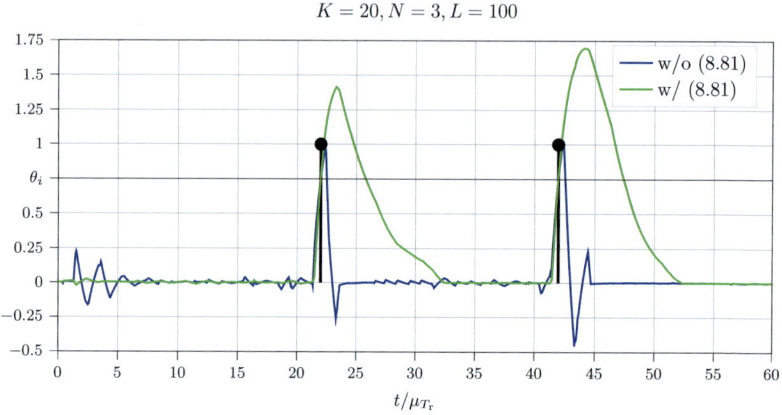

Figure 8.5: Open loop score signal of ξ_i with learnt weights as in (8.69) without (8.81) (blue) and with (8.81) (green), for $h_{\text{bio},\beta}(\cdot)$, $\beta = T_r/8$, and $\tau_{\min} = 0.3\mu_{T_r}$.

8.5 Memorization Capacity

In this section we study the (asymptotic) memorization capacity of a recurrent network which memorizes firing signals as defined in Section 8.1. To this end let us assume that the network is able to perfectly memorize all firing signals $\boldsymbol{Y}_N^{(K)} = (\tilde{\boldsymbol{y}}_1, \ldots, \tilde{\boldsymbol{y}}_L)^\mathsf{T}$ with $\tilde{\boldsymbol{y}}_\ell \in \mathcal{Y}_N^{(K)}$, for $\ell \in \{1, \ldots, L\}$. Then, the memorization capacity (measured in different units) is given by (cf. Chapter 5)

$$C_{\text{tot}} = L \log_2\left(\left|\mathcal{Y}_N^{(K)}\right|\right) \quad [\text{bits}], \tag{8.82}$$

$$C_{\text{neuron}} = \log_2\left(\left|\mathcal{Y}_N^{(K)}\right|\right) \quad [\text{bits per neuron}], \tag{8.83}$$

$$C_{\text{synapse}} = \frac{1}{L} \log_2\left(\left|\mathcal{Y}_N^{(K)}\right|\right) \quad [\text{bits per connection}], \tag{8.84}$$

where $\mathcal{Y}_N^{(K)} \subset \{0,1\}^{NK+1}$ is the set as defined in (8.12) and its cardinality is given by

$$\left|\mathcal{Y}_N^{(K)}\right| = \left(\boldsymbol{e}_1^\mathsf{T} + K\boldsymbol{e}_K^\mathsf{T}\right)\left(\boldsymbol{A}_\text{f}^K\right)^N \boldsymbol{e}_1 \tag{8.85}$$

with $\boldsymbol{A}_\text{f}^K \in \{0,1,2\}^{K \times K}$ defined as in (B.256), which is proved in Appendix B.7. Let

$$\boldsymbol{A}_\text{f}^K = \boldsymbol{Q}\boldsymbol{\Lambda}\boldsymbol{Q}^{-1} \tag{8.86}$$

be the eigendecomposition of $\boldsymbol{A}_\mathrm{f}^K$, which we insert into (8.85)

$$\begin{aligned}
\left|\mathcal{Y}_N^{(K)}\right| &= (\boldsymbol{e}_1^\mathsf{T} + K\boldsymbol{e}_K^\mathsf{T})\boldsymbol{Q}\boldsymbol{\Lambda}^N\boldsymbol{Q}^{-1}\boldsymbol{e}_1 && (8.87)\\
&= (\boldsymbol{e}_1^\mathsf{T} + K\boldsymbol{e}_K^\mathsf{T})\boldsymbol{Q}\boldsymbol{\Lambda}^N\tilde{\boldsymbol{q}}_1 && (8.88)\\
&= (\boldsymbol{e}_1^\mathsf{T} + K\boldsymbol{e}_K^\mathsf{T})\boldsymbol{Q}\boldsymbol{\Lambda}^N\sum_{k=1}^{K}\tilde{q}_{k,1}\boldsymbol{e}_k && (8.89)\\
&= \sum_{k=1}^{K}\tilde{q}_{k,1}(\boldsymbol{e}_1^\mathsf{T} + K\boldsymbol{e}_K^\mathsf{T})\boldsymbol{Q}\boldsymbol{\Lambda}^N\boldsymbol{e}_k && (8.90)\\
&= \sum_{k=1}^{K}\tilde{q}_{k,1}(\boldsymbol{e}_1^\mathsf{T} + K\boldsymbol{e}_K^\mathsf{T})\boldsymbol{Q}\lambda_k^N\boldsymbol{e}_k && (8.91)\\
&= \sum_{k=1}^{K}\tilde{q}_{k,1}(\boldsymbol{e}_1^\mathsf{T} + K\boldsymbol{e}_K^\mathsf{T})\boldsymbol{q}_k\,\lambda_k^N && (8.92)\\
&= \sum_{k=1}^{K}\underbrace{\tilde{q}_{k,1}(q_{1,k} + Kq_{K,k})}_{=:\,\alpha_k}\lambda_k^N, && (8.93)
\end{aligned}$$

where $q_{\ell,k}$ and $\tilde{q}_{\ell,k}$ denote the entries in row ℓ and column k of $\boldsymbol{Q}$ and $\boldsymbol{Q}^{-1}$, respectively. Without loss of generality we assume

$$|\lambda_1| > |\lambda_2| \geq \cdots \geq |\lambda_K|, \tag{8.94}$$

which implies

$$\lim_{N\to\infty}\frac{\left|\mathcal{Y}_N^{(K)}\right|}{\lambda_1^N} = \alpha_1. \tag{8.95}$$

Thus, we have

$$\begin{aligned}
\log_2\left(\left|\mathcal{Y}_N^{(K)}\right|\right) &= \alpha_1 + N\log_2(\lambda_1) && (8.96)\\
&\propto N\log_2(\lambda_1), && (8.97)
\end{aligned}$$

for N sufficiently large. Some values of $\log_2(\lambda_1)$ are given in Table 8.2.

Choosing $L = (NK+1) + L_\mathrm{m}$ with "margin"

$$L_\mathrm{m} \propto N^\nu, \tag{8.98}$$

K	$\max_{k\in\{1,\dots,K\}} \log_2\big(\lambda_k(\boldsymbol{A}_\mathrm{f}^K)\big)$	$\log_2(K)$
2	1.388	1.000
3	1.654	1.585
4	1.860	2.000
5	2.028	2.322
6	2.172	2.585
7	2.297	2.807
8	2.409	3.000
9	2.509	3.170
10	2.601	3.322
100	4.903	6.644
1 000	7.577	9.966
10 000	10.434	13.288

Table 8.2: Binary logarithm of the most dominant eigenvalue of $\boldsymbol{A}_\mathrm{f}^K$.

for $0 < \nu < 1$, yields an asymptotic capacity with a nonvanishing number of bits per connection/synapse, because

$$\lim_{N\to\infty} C_\text{synapse} = \lim_{N\to\infty} \frac{1}{L}\log_2\big(\big|\mathcal{Y}_N^{(K)}\big|\big) \tag{8.99}$$

$$= \lim_{N\to\infty} \frac{1}{L}\big(\alpha_1 + N\log_2(\lambda_1)\big) \tag{8.100}$$

$$= \lim_{N\to\infty} \frac{N}{NK+1+N^\nu}\log_2(\lambda_1) \tag{8.101}$$

$$= \lim_{N\to\infty} \frac{1}{K+1/N+1/N^{1-\nu}}\log_2(\lambda_1) \tag{8.102}$$

$$= \frac{1}{K}\log_2(\lambda_1). \tag{8.103}$$

The step from (8.100) to (8.101) holds since α_1 is independent of N and $L\to\infty$ as $N\to\infty$.

The quantity on the right-hand side of (8.103) is decreasing with K (cf. Table 8.2) and maximized for $K=2$:

$$\frac{1}{K}\log_2(\lambda_1)\bigg|_{K=2} = \frac{1}{2}\log_2\left(\frac{1}{2}\big(3+\sqrt{5}\big)\right) \tag{8.104}$$

$$\approx 0.694 \tag{8.105}$$

Chapter 9

Timing Robustness

In this chapter we examine the timing robustness of the firing signals introduced in Section 8.1 (i.e., of the firing signals with firings only on a regular grid) in genuine continuous-time (mainly by means of simulations). To this end we allow certain disturbances $\eta_i(\cdot)$ as in Section 7.1, which can be seen as a model for any form of imperfection. We once more remark that all disturbances essentially result either in

- shifted (i.e., too early or too late) firings
- false firings
- missing firings

We consider three forms of imperfections/disturbances: delay mismatch, firing-time jitter, and additive noise (on the neuron's score signals). The regime, where these disturbances cause false or missing firings, falls into the category where the memorization is not perfect. An analysis of this scenario can be done similarly as in the discrete-time model. In continuous-time the new regime (which does not exist in discrete-time) of shifted firings emerges. Thus, our analysis is focused on disturbances that cause shifted firings.

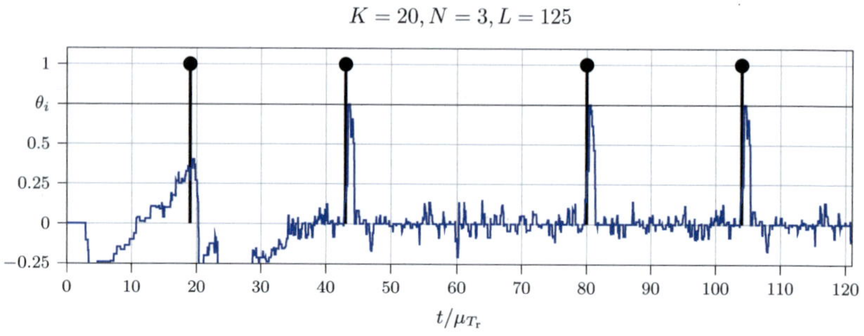

Figure 9.1: Open loop score signal of ξ_i as in Figure 8.3a but with delay mismatches $\Delta\tau_{\ell,i}$ drawn at random i.i.d. uniformly from $[-0.4\mu_{T_r}, 0.4\mu_{T_r}]$.

9.1 Delay Mismatch – Open Loop Analysis

Throughout this section let $i \in \{1, \ldots, L\}$ be fixed but arbitrary.

The imperfection considered now concerns the connection delays. After having determined the weights using the given (and known) delays $\tau_{\ell,i} \in \mathbb{R}_{>0}$ as described in Section 8.2, the network is run with actual delays

$$\tilde{\tau}_{\ell,i} = \tau_{\ell,i} + \Delta\tau_{\ell,i}, \tag{9.1}$$

for $\ell \in \{1, \ldots, L\}$, where $\Delta\tau_{\ell,i} \in \mathbb{R}$ models the delay mismatch of connection/synapse from ξ_ℓ to ξ_i. For the sake of convenience let us define

$$\Delta\boldsymbol{\tau}_i := \left(\Delta\tau_{1,i}, \ldots, \Delta\tau_{L,i}\right)^{\mathsf{T}} \in \mathbb{R}^L. \tag{9.2}$$

This can be seen as a model for the case where the delays are not exactly but approximately known.

The open loop score signal $z_i(\cdot)$ of Figure 8.3a with delay mismatch

$$\Delta\tau_{\ell,i} \overset{\text{i.i.d.}}{\sim} \mathcal{U}\big([-0.4\mu_{T_r}, 0.4\mu_{T_r}]\big), \qquad \ell \in \{1, \ldots, L\}, \tag{9.3}$$

is shown in Figure 9.1. Being precisely, the mismatches are choosen (once) beforehand randomly according to (9.3). In Figure 9.2, the effects of different delay mismatches $\Delta\boldsymbol{\tau}_i \in \mathbb{R}^L$ on the (open loop) score signal are depicted, for $h(\cdot) = h_{\text{rect}}(\cdot)$. Finally, Figure 9.3 shows examples of the score signal with delay mismatches (9.3) for both impulse responses $h_{\text{rect},\alpha}(\cdot)$ and $h_{\text{bio},\beta}(\cdot)$.

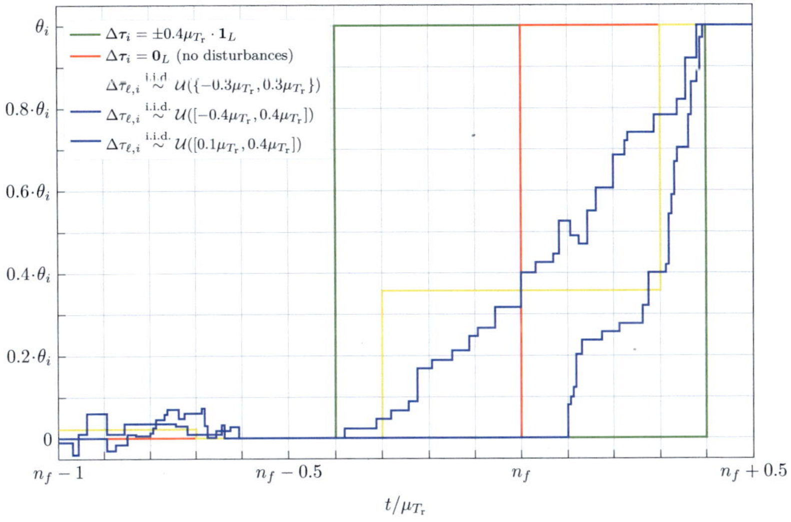

Figure 9.2: Open loop score signals of ξ_i around firing time $t_f^{(i)} = n_f \mu_{T_r}$, $n_f \in \mathbb{N}$, for different delay mismatches, and $h_{\text{rect}}(\cdot)$, for $L = 100$.

First Order Approximation

Let us assume that there is a firing at $t = n\mu_{T_r}$, $n \in \mathbb{N}$, i.e., the weight vector $\boldsymbol{w}_i \in \mathbb{R}^L$ is chosen/learnt such that

$$z_i(n\mu_{T_r}) = \theta_i, \tag{9.4}$$

(and $z_i'(n\mu_{T_r}) > 0$) where $z_i(\cdot)$ is the score signal of ξ_i with delays $\tau_{\ell,i}$. Then, we try to estimate the deviation $\Delta t_f^{(i)} \in \mathbb{R}$ such that

$$\tilde{z}_i\big(n\mu_{T_r} + \Delta t_f^{(i)}\big) = \theta_i, \tag{9.5}$$

where $\tilde{z}_i(\cdot)$ is the score signal of ξ_i with delays $\tilde{\tau}_{\ell,i}$ defined as in (9.1).

In order to determine $\Delta t_f^{(i)}$ from (9.5), we approximate the open loop score signal $\tilde{z}_i(\cdot)$ (cf. (8.46)) as follows. Let

$$g_{\ell,i}(t) := \big(h * \delta_{\tau_{\ell,i}} * y_\ell\big)(t), \qquad t \in \mathbb{R}, \tag{9.6}$$

which we linearly approximate around $t = n\mu_{T_r}$ by

$$\breve{g}_{\ell,i}(t) := a_{\ell,i} + b_{\ell,i} \cdot (t - n\mu_{T_r}), \qquad t \in \mathbb{R}, \tag{9.7}$$

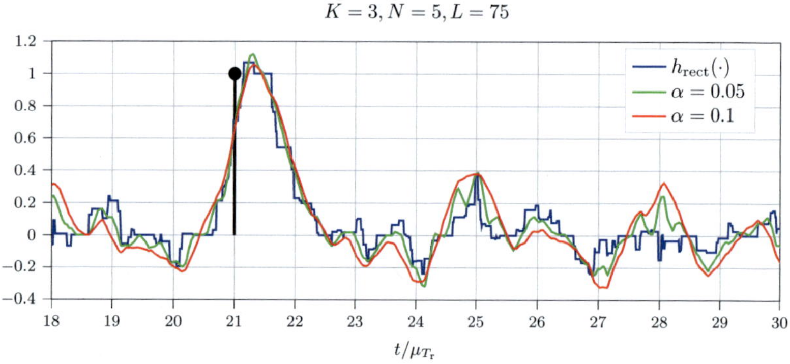

(a) For $h_{\mathrm{rect}}(\cdot)$ and $h_{\mathrm{rect},\alpha}(\cdot)$ with delays $\tau_{\ell,i} \in \{\mu_{T_r}, \ldots, K\mu_{T_r}\}$, and $\theta_i = 1$.

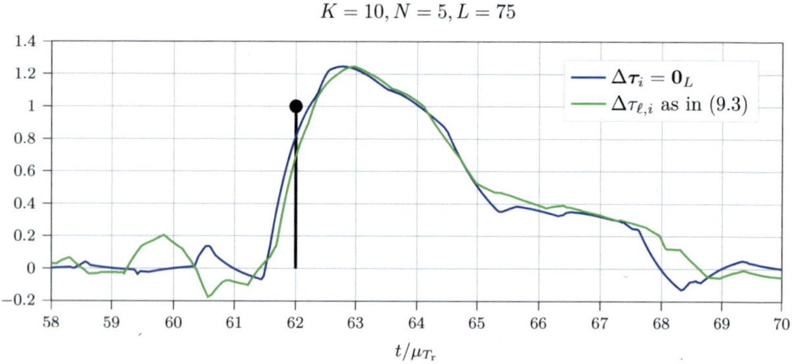

(b) For $h_{\mathrm{bio},\beta}(\cdot)$, $\beta = T_r/8$, with delays $\tau_{\ell,i} \in [0.3\mu_{T_r}, 0.7\mu_{T_r}]$, and $\theta_i = 0.8$.

Figure 9.3: Open loop score signals of ξ_i around a firing with delay mismatch (9.3), using different impulse responses.

with constants

$$a_{\ell,i} := g_{\ell,i}(n\mu_{T_\mathrm{r}}), \tag{9.8}$$

$$b_{\ell,i} := g'_{\ell,i}(n\mu_{T_\mathrm{r}}) := \frac{d}{dt}\, g_{\ell,i}(t)\bigg|_{t=n\mu_{T_\mathrm{r}}} . \tag{9.9}$$

Thus, we approximate

$$\begin{aligned} \tilde{z}_i(t) &= \sum_{\ell=1}^{L} w_{\ell,i} \left(h * \delta_{\tau_{\ell,i}+\Delta\tau_{\ell,i}} * y_\ell\right)(t) && (9.10)\\ &= \sum_{\ell=1}^{L} w_{\ell,i} \left(h * \delta_{\tau_{\ell,i}} * y_\ell\right)(t - \Delta\tau_{\ell,i}) && (9.11)\\ &= \sum_{\ell=1}^{L} w_{\ell,i}\, g_{\ell,i}(t - \Delta\tau_{\ell,i}), && (9.12) \end{aligned}$$

for $t \in \mathbb{R}$, by the linear function

$$\tilde{z}_{\mathrm{lin},i}(t) := \sum_{\ell=1}^{L} w_{\ell,i}\, \breve{g}_{\ell,i}(t - \Delta\tau_{\ell,i}), \qquad t \in \mathbb{R}, \tag{9.13}$$

with $\breve{g}_{\ell,i}(\cdot)$ defined as in (9.7). Then, instead of using (9.5) we use

$$\tilde{z}_{\mathrm{lin},i}\big(n\mu_{T_\mathrm{r}} + \Delta t_f^{(i)}\big) = \theta_i \tag{9.14}$$

for estimating $\Delta t_f^{(i)}$. From (9.14) and (9.13) we obtain

$$\begin{aligned} & \sum_{\ell=1}^{L} w_{\ell,i}\, \breve{g}_{\ell,i}\big(n\mu_{T_\mathrm{r}} + \Delta t_f^{(i)} - \Delta\tau_{\ell,i}\big) = \theta_i && (9.15)\\ \iff\ & \sum_{\ell=1}^{L} w_{\ell,i} \Big(a_{\ell,i} + b_{\ell,i}\left(\Delta t_f^{(i)} - \Delta\tau_{\ell,i}\right)\Big) = \theta_i && (9.16)\\ \iff\ & \sum_{\ell=1}^{L} w_{\ell,i}\, a_{\ell,i} + \Delta t_f^{(i)} \sum_{\ell=1}^{L} w_{\ell,i}\, b_{\ell,i} - \sum_{\ell=1}^{L} w_{\ell,i}\, b_{\ell,i}\, \Delta\tau_{\ell,i} = \theta_i && (9.17)\\ \iff\ & \Delta t_f^{(i)} = \frac{\sum_{\ell=1}^{L} w_{\ell,i}\, b_{\ell,i}\, \Delta\tau_{\ell,i}}{\sum_{\ell=1}^{L} w_{\ell,i}\, b_{\ell,i}} . && (9.18) \end{aligned}$$

The step from (9.14) to (9.15) follows from (9.13), and (9.16) follows from (9.7). Finally, (9.18) holds because

$$\begin{aligned}\sum_{\ell=1}^{L} w_{\ell,i}\, a_{\ell,i} &= \sum_{\ell=1}^{L} w_{\ell,i}\, g_{\ell,i}(n\mu_{T_\mathrm{r}}) &(9.19)\\ &= \sum_{\ell=1}^{L} w_{\ell,i}\,\big(h * \delta_{\tau_{\ell,i}} * y_\ell\big)(n\mu_{T_\mathrm{r}}) &(9.20)\\ &= z_i(n\mu_{T_\mathrm{r}}) &(9.21)\\ &= \theta_i, &(9.22)\end{aligned}$$

where (9.21) follows from (8.46), and (9.22) follows from (9.4).

The estimate in (9.18) clearly satisfies the inequalities

$$\min_{\ell\in\{1,\ldots,L\}} \Delta\tau_{\ell,i} \le \Delta t_f^{(i)} \le \max_{\ell\in\{1,\ldots,L\}} \Delta\tau_{\ell,i} \tag{9.23}$$

and

$$\frac{(wb)_{\min,i}}{(wb)_{\max,i}} \cdot \frac{1}{L}\sum_{\ell=1}^{L} \Delta\tau_{\ell,i} \le \Delta t_f^{(i)} \le \frac{(wb)_{\max,i}}{(wb)_{\min,i}} \cdot \frac{1}{L}\sum_{\ell=1}^{L} \Delta\tau_{\ell,i}\,, \tag{9.24}$$

where

$$\begin{aligned}(wb)_{\min,i} &:= \min_{\ell\in\{1,\ldots,L\}} w_{\ell,i}\, b_{\ell,i}\,, &(9.25)\\ (wb)_{\max,i} &:= \max_{\ell\in\{1,\ldots,L\}} w_{\ell,i}\, b_{\ell,i}\,. &(9.26)\end{aligned}$$

9.1.1 General Linear Estimate for $\Delta t_f^{(i)}$

Let

$$\mathcal{L}_{t_f} := \Big\{ i \in \{1,\ldots,L\} : t_f - T_\mathrm{r} < t_j^{(i)} \le t_f, \quad \text{for some } j \in \{1,\ldots,J_i\} \Big\} \tag{9.27}$$

be the set of all channel-indices which have a firing in the time interval $]t_f - T_\mathrm{r}, t_f]$, i.e., in the receptive field w.r.t. the time instant $t = t_f$. E.g., in Figure 9.4 below, we have $\mathcal{L}_{n\mu_{T_\mathrm{r}}} = \{1,2,3,4\}$.

Now, we assume that $\mathcal{L}_{t_f} = \{\ell_1, \ldots, \ell_q\}$, for $1 \leq q \leq L$. Then, the estimate in (9.18) can be generalized to

$$\begin{aligned} \Delta t_f^{(i)} & \\ &= \frac{1}{\sum_{\ell \in \mathcal{L}_{t_f}} w_{\ell,i}\, b_{\ell,i}} \sum_{\ell \in \mathcal{L}_{t_f}} w_{\ell,i}\, b_{\ell,i} \sum_{j=1}^{J_\ell} \Delta t_j^{(\ell)}\, \mathrm{I}\big[t_f - T_\mathrm{r} < t_j^{(\ell)} \leq t_f\big] \quad (9.28) \\ &= \frac{1}{\sum_{\ell \in \mathcal{L}_{t_f}} w_{\ell,i}\, b_{\ell,i}} \big(w_{\ell_1,i}\, b_{\ell_1,i} \quad \cdots \quad w_{\ell_q,i}\, b_{\ell_q,i}\big) \begin{pmatrix} \Delta t_{j_{\ell_1}}^{(\ell_1)} \\ \vdots \\ \Delta t_{j_{\ell_q}}^{(\ell_q)} \end{pmatrix}, \quad (9.29) \end{aligned}$$

where the delay mismatches $\Delta\tau_{\ell,i}$ in (9.18) are replaced by arbitrary "firing-time jitters" $\Delta t_j^{(\ell)}$. Thus, the (linear) estimate in (9.29) holds for any disturbance model which results in the jitters $\Delta t_j^{(\ell)}$. We note that the expression in (9.29) does not necessarily require the firings to be on a regular grid.

In order to justify the generalization from (9.18) to (9.29), let us assume that

$$\begin{aligned} y_\ell(t) &:= \delta_{t_1^{(\ell)} + \Delta t_1^{(\ell)}}(t) && (9.30) \\ &= \big(\delta_{t_1^{(\ell)}} * \delta_{\Delta t_1^{(\ell)}}\big)(t), \qquad t \in \mathbb{R}, && (9.31) \end{aligned}$$

for $\ell \in \{1, \ldots, L\}$. I.e., in each channel there is only a single firing with desired firing time $t_1^{(\ell)} \in \mathbb{R}_{>0}$, and the quantity $\Delta t_1^{(\ell)} \in \mathbb{R}$ represents some jitter on that firing time. Then, the open-loop score signal can be rewritten as

$$\begin{aligned} z_i(t) &= \sum_{\ell=1}^{L} w_{\ell,i}\, \big(h * \delta_{\tau_{\ell,i}} * y_\ell\big)(t) && (9.32) \\ &= \sum_{\ell=1}^{L} w_{\ell,i}\, \big(h * \delta_{\tau_{\ell,i}} * \delta_{t_1^{(\ell)}} * \delta_{\Delta t_1^{(\ell)}}\big)(t) && (9.33) \\ &= \sum_{\ell=1}^{L} w_{\ell,i}\, \big(h * \delta_{\tau_{\ell,i} + \Delta t_1^{(\ell)}} * \delta_{t_1^{(\ell)}}\big)(t), && (9.34) \end{aligned}$$

for $t \in \mathbb{R}$, which is of the same form as (9.10), and thus the analysis leading to (9.18) can be applied.

9.2 Shifted Firings – Time Correction

As mentioned at the beginning of this chapter, in any real system shifted firings are inevitable. Thus, the firing signal produced by the recurrent network will somehow drift away from its original target firing signal. (This happens in any real-world scenario, also if the firing signal is perfectly memorized by the network.) However, we are not especially interested in the absolute firing times. What we want is that the relative occurrence of the firings is preserved to a certain extent. To this end we introduce a "time correction" (for the firing signals considered in Section 8.1), which allows us to evaluate whether the firings remain together relative to each other over a long time span or not.

Given a firing signal $\mathbf{Y}_N^{(K)} \in \{0,1\}^{L\times(NK+1)}$ as introduced in Section 8.1, we define

$$\mathcal{R}_n := \big\{t \in \mathbb{R} : (n-K)\mu_{T_\mathrm{r}} \le t < n\mu_{T_\mathrm{r}}\big\}, \qquad n \in \mathbb{N}, \tag{9.35}$$

to be the *receptive field* at time $t = n\mu_{T_\mathrm{r}}$. Note the length of the interval $\mathcal{R}_n$ is equal to T_r. For every time point on the grid, we compute the time correction in $\mathcal{R}_n$ as

$$t_{\mathrm{corr},n} := \frac{1}{J_{\mathcal{R}_n}} \sum_{\ell=1}^{L} \sum_{j=1}^{J_\ell} \big(\tilde{t}_j^{(\ell)} - t_j^{(\ell)}\big)\,\mathrm{I}\big[t_j^{(\ell)} \in \mathcal{R}_n\big], \qquad n \in \mathbb{N}, \tag{9.36}$$

where $t_j^{(\ell)}$ denotes the firing time of the j-th desired/target firing in channel ℓ and $\tilde{t}_j^{(\ell)}$ denotes the firing time of the corresponding generated firing, and

$$J_{\mathcal{R}_n} := \sum_{\ell=1}^{L} \sum_{j=1}^{J_\ell} \mathrm{I}\big[t_j^{(\ell)} \in \mathcal{R}_n\big] \tag{9.37}$$

is the total number of desired firings in $\mathcal{R}_n$, cf. Figure 9.4. Because of the neuron's refractory period $T_\mathrm{r} = K\mu_{T_\mathrm{r}}$, we have $\sum_{j=1}^{J_\ell} \mathrm{I}\big[t_j^{(\ell)} \in \mathcal{R}_n\big] \in \{0,1\}$, which implies $J_{\mathcal{R}_n} \le L$. For a memorizable firing signal, at least one firing has to occur in $\mathcal{R}_n$, thus we have $J_{\mathcal{R}_n} > 0$ and (9.36) is well defined. Then, we also compute

$$\sigma^2_{\mathrm{corr},n} := \frac{1}{J_{\mathcal{R}_n}} \sum_{\ell=1}^{L} \sum_{j=1}^{J_\ell} \Big(\tilde{t}_j^{(\ell)} - t_j^{(\ell)} - t_{\mathrm{corr},n}\Big)^2\,\mathrm{I}\big[t_j^{(\ell)} \in \mathcal{R}_n\big], \tag{9.38}$$

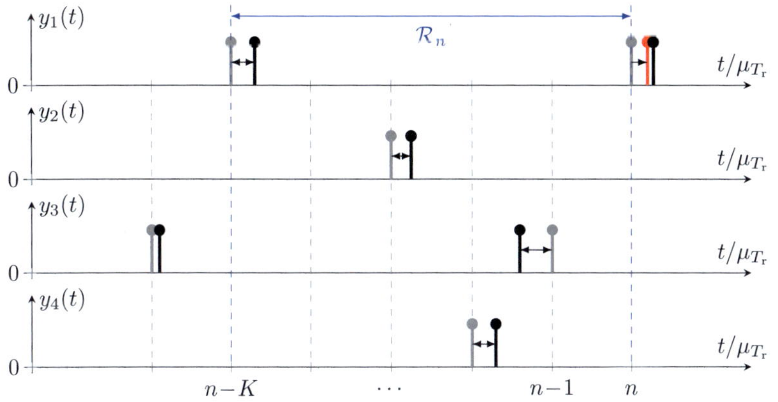

Figure 9.4: Illustration of $t_{\text{corr},n}$ as in (9.36) for a 4-channel local receptive field $\mathcal{R}_n$. The time correction $t_{\text{corr},n}$ at $t = n\mu_{T_r}$, $n \in \mathbb{N}$, is the average deviation of the generated firings at $\tilde{t}_j^{(\ell)}$ (black) from the desired firings at $t_j^{(\ell)}$ on the grid (grey) in $\mathcal{R}_n$. The red firing at $t = n\mu_{T_r} + t_{\text{corr},n}$ indicates the corrected (desired) firing.

which can be seen as the sample variance of $t_{\text{corr},n}$. Thus, the quantity $\sigma^2_{\text{corr},n}$ gives a measure for the average deviation between the generated firings at $\tilde{t}_j^{(\ell)}$ (black) and the "expected" firings at $t_j^{(\ell)} + t_{\text{corr},n}$ (red) in $\mathcal{R}_n$. A bounded evolution of $\sigma^2_{\text{corr},n}$, for $n \in \mathbb{N}$, indicates that the firings do not drift away relative from each other.

9.3 Simulation Results

Given the recurrent network (with all its parameters), we simulate its "real-time" behaviour according to Algorithm 1 below. From Line 8 to Line 12, we compute

$$z_i[k] := z_i(t_k) = \sum_{\ell=1}^{L} w_{\ell,i} \left(h * \delta_{\tau_{\ell,i}} * y_\ell\right)(t_k) \tag{9.39}$$

with

$$y_\ell(t) = \sum_{t_f \in \mathcal{T}_f^{(\ell)}} \delta(t - t_f), \qquad t \in \mathbb{R}, \tag{9.40}$$

where $\mathcal{T}_f^{(\ell)}$ contains all firing-times smaller than or equal to t_k of the ℓ-th channel. Algorithm 1 determines the firing times, i.e., $\mathcal{T}_f^{(i)}$, $i \in \{1, \ldots, L\}$, and the (closed-loop) score signals by means of a sample-based (forward) simulation, where the continuous-time signals in the network are represented by S samples per grid size μ_{T_r}. In all simulations the parameter S is chosen with care. It is a trade-off between the computational complexity and the precision of the simulation. Clearly, this type of simulation is not able to determine the firing times with unlimited precision. The time resolution of this method is limited by the number of samples:

$$t_{k+1} - t_k = \frac{\mu_{T_\text{r}}}{S}, \tag{9.41}$$

for all k, i.e., the larger S the better the time resolution of the simulation.

Figure 9.5 shows an excerpt at the beginning of the score signals obtained by Algorithm 1, for $h(\cdot) = h_{\text{bio},\beta}(\cdot)$, $\beta = T_\text{r}/8$, and $\tau_\text{min} = 0.3\mu_{T_\text{r}}$. The produced firings (black) are shifted compared to the desired/target firings (grey) despite no disturbances are taken into account. This effect arises from the limited time-resolution, which thus can be seen as a systematic drift yielding a small $\sigma^2_{\text{corr},n}$. In Figure 9.6 the evolution of the quantities

$$\Delta t_{\text{corr},n} := t_{\text{corr},n} - t_{\text{corr},n-1}, \qquad n \in \mathbb{N}, \tag{9.42}$$

and $\sigma^2_{\text{corr},n}$ of the simulation in Figure 9.5 are depicted, for 10 periods.

In all simulations presented in this section, we use (for the sake of comparison) the same firing signal and the same parameters as in Figure 9.5 but with different disturbances.

Algorithm 1: Sample-based Firing-times Reconstruction

Input : $\boldsymbol{w}_1, \ldots, \boldsymbol{w}_L \in \mathbb{R}^L$,
$\theta_1, \ldots, \theta_L \in \mathbb{R}$,
$\boldsymbol{\tau}_1, \ldots, \boldsymbol{\tau}_L \in [\tau_{\min}, \mu_{T_\mathrm{r}} - \tau_{\min}]^L$, where $0 < \tau_{\min} < \mu_{T_\mathrm{r}}/2$,
$t_1^{(1)}, \ldots, t_1^{(L)} \in [0, NT_\mathrm{r}]$, with $t_1^{(\ell)} := \min\{t \in \mathbb{R} : y_\ell(t) \neq 0\}$.

Output: Firing times: $\mathcal{T}_f^{(1)}, \ldots, \mathcal{T}_f^{(L)} \subseteq \mathbb{R}_{\geq 0}$.

Parameters: $S \in \mathbb{N}$, (number of samples per grid unit μ_{T_r})
$T_\mathrm{r} > 0$. (neuron refractory period, i.e., minimal time between two consecutive firings)

Initializations: $\mathcal{T}_f^{(1)} = \{t_1^{(1)}\}, \ldots, \mathcal{T}_f^{(L)} = \{t_1^{(L)}\}$. (first firing in each channel)

for $k = 1, 2, \ldots$ **do**
  $t_k = k\frac{\mu_{T_\mathrm{r}}}{S}$. (sampling points)
  for $i = 1, 2, \ldots, L$ **do**
    Computation of $z_i[k]$
    $z_i[k] = 0$.
    for $\ell = 1, 2, \ldots, L$ **do**
      $t_f^{(\ell)} = \max \mathcal{T}_f^{(\ell)}$.
      if $t_k \geq \tau_{\ell,i} + t_f^{(\ell)}$ **then**
        $z_i[k] \leftarrow z_i[k] + w_{\ell,i}\, h\big(t_k - \tau_{\ell,i} - t_f^{(\ell)}\big)$.
    Update firing time
    if $z_i[k] \geq \theta_i$ **and** $t_k \geq t_f^{(i)} + T_\mathrm{r}$ **then**
      $\mathcal{T}_f^{(i)} \leftarrow \mathcal{T}_f^{(i)} \cup \{t_k\}$.

Return: $\mathcal{T}_f^{(1)}, \ldots, \mathcal{T}_f^{(L)}$.

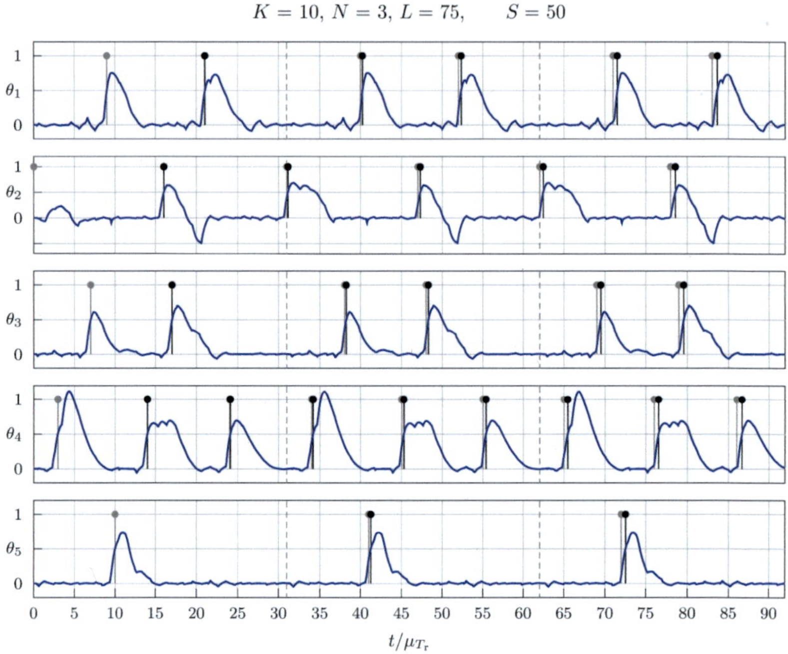

Figure 9.5: Score signals $z_1[\cdot]$ (top) to $z_5[\cdot]$ (bottom) obtained by the sample-based simulation given in Algorithm 1 and its corresponding firings: desired firings (grey) on the grid and produced firings (black).

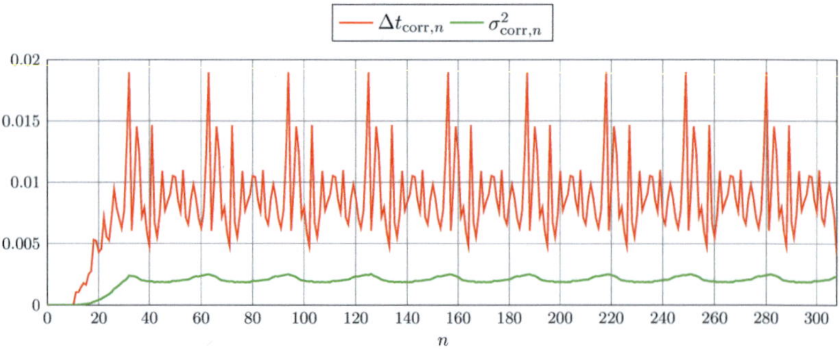

Figure 9.6: Plots of $\Delta t_{\mathrm{corr},n}$ and $\sigma^2_{\mathrm{corr},n}$ without disturbance.

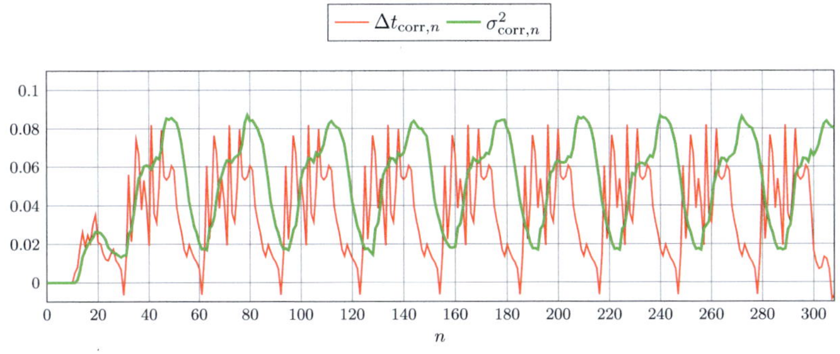

(a) $\Delta\tau = 0.15\mu_{T_r}$

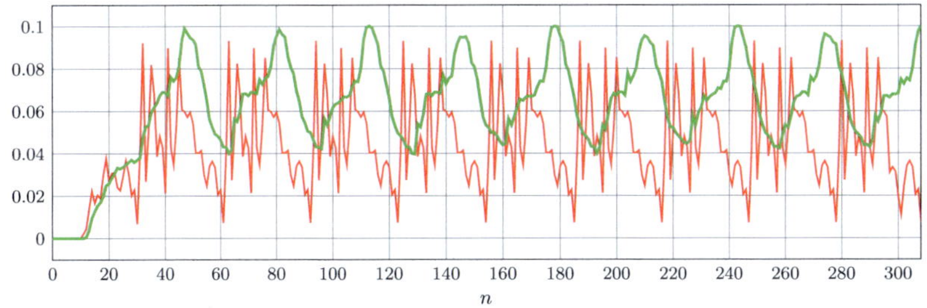

(b) $\Delta\tau = 0.3\mu_{T_r}$

Figure 9.7: Plots of $\Delta t_{\mathrm{corr},n}$ and $\sigma^2_{\mathrm{corr},n}$ with delay mismatch.

9.3.1 Delay Mismatch

The results of the simulation in Figure 9.5 with delay mismatch, as in Section 9.1, are plotted in Figure 9.7. The delay mismatches are choosen randomly according to

$$\Delta\tau_{\ell,i} \overset{\text{i.i.d.}}{\sim} \mathcal{U}\big([-\Delta\tau, \Delta\tau]\big), \qquad (\ell, i) \in \{1, \dots, L\}^2. \tag{9.43}$$

The plots in Figure 9.7 show two examples where the network successfully reproduces the given firing signal with $\sigma^2_{\mathrm{corr},n} \leq 0.1$, for all n. The simulations also indicate that for $\Delta\tau > 0.4\mu_{T_r}$ the network typically fails to reproduce the firing signal in the sense that $z_i[k] = 0$, $k \geq k_0$, for some $k_0 \in \mathbb{N}$, i.e., no firings are produced after some time analog to Figure 9.8c.

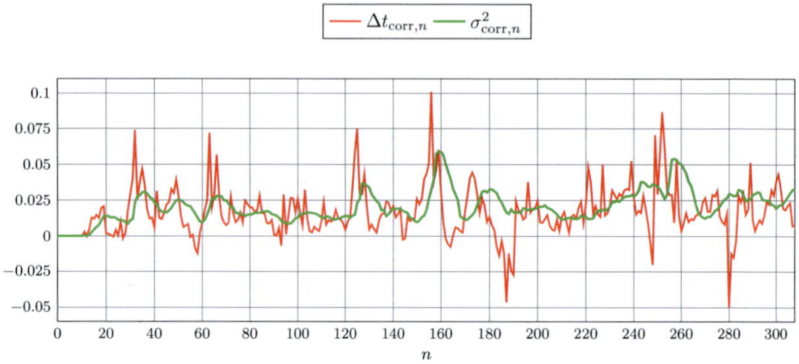

(a) $\Delta t_f = 0.15\mu_{T_\mathrm{r}}$

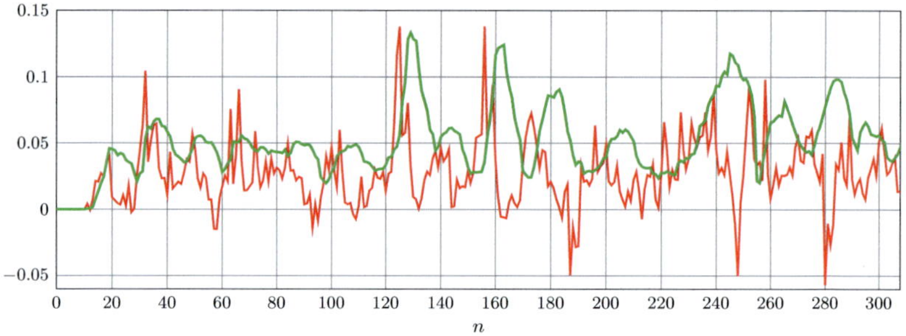

(b) $\Delta t_f = 0.25\mu_{T_\mathrm{r}}$

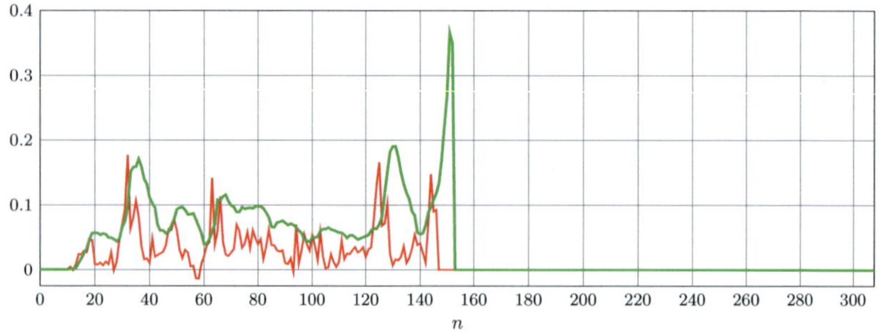

(c) $\Delta t_f = 0.3\mu_{T_\mathrm{r}}$

Figure 9.8: Plots of $\Delta t_{\text{corr},n}$ and $\sigma^2_{\text{corr},n}$ with firing-time jitter.

9.3.2 Firing-time Jitter

The results of the simulation in Figure 9.5 with firing-time jitter are plotted in Figure 9.8, where the jitter is modeled as follows. In Algorithm 1 Line 15 is replaced by

$$\mathcal{T}_f^{(i)} \leftarrow \mathcal{T}_f^{(i)} \cup \{t_k + \Delta t_k\}, \tag{9.44}$$

where

$$\Delta t_k \overset{\text{i.i.d.}}{\sim} \mathcal{U}\big([-\Delta t_f, \Delta t_f]\big), \tag{9.45}$$

for all k, i.e., every firing time (produced by the simulated score signals) is randomly shifted, where all time shifts Δt_k are independent. Thus, the temporal evolution of $\Delta t_{\text{corr},n}$ and $\sigma^2_{\text{corr},n}$ is not periodic anymore as it is for the delay-mismatch case, cf. Figure 9.7. There the disturbance, i.e., the delays do not change during run-time, whereas the jitter model (9.45) causes a random behaviour of the simulation and the curves of $\Delta t_{\text{corr},n}$ and $\sigma^2_{\text{corr},n}$ in Figure 9.8 are sample paths of a stochastic process. Thus, we have no guarantee that the examples in Figure 9.8a and 9.8b do not fail for $n \geq 310$ as it does in Figure 9.8c.

Because of this randomness an adversarial constellation could potentially occur at any point in time implying that the model with firing-time jitter could potentially fail at any point in time. In Figure 9.8c it fails in the fifth period. By contrast, in the case of delay mismatch, if the simulation fails, it does always fail in the second period, i.e., for $n \in \{31, \ldots, 61\}$.

9.3.3 Additive Noise

In Line 13 of Algorithm 1 we insert the command

$$z_i[k] \leftarrow z_i[k] + \eta_k, \tag{9.46}$$

with either uniform noise

$$\eta_k \overset{\text{i.i.d.}}{\sim} \mathcal{U}\big([-\eta, \eta]\big) \tag{9.47}$$

in Figure 9.9, or Gaussian noise

$$\eta_k \overset{\text{i.i.d.}}{\sim} \mathcal{N}\big(0, \sigma_\eta^2\big) \tag{9.48}$$

in Figure 9.10, to model additive i.i.d. noise on the score signals.

For this type of disturbance the curves of Figure 9.9 and 9.10 are sample paths of the stochastic process obtained by Algorithm 1 as discussed in the case of firing-time jitter, cf. Section 9.3.2.

Note that the produced firings have a trend to be earlier than they are supposed to be (especially for Gaussian noise). In order to understand this observation let us consider the corresponding score signals in Figure 9.11. Metaphorically speaking a "wider" score signal potentially hits the threshold level earlier.

Figure 9.9c and 9.10c show examples where $\sigma^2_{\mathrm{corr},n}$ attains large values and is growing in every period, i.e., the firing occurrences are drifting away and seem to appear randomly (without any relation to each other). Thus, the network fails to reproduce the given firing signal in these cases by producing unrelated "random" firings. This failure mode is in contrast to the failure mode described in Section 9.3.2, which ends up in stopping produce any firings. Clearly, if the noise level is too large, i.e., $\eta_k \approx \theta_i$, the network will keep producing firings.

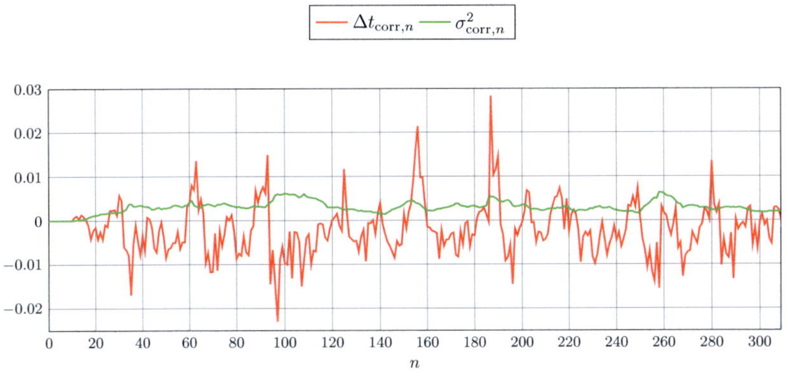

(a) $\eta = 0.05$

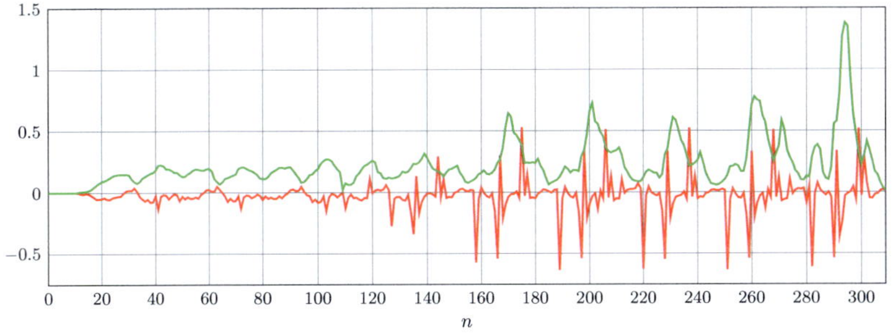

(b) $\eta = 0.2$

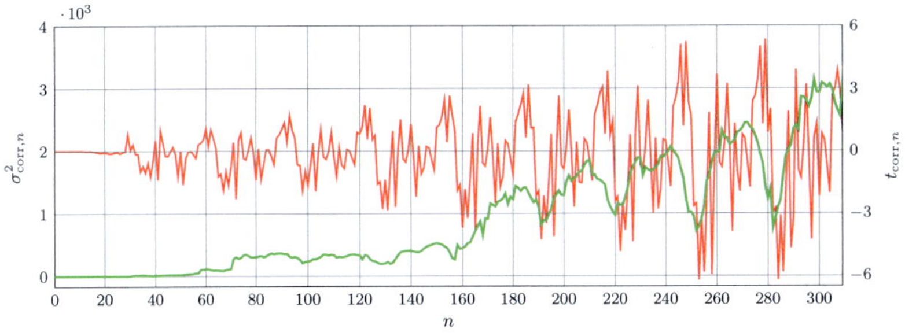

(c) $\eta = 0.3$

Figure 9.9: Plots of $\Delta t_{\mathrm{corr},n}$ and $\sigma^2_{\mathrm{corr},n}$ with additive uniform noise.

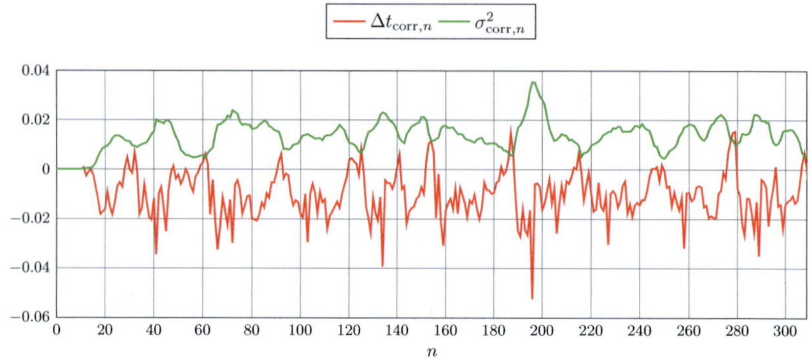

(a) $\sigma_\eta^2 = 0.05$

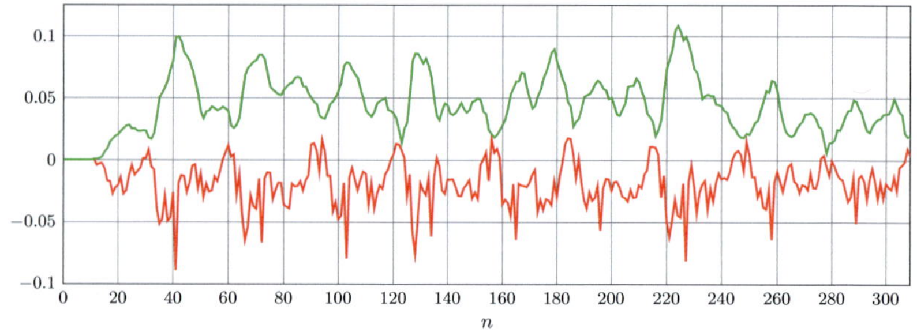

(b) $\sigma_\eta^2 = 0.075$

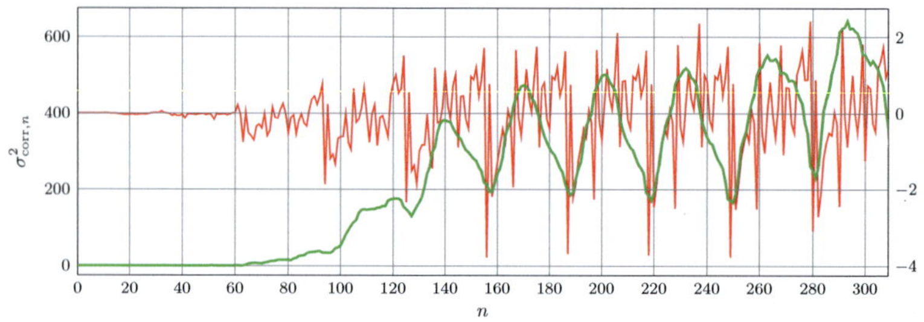

(c) $\sigma_\eta^2 = 0.1$

Figure 9.10: Plots of $\Delta t_{\mathrm{corr},n}$ and $\sigma^2_{\mathrm{corr},n}$ with additive Gaussian noise.

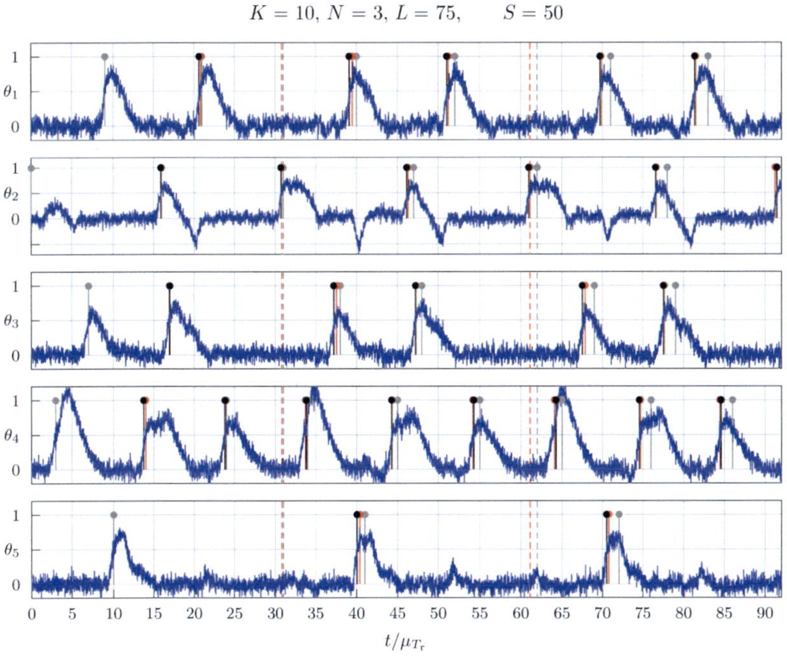

Figure 9.11: Score signals $z_1[\cdot]$ (top) to $z_5[\cdot]$ (bottom) as in Figure 9.5 with additive Gaussian noise, for $\sigma_\eta^2 = 0.075$, and its corresponding firings: desired firings (grey) on the grid, corrected desired firings (red), and produced firings (black).

Chapter 10

Conclusion

In this thesis, we have studied the capability of recurrently connected networks of spiking neurons to memorize (dynamical) firing signals by a form of quasi-Hebbian (i.e., supervised) learning.

In a first part, we analyzed the performance of a discrete-time model to perfectly memorize random firing sequences. Our main result was an upper bound on the probability that instantaneous (or one-shot) memorization is not perfect. From this bound, the instantaneous-memorization capacity of a network with L neurons is (at least) $O\big(L/\ln(L)\big)$ bits per neuron. By contrast, iterative (i.e., multi-pass) learning was shown to achieve a capacity of $O(L)$ bits per neuron and $O(1)$ bits per connection/synapse.

In a second part, we defined a special class of continuous-time firing signals. Then, we showed (for the ideal case) how those firing signals can be memorized with a spiking RNN model. The corresponding weights can potentially be determined by quasi-Hebbian multi-pass learning. The aspect of timing robustness (which does not exist in discrete-time) was addressed and it was illustrated (by means of simulations) under which conditions the memorized firing signals were stable w.r.t. their relative firing-times. We did not consider the important ability of single-pass/one-shot learning in continuous-time. This might be a topic for further theoretical investigation of the continuous-time model.

The proposed networks seem to be ready to be used as building blocks for associative memory and other tasks in "real-world" applications. As a long-term goal we envisage neuromorphic hardware realizations, cf. [5, 46, 55, 69].

Appendices

Appendix A

Toy Examples

The goal of this chapter is to illustrate the operating mode of the different models analyzed in this thesis on the basis of simple toy examples. For such rather "small" examples, learning can be done by hand, which hopefully helps to establish understanding.

A.1 Hopfield Network

The classic model for an associative memory that is built up of neurons is the Hopfield network [29], [40, Chapter 42]. The Hopfield network is a recurrent (artificial) neural network which memorizes vectors as static attractors of the network.

The neurons $\xi_1, \dots, \xi_L$ in a Hopfield network are mappings defined as

$$\xi_i \colon \mathbb{R}^L \to \{-1, 1\}, \quad \boldsymbol{y} \mapsto \xi_i(\boldsymbol{y}) := \begin{cases} 1, & \text{if } \langle \boldsymbol{y}, \boldsymbol{w}_i \rangle \geq \theta_i \\ -1, & \text{otherwise,} \end{cases} \tag{A.1}$$

with weight vector $\boldsymbol{w}_i \in \mathbb{R}^L$, threshold $\theta_i \in \mathbb{R}$ (typically $\theta_i := 0$), and where $\langle \boldsymbol{y}, \boldsymbol{w}_i \rangle := \boldsymbol{w}_i^\mathsf{T} \boldsymbol{y}$. The right-hand side of (A.1) can also be written as

$$\xi_i(\boldsymbol{y}) = 2\,\sigma_{\theta_i}\big(\langle \boldsymbol{y}, \boldsymbol{w}_i \rangle\big) - 1, \tag{A.2}$$

where $\sigma_{\theta_i}(x) := \mathrm{I}[x \geq \theta_i]$, $x \in \mathbb{R}$, denotes the thresholding function.

These neurons are fully connected as shown in Figure A.1, for an example with $L = 3$ neurons. The state of the Hopfield network is

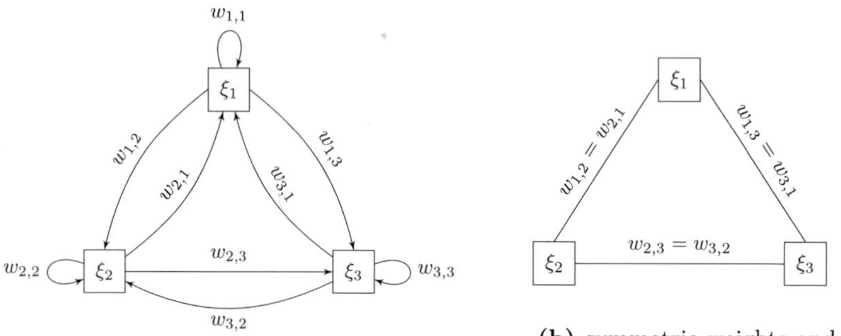

(a) arbitrary weights

(b) symmetric weights and no self-connections

Figure A.1: Hopfield network consisting of $L = 3$ neurons.

defined by the vector

$$\big(\xi_1(\boldsymbol{y}), \dots, \xi_L(\boldsymbol{y})\big)^\mathsf{T} \in \{-1, 1\}^L, \tag{A.3}$$

which represents L bits of information. All stable states (or fixed points) $\boldsymbol{y} \in \{-1, 1\}^L$ such that

$$\big(\xi_1(\boldsymbol{y}), \dots, \xi_L(\boldsymbol{y})\big)^\mathsf{T} = \boldsymbol{y} \tag{A.4}$$

are the different memories of the Hopfield network.

A.1.1 Learning of the Weights

Given N vectors (memories) $\boldsymbol{y}_1, \dots, \boldsymbol{y}_N \in \{-1, 1\}^L$, which represent the patterns to be memorized by the network, the weights are defined by the Hebbian learning rule

$$\boldsymbol{W} = \sum_{n=1}^{N} \boldsymbol{y}_n \boldsymbol{y}_n^\mathsf{T} - N \boldsymbol{I}_L, \tag{A.5}$$

where

$$\boldsymbol{W} := (\boldsymbol{w}_1, \dots, \boldsymbol{w}_L) \in \mathbb{R}^{L \times L} \tag{A.6}$$

with column vector $\boldsymbol{w}_i \in \mathbb{R}^L$ denoting the weight vector of neuron ξ_i. We note that (A.5) implies i.) $\boldsymbol{W}$ is symmetric, i.e., $\boldsymbol{W}^{\mathsf{T}} = \boldsymbol{W}$

ii.) $\boldsymbol{W}$ has zero diagonal, i.e., $\mathrm{diag}(\boldsymbol{W}) = \mathbf{0}_L$

which means $w_{i,j} = w_{j,i}$ and there are no self-connections, i.e., $w_{i,i} = 0$, cf. Figure A.1b.

A.1.2 Retrieval Phase

Having determined the weights, there are two modes of retrieval. First, an initial vector $\boldsymbol{y} \in \{-1, 1\}^L$ is imposed on the Hopfield network as its state. Then, the state of the network is updated by

- **Asynchronous updating:** In this mode only one neuron is updated at a time. This neuron can either be choosen at random, or in a pre-defined (deterministic) updating order.

- **Synchronous updating:** All neurons are updated at the very same time.

Asynchronous updating is most common since it does not need a global clock signal, and thus is biologically more plausible than synchronous updating. Moreover, it can be shown [29], if the neurons are updated asynchronously, then the Hopfield network with weight matrix (A.5) will always converge to a stable state (or fixed point) satisfying (A.4).

A.1.3 Example: Hopfield Network with $L = 3$ Neurons

We illustrate the behaviour of a Hopfield network by means of a network consisting of $L = 3$ neurons as shown in Figure A.1, cf. [24, Chapter 14]. Now, we want the Hopfield network to memorize (or store) $N = 2$ vectors (patterns)

$$\boldsymbol{y}_1 = (1, -1, 1)^{\mathsf{T}}, \tag{A.7}$$

$$\boldsymbol{y}_2 = (-1, 1, -1)^{\mathsf{T}}. \tag{A.8}$$

The thresholds are choosen to be

$$\theta_i := 0, \qquad i \in \{1, 2, 3\}, \tag{A.9}$$

and the Hebbian learning rule (A.5) yields the weight matrix

$$\boldsymbol{W} = \boldsymbol{y}_1\boldsymbol{y}_1^\mathsf{T} + \boldsymbol{y}_2\boldsymbol{y}_2^\mathsf{T} - 2\boldsymbol{I}_3 \tag{A.10}$$

$$= \begin{pmatrix} 1 & -1 & 1 \\ -1 & 1 & -1 \\ 1 & -1 & 1 \end{pmatrix} + \begin{pmatrix} 1 & -1 & 1 \\ -1 & 1 & -1 \\ 1 & -1 & 1 \end{pmatrix} - 2\boldsymbol{I}_3 \tag{A.11}$$

$$= \begin{pmatrix} 0 & -2 & 2 \\ -2 & 0 & -2 \\ 2 & -2 & 0 \end{pmatrix}. \tag{A.12}$$

We note that both $\boldsymbol{y}_1$ and $\boldsymbol{y}_2$ are stable states. For $\boldsymbol{y}_1$, we have

$$\begin{pmatrix} \xi_1(\boldsymbol{y}_1) \\ \xi_2(\boldsymbol{y}_1) \\ \xi_3(\boldsymbol{y}_1) \end{pmatrix} = \begin{pmatrix} 2\,\sigma_0(\boldsymbol{w}_1^\mathsf{T}\boldsymbol{y}_1) - 1 \\ 2\,\sigma_0(\boldsymbol{w}_2^\mathsf{T}\boldsymbol{y}_1) - 1 \\ 2\,\sigma_0(\boldsymbol{w}_3^\mathsf{T}\boldsymbol{y}_1) - 1 \end{pmatrix} \tag{A.13}$$

$$= \begin{pmatrix} 2\,\sigma_0(4) - 1 \\ 2\,\sigma_0(-4) - 1 \\ 2\,\sigma_0(4) - 1 \end{pmatrix} \tag{A.14}$$

$$= \begin{pmatrix} 1 \\ -1 \\ 1 \end{pmatrix} = \boldsymbol{y}_1, \tag{A.15}$$

and similarly for $\boldsymbol{y}_2$, we have

$$\begin{pmatrix} \xi_1(\boldsymbol{y}_2) \\ \xi_2(\boldsymbol{y}_2) \\ \xi_3(\boldsymbol{y}_2) \end{pmatrix} = \boldsymbol{y}_2. \tag{A.16}$$

Moreover, $\boldsymbol{y}_1$ and $\boldsymbol{y}_2$ are in fact the only stable states out of all the $2^3 = 8$ possible states. The other 6 states are all unstable and will converge either to $\boldsymbol{y}_1 = (1, -1, 1)^\mathsf{T}$ or $\boldsymbol{y}_2 = (-1, 1, -1)^\mathsf{T}$ depending on the neuron updating order. E.g., if we initialize the network with state

$$\boldsymbol{y}^{(0)} := (-1, 1, 1)^\mathsf{T}, \tag{A.17}$$

then we either obtain the following sequence of network states

$$\boldsymbol{y}^{(0)} = \begin{pmatrix} -1 \\ 1 \\ 1 \end{pmatrix} \xrightarrow{\text{update } \xi_1} \begin{pmatrix} 1 \\ 1 \\ 1 \end{pmatrix} \xrightarrow{\text{update } \xi_2} \begin{pmatrix} 1 \\ -1 \\ 1 \end{pmatrix} = \boldsymbol{y}_1, \tag{A.18}$$

or

$$\boldsymbol{y}^{(0)} = \begin{pmatrix} -1 \\ 1 \\ 1 \end{pmatrix} \xrightarrow{\text{update } \xi_2} \begin{pmatrix} -1 \\ 1 \\ 1 \end{pmatrix} \xrightarrow{\text{update } \xi_3} \begin{pmatrix} -1 \\ 1 \\ -1 \end{pmatrix} = \boldsymbol{y}_2. \tag{A.19}$$

A.2 Discrete-time Autonomous RNN Model

We consider a discrete-time recurrent neural network consisting of $L = 4$ neurons as introduced in Chapter 2. The network is shown in Figure A.2, which is equivalent to the network shown in Figure 2.2 for $L = 4$. In Figure A.2 the branching points are after the delay cells, whereas in Figure 2.2 the branching points are before the delay cells. Moving the branching points behind the delay cells is feasible since all connections possess the same unit-delay, and at the same time it reduces the number of delay cells by a factor $1/L$.

Now, we want the network to memorize (a periodic extension of) the discrete-time firing signal (cf. Figure A.3 below)

$$\boldsymbol{Y} := \big(\boldsymbol{y}[0], \boldsymbol{y}[1], \boldsymbol{y}[2]\big) \tag{A.20}$$

$$= \begin{pmatrix} 0 & 1 & 1 \\ 1 & 0 & 0 \\ 0 & 1 & 0 \\ 1 & 1 & 1 \end{pmatrix} \in \{0,1\}^{4\times 3} \tag{A.21}$$

of length $N = 3$ as described in Section 2.3. For the sake of convenience we consider the disturbance-free case, i.e., $\eta := 0$. We are now going to show that $\boldsymbol{Y} \in \{0,1\}^{4\times 3}$ can be memorized, e.g, by the single-pass learning rule (cf. Sections 3.1 and 4.1)

$$\boldsymbol{w}_\ell := \sum_{n=0}^{N-1} \big(2y_\ell[n] - 1\big)\boldsymbol{y}[n-1], \qquad \ell \in \{1,2,3,4\}, \tag{A.22}$$

which has the same form as (3.4) (or (4.47)). Applying (A.22) to the firing signal given in (A.21) yields

$$\boldsymbol{w}_1 = \quad \boldsymbol{y}[0] + \boldsymbol{y}[1] - \boldsymbol{y}[2], \tag{A.23}$$

$$\boldsymbol{w}_2 = -\boldsymbol{y}[0] - \boldsymbol{y}[1] + \boldsymbol{y}[2], \tag{A.24}$$

$$\boldsymbol{w}_3 = \quad \boldsymbol{y}[0] - \boldsymbol{y}[1] - \boldsymbol{y}[2], \tag{A.25}$$

$$\boldsymbol{w}_4 = \quad \boldsymbol{y}[0] + \boldsymbol{y}[1] + \boldsymbol{y}[2], \tag{A.26}$$

and the inner products $\langle \boldsymbol{y}[n], \boldsymbol{w}_1 \rangle$, for $n \in \{0,1,2\}$, evaluate to

$$\langle \boldsymbol{y}[0], \boldsymbol{w}_1 \rangle = \|\boldsymbol{y}[0]\|^2 + \langle \boldsymbol{y}[0], \boldsymbol{y}[1] \rangle - \langle \boldsymbol{y}[0], \boldsymbol{y}[2] \rangle \tag{A.27}$$

$$= 2 + 1 - 1 \tag{A.28}$$

$$= 2, \tag{A.29}$$

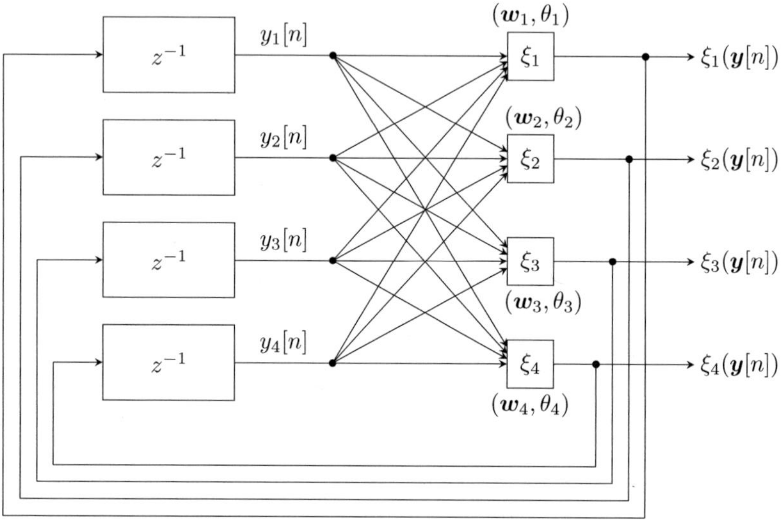

Figure A.2: Discrete-time RNN consisting of $L = 4$ neurons at time step $n \in \mathbb{N}$.

$$\begin{aligned}
\langle \boldsymbol{y}[1], \boldsymbol{w}_1 \rangle &= \langle \boldsymbol{y}[1], \boldsymbol{y}[0] \rangle + \|\boldsymbol{y}[1]\|^2 - \langle \boldsymbol{y}[1], \boldsymbol{y}[2] \rangle && \text{(A.30)} \\
&= 1 + 3 - 2 && \text{(A.31)} \\
&= 2, && \text{(A.32)}
\end{aligned}$$

and

$$\begin{aligned}
\langle \boldsymbol{y}[2], \boldsymbol{w}_1 \rangle &= \langle \boldsymbol{y}[2], \boldsymbol{y}[0] \rangle + \langle \boldsymbol{y}[2], \boldsymbol{y}[1] \rangle - \|\boldsymbol{y}[2]\|^2 && \text{(A.33)} \\
&= 1 + 2 - 2 && \text{(A.34)} \\
&= 1. && \text{(A.35)}
\end{aligned}$$

By choosing, e.g., $\theta_1 := 3/2$, we obtain from (2.3) with $\eta_1 = 0$

$$\begin{aligned}
\xi_1(\boldsymbol{y}[2]) &= \sigma_{\theta_1}(\langle \boldsymbol{y}[2], \boldsymbol{w}_1 \rangle) && \text{(A.36)} \\
&= 0 && \text{(A.37)} \\
&= y_1[0], && \text{(A.38)} \\
\xi_1(\boldsymbol{y}[0]) &= \sigma_{\theta_1}(\langle \boldsymbol{y}[0], \boldsymbol{w}_1 \rangle) && \text{(A.39)} \\
&= 1 && \text{(A.40)} \\
&= y_1[1], && \text{(A.41)}
\end{aligned}$$

and

$$\begin{aligned} \xi_1(\boldsymbol{y}[1]) &= \sigma_{\theta_1}(\langle \boldsymbol{y}[1], \boldsymbol{w}_1 \rangle) && \text{(A.42)} \\ &= 1 && \text{(A.43)} \\ &= y_1[2]. && \text{(A.44)} \end{aligned}$$

Thus, we have

$$\xi_1(\boldsymbol{y}[n-1]) = y_1[n], \qquad n \in \{0, 1, 2\}. \tag{A.45}$$

Recall, the time indices n are taken modulo $N-1$. Similarly for ξ_2, we have

$$\begin{aligned} \langle \boldsymbol{y}[0], \boldsymbol{w}_2 \rangle &= -2, && \text{(A.46)} \\ \langle \boldsymbol{y}[1], \boldsymbol{w}_2 \rangle &= -2, && \text{(A.47)} \\ \langle \boldsymbol{y}[2], \boldsymbol{w}_2 \rangle &= -1, && \text{(A.48)} \end{aligned}$$

and thus by choosing, e.g., $\theta_2 := -3/2$, we obtain

$$\xi_2(\boldsymbol{y}[n-1]) = y_2[n], \qquad n \in \{0, 1, 2\}. \tag{A.49}$$

Since

$$\begin{aligned} \langle \boldsymbol{y}[0], \boldsymbol{w}_3 \rangle &= 0, && \text{(A.50)} \\ \langle \boldsymbol{y}[1], \boldsymbol{w}_3 \rangle &= -4, && \text{(A.51)} \\ \langle \boldsymbol{y}[2], \boldsymbol{w}_3 \rangle &= -3, && \text{(A.52)} \end{aligned}$$

we choose $\theta_3 := -3/2$, and every

$$\begin{aligned} \theta_4 &\leq \min_{n \in \{0,1,2\}} \langle \boldsymbol{y}[n], \boldsymbol{w}_4 \rangle && \text{(A.53)} \\ &= 4 && \text{(A.54)} \end{aligned}$$

suffices to ensure

$$\xi_\ell(\boldsymbol{y}[n-1]) = y_\ell[n], \qquad n \in \{0, 1, 2\}, \tag{A.55}$$

for $\ell = 4$.

Thus, we have shown that the weight vectors (A.23) – (A.26), and thresholds

$$\begin{aligned} \theta_1 &= 3/2, && \text{(A.56)} \\ \theta_2 &= -3/2, && \text{(A.57)} \\ \theta_3 &= -3/2, && \text{(A.58)} \\ \theta_4 &= 0, && \text{(A.59)} \end{aligned}$$

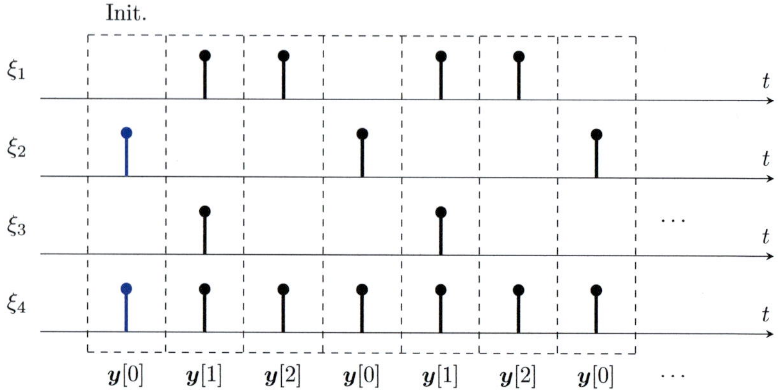

Figure A.3: Discrete-time firing signal produced by the RNN in Figure A.2 if initialized with $\boldsymbol{y}[0] = (0, 1, 0, 1)^\mathsf{T}$.

imply (A.55), for all $\ell \in \{1, 2, 3, 4\}$, which proves that if the network is initialized with any $\boldsymbol{y}[k]$, $k \in \{0, 1, 2\}$, then it will produce the (firing) sequence

$$\big(\boldsymbol{y}[(n+k) \bmod 3]\big)_{n \in \mathbb{N}}. \tag{A.60}$$

The sequence (A.60), for $\boldsymbol{y}[0] := (0, 1, 0, 1)^\mathsf{T}$, is illustrated in Figure A.3.

We now check the first step. From (A.21) and (A.23) – (A.26) it follows that

$$\begin{pmatrix} \langle \boldsymbol{y}[0], \boldsymbol{w}_1 \rangle \\ \langle \boldsymbol{y}[0], \boldsymbol{w}_2 \rangle \\ \langle \boldsymbol{y}[0], \boldsymbol{w}_3 \rangle \\ \langle \boldsymbol{y}[0], \boldsymbol{w}_4 \rangle \end{pmatrix} = \begin{pmatrix} \boldsymbol{w}_1^\mathsf{T} \\ \boldsymbol{w}_2^\mathsf{T} \\ \boldsymbol{w}_3^\mathsf{T} \\ \boldsymbol{w}_4^\mathsf{T} \end{pmatrix} \boldsymbol{y}[0] = \begin{pmatrix} 0 & 1 & 1 & 1 \\ 0 & -1 & -1 & -1 \\ -2 & 1 & -1 & -1 \\ 2 & 1 & 1 & 3 \end{pmatrix} \begin{pmatrix} 0 \\ 1 \\ 0 \\ 1 \end{pmatrix} = \begin{pmatrix} 2 \\ -2 \\ 0 \\ 4 \end{pmatrix}, \tag{A.61}$$

and thus by (A.56) – (A.59), we obtain

$$\begin{pmatrix} \xi_1(\boldsymbol{y}[0]) \\ \xi_2(\boldsymbol{y}[0]) \\ \xi_3(\boldsymbol{y}[0]) \\ \xi_4(\boldsymbol{y}[0]) \end{pmatrix} = \begin{pmatrix} \sigma_{3/2}(\langle \boldsymbol{y}[0], \boldsymbol{w}_1 \rangle) \\ \sigma_{-3/2}(\langle \boldsymbol{y}[0], \boldsymbol{w}_2 \rangle) \\ \sigma_{-3/2}(\langle \boldsymbol{y}[0], \boldsymbol{w}_3 \rangle) \\ \sigma_0(\langle \boldsymbol{y}[0], \boldsymbol{w}_4 \rangle) \end{pmatrix} = \begin{pmatrix} 1 \\ 0 \\ 1 \\ 1 \end{pmatrix} = \boldsymbol{y}[1]. \tag{A.62}$$

A.3 Continuous-time Autonomous RNN Model

For $K = N = 2$, we are given the continuous-time firing signal $\boldsymbol{y}(t) \in \mathbb{R}^4$, $t \in \mathbb{R}$, characterized by (cf. Section 8.1)

$$\boldsymbol{Y}_2^{(2)} = \big(\boldsymbol{y}[0], \ldots, \boldsymbol{y}[4]\big) = \begin{pmatrix} \tilde{\boldsymbol{y}}_1^{\mathsf{T}} \\ \vdots \\ \tilde{\boldsymbol{y}}_4^{\mathsf{T}} \end{pmatrix} = \begin{pmatrix} 0 & 1 & 0 & 1 & 0 \\ 0 & 0 & 1 & 0 & 0 \\ 1 & 0 & 0 & 1 & 0 \\ 0 & 0 & 0 & 0 & 1 \end{pmatrix} \tag{A.63}$$

as shown in Figure A.4.

We want to memorize the given firing signal $\boldsymbol{Y}_2^{(2)}$ by means of a recurrent network model, introduced in Sections 7.1 and 7.2, consisting of $L = 4$ neurons, and delays given by

$$\boldsymbol{\tau}_1 = (1, 1, 2, 2)^{\mathsf{T}} \mu_{T_\mathrm{r}}, \tag{A.64}$$

$$\boldsymbol{\tau}_2 = (2, 1, 1, 2)^{\mathsf{T}} \mu_{T_\mathrm{r}}, \tag{A.65}$$

$$\boldsymbol{\tau}_3 = (2, 2, 1, 1)^{\mathsf{T}} \mu_{T_\mathrm{r}}, \tag{A.66}$$

$$\boldsymbol{\tau}_4 = (1, 1, 1, 2)^{\mathsf{T}} \mu_{T_\mathrm{r}}. \tag{A.67}$$

For the sake of convenience, we use a rectangular impulse response, cf. Figure 7.2a. Note that the number of samples (of a channel) is larger than the number of neurons, i.e., $L < NK + 1$.

We determine $\Delta \boldsymbol{w}_i^{(n)} \in \mathbb{R}^4$ according to (8.63), i.e.,

$$\Delta \boldsymbol{w}_i^{(n)} = \sum_{k=0}^{K-1} \begin{pmatrix} y_1[n - k_{1,i} - k] \\ \vdots \\ y_L[n - k_{L,i} - k] \end{pmatrix}, \tag{A.68}$$

where

$$k_{\ell,i} := \frac{\tau_{\ell,i}}{\mu_{T_\mathrm{r}}}, \qquad (\ell, i) \in \{1, \ldots, L\}^2. \tag{A.69}$$

For $i = 1$, $n = 0$, (A.68) yields

$$\Delta \boldsymbol{w}_1^{(0)} = \sum_{k=0}^{1} \begin{pmatrix} y_1[0 - 1 - k] \\ y_2[0 - 1 - k] \\ y_3[0 - 2 - k] \\ y_4[0 - 2 - k] \end{pmatrix} = \begin{pmatrix} y_1[4] + y_1[3] \\ y_2[4] + y_2[3] \\ y_3[3] + y_3[2] \\ y_4[3] + y_4[2] \end{pmatrix} = \begin{pmatrix} 1 \\ 0 \\ 1 \\ 0 \end{pmatrix}, \tag{A.70}$$

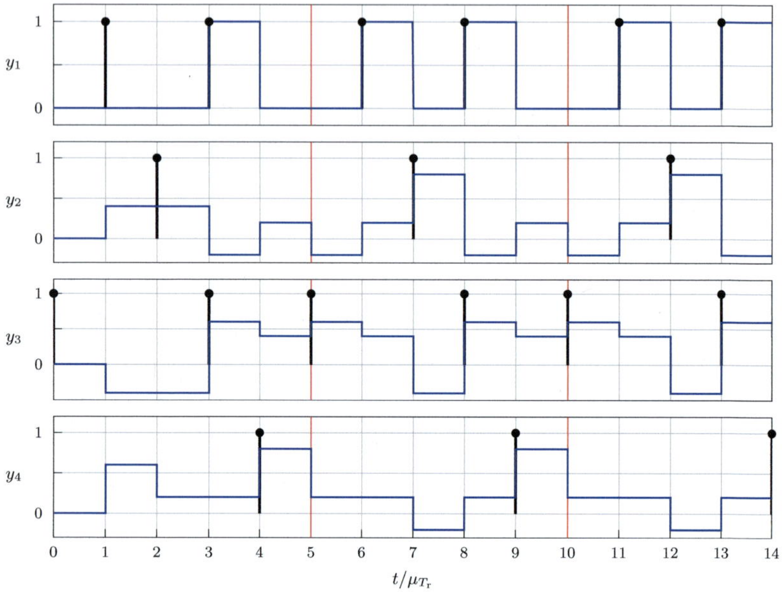

Figure A.4: First three periods of the firing signal (A.63), and the corresponding score signals (blue) obtained by the optimal weights and initialized with zero.

where the indices of $y_\ell[\cdot]$ are taken modulo $NK + 1 = 5$. Similarly, we obtain

$$\Delta \boldsymbol{w}_1^{(1)} = \begin{pmatrix} 0 \\ 0 \\ 1 \\ 1 \end{pmatrix}, \; \Delta \boldsymbol{w}_1^{(2)} = \begin{pmatrix} 1 \\ 0 \\ 1 \\ 1 \end{pmatrix}, \; \Delta \boldsymbol{w}_1^{(3)} = \begin{pmatrix} 1 \\ 1 \\ 1 \\ 0 \end{pmatrix}, \; \Delta \boldsymbol{w}_1^{(4)} = \begin{pmatrix} 1 \\ 1 \\ 0 \\ 0 \end{pmatrix}, \tag{A.71}$$

which yields

$$\Delta \boldsymbol{W}_1 = \begin{pmatrix} \left(\Delta \boldsymbol{w}_1^{(0)}\right)^{\mathsf{T}} \\ \vdots \\ \left(\Delta \boldsymbol{w}_1^{(4)}\right)^{\mathsf{T}} \end{pmatrix} = \begin{pmatrix} 1 & 0 & 1 & 0 \\ 0 & 0 & 1 & 1 \\ 1 & 0 & 1 & 1 \\ 1 & 1 & 1 & 0 \\ 1 & 1 & 0 & 0 \end{pmatrix}. \tag{A.72}$$

Thus, the weights of ξ_1 are given by

$$\boldsymbol{w}_1 = \Delta \boldsymbol{W}_1^{\dagger} \tilde{\boldsymbol{y}}_1 = (-1, 1, 1, 0)^{\mathsf{T}}, \tag{A.73}$$

where $\Delta \boldsymbol{W}_1^{\dagger}$ denotes the pseudoinverse of $\Delta \boldsymbol{W}_1$, cf. (8.70) on page 97. Note that (cf. Figure A.4)

$$\Delta \boldsymbol{W}_1 \boldsymbol{w}_1 = \tilde{\boldsymbol{y}}_1 \tag{A.74}$$

in accordance with (8.24) from Proposition 8.1, because

$$\Delta \boldsymbol{W}_i \, \boldsymbol{w}_i = \big(z_i(0), \ldots, z_i(4\mu_{T_{\mathrm{r}}})\big)^{\mathsf{T}}, \tag{A.75}$$

for all i, as shown in (8.60).

The same procedure yields

$$\boldsymbol{w}_2 = \frac{1}{5}(-3, 2, 2, 2)^{\mathsf{T}}, \tag{A.76}$$

and

$$\Delta \boldsymbol{W}_2 \, \boldsymbol{w}_2 = \frac{1}{5}(-1, 1, 4, -1, 1)^{\mathsf{T}} \neq \tilde{\boldsymbol{y}}_2. \tag{A.77}$$

However, choosing, e.g., $\theta_2 := 1/2$ results in perfect memorization of $\tilde{\boldsymbol{y}}_2$ as illustrated in Figure A.4. This holds also for the remaining channels:

$$\boldsymbol{w}_3 = \frac{1}{5}(3, 1, -2, 1)^{\mathsf{T}}, \tag{A.78}$$

$$\boldsymbol{w}_4 = \frac{1}{5}(-2, 3, 3, -2)^{\mathsf{T}}, \tag{A.79}$$

resulting in

$$\Delta \boldsymbol{W}_3 \, \boldsymbol{w}_3 = \frac{1}{5}(3, 2, -2, 3, 2)^{\mathsf{T}} \neq \tilde{\boldsymbol{y}}_3, \tag{A.80}$$

$$\Delta \boldsymbol{W}_4 \, \boldsymbol{w}_4 = \frac{1}{5}(1, 1, -1, 1, 4)^{\mathsf{T}} \neq \tilde{\boldsymbol{y}}_4. \tag{A.81}$$

Thus, e.g., $\theta_3 := 1/2$ and $\theta_4 := 1/2$ yields perfect memorization overall, albeit $L < NK + 1$. This example shows that the condition (8.22) in Proposition 8.1 is not necessary.

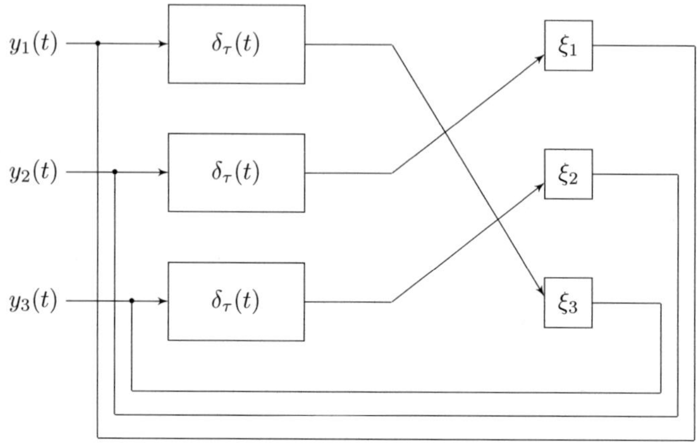

Figure A.5: RNN which is not fully connected.

A.3.1 Applications: Permutation & Pattern Detection

Let us consider the continuous-time RNN given in Figure A.5, i.e.,

$$\boldsymbol{w}_1 = (0, 1, 0)^\mathsf{T}, \tag{A.82}$$

$$\boldsymbol{w}_2 = (0, 0, 1)^\mathsf{T}, \tag{A.83}$$

$$\boldsymbol{w}_3 = (1, 0, 0)^\mathsf{T}, \tag{A.84}$$

and all delays are equal to $\tau \in \mathbb{R}$, $\tau > T_\mathrm{r}$.

If we initialize this network with a (local) monomial pattern (i.e., exactly one pulse in each channel), then the network produces another monomial pattern, after a time span of τ seconds, according to the permutation

$$\pi_\text{channel} = \begin{pmatrix} 1 & 2 & 3 \\ 3 & 1 & 2 \end{pmatrix}. \tag{A.85}$$

The meaning of π_channel is that a pulse in channel 1 causes a pulse in channel 3, a pulse in channel 2 causes a pulse in channel 1, and a pulse in channel 3 causes a pulse in channel 1. Where each produced pulse is delayed by τ seconds w.r.t. its causing input pulse. (This implicitly assumes, e.g., $\theta_i = 0$, for all i.)

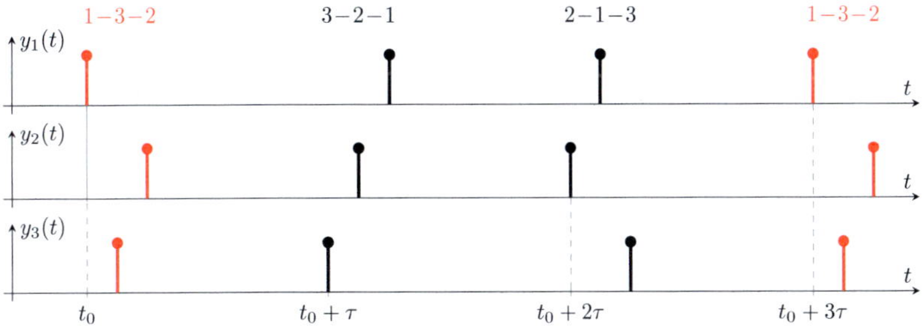

Figure A.6: Periodic sequence of quasi-monomial pulse patterns.

Thus, if we initialize the network in Figure A.5, e.g., with the monomial pattern $1-3-2$ at $t = t_0$, then the network produces the pattern $\pi_{\text{channel}}(1) - \pi_{\text{channel}}(3) - \pi_{\text{channel}}(2) = 3-2-1$ at $t = t_0 + \tau$, cf. Figure A.6. The pattern $3-2-1$ then produces $2-1-3$ at $t = t_0 + 2\tau$ and so on. Overall, the network produces a periodic sequence of (monomial) patterns with cycle

$$1-3-2 \longrightarrow 3-2-1 \longrightarrow 2-1-3 \longrightarrow 1-3-2 \longrightarrow \cdots \tag{A.86}$$

as illustrated in Figure A.6.

Pattern Detection Capability of a Single Neuron Using the Synaptic Delays

Let us consider a single neuron as in Figure A.7 with $L = 3$ inputs, weights

$$w_{1,i} = w_{2,i} = w_{3,i} = 1, \tag{A.87}$$

and delays

$$\tau_{1,i} = 2T_{\text{r}}, \qquad \tau_{2,i} = 0, \qquad \tau_{3,i} = T_{\text{r}}. \tag{A.88}$$

The given delays clearly imply that the pattern 1–3–2 generates the score signal $z_i(\cdot)$ having the largest peak, cf. Figure A.8. Thus, with a suitable threshold θ_i, the neuron is able to detect the preferred pattern $1-3-2$ out of all possible 3-channel input patterns as demonstrated in Figure A.8.

By choosing the delays appropriately, any of the 6 possible patterns can become the preferred pattern.

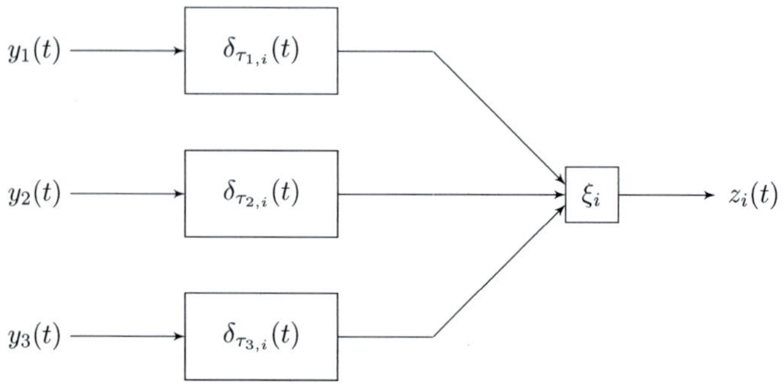

Figure A.7: A single neuron with $L = 3$ inputs.

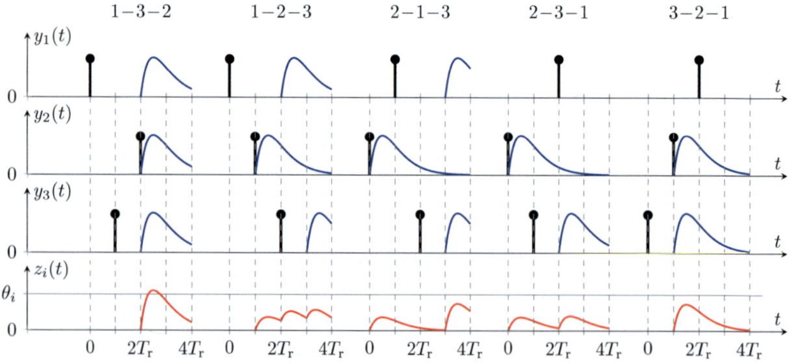

Figure A.8: Score signal of a single neuron for all possible 3-channel input patterns. The pattern 3–1–2 (which is not plotted) produces the same score signal as the pattern 1–2–3.

Appendix B

Proofs

For the sake of completeness we give proofs of some statements which are relevant in this thesis. This appendix contains supplementary material which is mainly self-contained.

Section B.1 is crucial for the proof of the main result of Part I. The last section of this appendix proves two inequalities which were encountered during this work, but which are not directly related to the rest of the thesis.

B.1 An Upper Bound on the Moment Generating Function of $S_{\ell,n}$

The main ingredient to prove the upper bound in (B.21) below is the inequality (B.1) [1] in the following lemma, which is illustrated in Figure B.1. Note that the left-hand side of (B.1) equals to $\mathrm{E}\left[e^{\lambda(X-p)}\right]$, for $X \sim \mathrm{Ber}(p)$, $0 < p < 1$.

Lemma B.1. *For all* $0 < p < 1$, $\lambda \in \mathbb{R}$,

$$pe^{(1-p)\lambda} + (1-p)e^{-p\lambda} \leq e^{\lambda^2/8}. \tag{B.1}$$

□

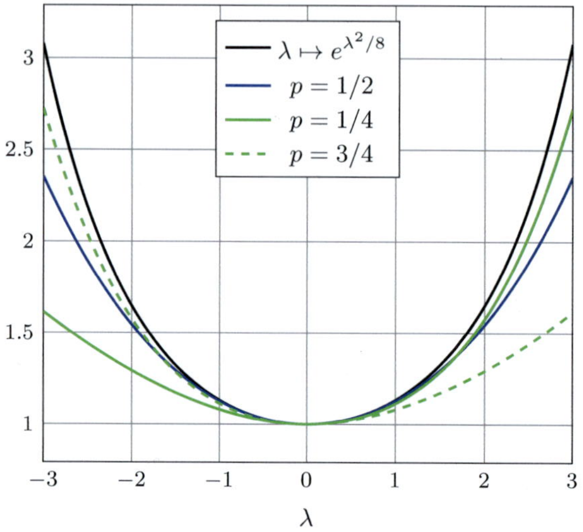

Figure B.1: Graphs of $\lambda \mapsto pe^{(1-p)\lambda} + (1-p)e^{-p\lambda}$, for $p \in \left\{\frac{1}{4}, \frac{1}{2}, \frac{3}{4}\right\}$, and $\lambda \mapsto e^{\lambda^2/8}$.

Proof of Lemma B.1. First, we rewrite (B.1)

$$pe^{(1-p)\lambda} + (1-p)e^{-p\lambda} \leq e^{\lambda^2/8} \tag{B.2}$$

$$pe^{\frac{\lambda}{2}} + (1-p)e^{-\frac{\lambda}{2}} \leq e^{\frac{\lambda^2}{8}+(p-\frac{1}{2})\lambda} \tag{B.3}$$

$$\frac{1}{2}\big(1+2p-1\big)e^{\frac{\lambda}{2}} + \frac{1}{2}\big(1-(2p-1)\big)e^{-\frac{\lambda}{2}} \leq e^{\frac{\lambda^2}{8}+(2p-1)\frac{\lambda}{2}} \tag{B.4}$$

$$\frac{1}{2}(1+\alpha)e^{x} + \frac{1}{2}(1-\alpha)e^{-x} \leq e^{\frac{x^2}{2}+\alpha x} \tag{B.5}$$

$$\frac{1}{2}(e^{x}+e^{-x}) + \frac{\alpha}{2}(e^{x}-e^{-x}) \leq e^{\frac{x^2}{2}+\alpha x} \tag{B.6}$$

$$\cosh(x) + \alpha\sinh(x) \leq e^{\frac{x^2}{2}+\alpha x}, \tag{B.7}$$

where in (B.5) we introduced the variables

$$\alpha := 2p-1, \tag{B.8}$$

and

$$x := \frac{\lambda}{2}. \tag{B.9}$$

Note $|\alpha| < 1$ and $x \in \mathbb{R}$.

Now, let us define

$$f(\alpha, x) := \cosh(x) + \alpha \sinh(x) - e^{\frac{x^2}{2}+\alpha x}. \tag{B.10}$$

For x sufficiently large, the term $e^{x^2/2}$ dominates and thus

$$\lim_{x\to\pm\infty} f(\alpha, x) = -\infty < 0, \qquad |\alpha| < 1. \tag{B.11}$$

In order to find the (global) maximum of $f(\cdot,\cdot)$, we set the partial derivatives equal to zero

$$\frac{\partial}{\partial\alpha} f(\alpha, x) = \sinh(x) - x e^{\frac{x^2}{2}+\alpha x} \overset{!}{=} 0, \tag{B.12}$$

$$\frac{\partial}{\partial x} f(\alpha, x) = \sinh(x) + \alpha \cosh(x) - (x+\alpha) e^{\frac{x^2}{2}+\alpha x} \overset{!}{=} 0. \tag{B.13}$$

Equation (B.12) is equivalent to

$$\sinh(x) = x e^{\frac{x^2}{2}+\alpha x}, \tag{B.14}$$

which inserted into (B.13) leads to

$$\cosh(x) = e^{\frac{x^2}{2}+\alpha x}, \tag{B.15}$$

and thus

$$\tanh(x) = \frac{\sinh(x)}{\cosh(x)} \tag{B.16}$$

$$= x, \tag{B.17}$$

which implies $x = 0$. Since

$$f(\alpha, 0) = 0, \tag{B.18}$$

for all α, we have shown that $f(\alpha, x) \le 0$, for all $|\alpha| < 1$, $x \in \mathbb{R}$, which implies (B.7). ∎

The next lemma states the key upper bound (B.21) needed in Section 4.2 to derive an appropriately tight bound on the single-pass (one-shot) memorization error-probability.

Lemma B.2. *Let* $X_{\ell,n} \overset{\text{i.i.d.}}{\sim} \mathrm{Ber}(p)$*, for* $(\ell, n) \in \{1, \ldots, L\} \times \{1, \ldots, N\}$*,* $0 < p < 1$*. Then, the random variable*

$$S_{\ell,n} := \sum_{n' \in \{1,\ldots,N\}\setminus\{n\}} X_{\ell,n'} \sum_{\ell'=1}^{L} X_{\ell',n-1}(X_{\ell',n'-1} - p) \tag{B.19}$$

has expectation zero, i.e.,

$$\mathrm{E}[S_{\ell,n}] = 0, \tag{B.20}$$

and its moment generating function is upper bounded by

$$\mathrm{E}\big[e^{\lambda S_{\ell,n}}\big] < e^{\frac{\lambda^2}{8} LN}, \tag{B.21}$$

for all $\lambda \in \mathbb{R}$*.* □

Proof of Lemma B.2. We first prove (B.20):

$$\begin{aligned}
\mathrm{E}[S_{\ell,n}] &= \sum_{n' \in \{1,\ldots,N\}\setminus\{n\}} \sum_{\ell'=1}^{L} \mathrm{E}\big[X_{\ell,n'} X_{\ell',n-1}(X_{\ell',n'-1} - p)\big] && \text{(B.22)}\\
&= \sum_{n' \in \{1,\ldots,N\}\setminus\{n\}} \sum_{\ell'=1}^{L} \mathrm{E}[X_{\ell,n'} X_{\ell',n-1}] \underbrace{\mathrm{E}[X_{\ell',n'-1} - p]}_{=0} && \text{(B.23)}\\
&= 0. && \text{(B.24)}
\end{aligned}$$

In (B.22) we used linearity of expectation, and (B.23) holds because the random variables $X_{\ell,n'} X_{\ell',n-1}$ and $X_{\ell',n'-1}$ are independent, for all $(\ell', n') \in \{1, \ldots, L\} \times \{1, \ldots, N\} \setminus \{n\}$.

For all $\lambda \in \mathbb{R}$, the moment generating function of $S_{\ell,n}$ can be written as

$$\begin{aligned}
&\mathrm{E}\big[e^{\lambda S_{\ell,n}}\big]\\
&= \mathrm{E}\left[\prod_{n' \in \{1,\ldots,N\}\setminus\{n\}} \prod_{\ell'=1}^{L} e^{\lambda X_{\ell,n'} X_{\ell',n-1}(X_{\ell',n'-1} - p)}\right] && \text{(B.25)}\\
&= \mathrm{E}\left[\prod_{n' \in \{1,\ldots,N\}\setminus\{n\}} e^{\lambda X_{\ell,n'} X_{\ell,n-1}(X_{\ell,n'-1} - p)}\right.\\
&\qquad \left.\cdot \prod_{\ell' \in \{1,\ldots,L\}\setminus\{\ell\}} e^{\lambda X_{\ell,n'} X_{\ell',n-1}(X_{\ell',n'-1} - p)}\right] && \text{(B.26)}
\end{aligned}$$

$$
\begin{aligned}
&= \prod_{n'=1}^{N} \sum_{x_{\ell,n'} \in \{0,1\}} P_X(x_{\ell,n'}) \prod_{\ell' \in \{1,\ldots,L\}\setminus\{\ell\}} \sum_{x_{\ell',n-1} \in \{0,1\}} P_X(x_{\ell',n-1}) \\
&\quad \cdot \mathrm{E}\Bigg[\prod_{n' \in \{1,\ldots,N\}\setminus\{n\}} e^{\lambda X_{\ell,n'} X_{\ell,n-1}(X_{\ell,n'-1}-p)} \\
&\qquad \cdot \prod_{\ell' \in \{1,\ldots,L\}\setminus\{\ell\}} e^{\lambda X_{\ell,n'} X_{\ell',n-1}(X_{\ell',n'-1}-p)} \,\Bigg|\, \mathcal{X}_{\ell,n-1} \Bigg] \qquad \text{(B.27)} \\
&= \prod_{n'=1}^{N} \sum_{x_{\ell,n'} \in \{0,1\}} P_X(x_{\ell,n'}) \prod_{\ell' \in \{1,\ldots,L\}\setminus\{\ell\}} \sum_{x_{\ell',n-1} \in \{0,1\}} P_X(x_{\ell',n-1}) \\
&\quad \cdot \mathrm{E}\Bigg[\prod_{n' \in \{1,\ldots,N\}\setminus\{n\}} e^{\lambda x_{\ell,n'} x_{\ell,n-1}(x_{\ell,n'-1}-p)} \\
&\qquad \cdot \prod_{\ell' \in \{1,\ldots,L\}\setminus\{\ell\}} e^{\lambda x_{\ell,n'} x_{\ell',n-1}(X_{\ell',n'-1}-p)} \Bigg] \qquad \text{(B.28)} \\
&= \prod_{n'=1}^{N} \sum_{x_{\ell,n'} \in \{0,1\}} P_X(x_{\ell,n'}) \prod_{\ell' \in \{1,\ldots,L\}\setminus\{\ell\}} \sum_{x_{\ell',n-1} \in \{0,1\}} P_X(x_{\ell',n-1}) \\
&\quad \cdot \prod_{n' \in \{1,\ldots,N\}\setminus\{n\}} e^{\lambda x_{\ell,n'} x_{\ell,n-1}(x_{\ell,n'-1}-p)} \\
&\qquad \cdot \prod_{\ell' \in \{1,\ldots,L\}\setminus\{\ell\}} \mathrm{E}\Big[e^{\lambda x_{\ell,n'} x_{\ell',n-1}(X_{\ell',n'-1}-p)} \Big]. \qquad \text{(B.29)}
\end{aligned}
$$

Equation (B.25) follows from the definition of $S_{\ell,n}$, cf. (B.19). In (B.26) we took the factor for $\ell' = \ell$ out of the product on the right-hand side. The step from (B.26) to (B.27) uses the law of total probability/expectation (where we conditioning on "channel" ℓ and "time step" $n-1$, cf. (B.31) below), together with the definitions

$$P_X:\ \{0,1\} \to [0,1],\ x \mapsto P_X(x) := p^x(1-p)^{1-x}, \qquad \text{(B.30)}$$

i.e., $P_X(\cdot)$ denotes the probability mass function of $X \sim \mathrm{Ber}(p)$, and

$$\mathcal{X}_{\ell,n-1} := \bigcap_{n'=1}^{N} \{X_{\ell,n'} = x_{\ell,n'}\} \cap \bigcap_{\ell' \in \{1,\ldots,L\}\setminus\{\ell\}} \{X_{\ell',n-1} = x_{\ell',n-1}\}. \qquad \text{(B.31)}$$

In (B.28) we inserted the values of condition $\mathcal{X}_{\ell,n-1}$ and used the fact that the remaining random variables $X_{\ell',n'-1}$ are independent of $\mathcal{X}_{\ell,n-1}$, for $(\ell',n') \in \{1,\ldots,L\} \setminus \{\ell\} \times \{1,\ldots,N\} \setminus \{n\}$. Finally, in (B.29) we applied linearity of expectation and again independence of the remaining random variables $X_{\ell',n'-1}$.

Now, by means of Lemma B.1 we can upper bound the expectation in (B.29) by

$$
\begin{aligned}
&\mathrm{E}\left[e^{\lambda x_{\ell,n'} x_{\ell',n-1}(X_{\ell',n'-1}-p)}\right] \\
&\quad = p e^{\lambda x_{\ell,n'} x_{\ell',n-1}(1-p)} + (1-p) e^{-\lambda x_{\ell,n'} x_{\ell',n-1} p} && \text{(B.32)} \\
&\quad \leq e^{(\lambda x_{\ell,n'} x_{\ell',n-1})^2/8} && \text{(B.33)} \\
&\quad \leq e^{\lambda^2/8}, && \text{(B.34)}
\end{aligned}
$$

where (B.32) holds since $X_{\ell',n'-1} \sim \mathrm{Ber}(p)$. Inequality (B.33) follows from (B.1), and (B.32) holds since $x_{\ell,n'}, x_{\ell',n-1} \in \{0,1\}$.

Thus, the right-hand side of (B.29) can be upper bounded by

$$
\begin{aligned}
&\mathrm{E}\left[e^{\lambda S_{\ell,n}}\right] \\
&\leq \prod_{n'=1}^{N} \sum_{x_{\ell,n'} \in \{0,1\}} P_X(x_{\ell,n'}) \prod_{\ell' \in \{1,\ldots,L\} \setminus \{\ell\}} \sum_{x_{\ell',n-1} \in \{0,1\}} P_X(x_{\ell',n-1}) \\
&\quad \cdot \prod_{n' \in \{1,\ldots,N\} \setminus \{n\}} e^{\lambda x_{\ell,n'} x_{\ell,n-1}(x_{\ell,n'-1}-p)} \cdot e^{\frac{\lambda^2}{8}(L-1)} && \text{(B.35)} \\
&= \prod_{n'=1}^{N} \sum_{x_{\ell,n'} \in \{0,1\}} P_X(x_{\ell,n'}) \prod_{\ell' \in \{1,\ldots,L\} \setminus \{\ell\}} \sum_{x_{\ell',n-1} \in \{0,1\}} P_X(x_{\ell',n-1}) \\
&\quad \cdot e^{\frac{\lambda^2}{8}(L-1)(N-1)} \prod_{n' \in \{1,\ldots,N\} \setminus \{n\}} e^{\lambda x_{\ell,n'} x_{\ell,n-1}(x_{\ell,n'-1}-p)} && \text{(B.36)} \\
&= e^{\frac{\lambda^2}{8}(L-1)(N-1)} \prod_{n'=1}^{N} \sum_{x_{\ell,n'} \in \{0,1\}} P_X(x_{\ell,n'}) \\
&\quad \cdot \prod_{n' \in \{1,\ldots,N\} \setminus \{n\}} e^{\lambda x_{\ell,n'} x_{\ell,n-1}(x_{\ell,n'-1}-p)} && \text{(B.37)} \\
&= e^{\frac{\lambda^2}{8}(L-1)(N-1)} \sum_{x_{\ell,n-1} \in \{0,1\}} P_X(x_{\ell,n-1}) \\
&\quad \cdot \sum_{x_{\ell,n-2} \in \{0,1\}} P_X(x_{\ell,n-2})\, e^{\lambda x_{\ell,n-1} x_{\ell,n-1}(x_{\ell,n-2}-p)}
\end{aligned}
$$

$$\vdots$$

$$\cdot \sum_{x_{\ell,1}\in\{0,1\}} P_X(x_{\ell,1})\, e^{\lambda x_{\ell,2} x_{\ell,n-1}(x_{\ell,1}-p)}$$

$$\cdot \sum_{x_{\ell,N}\in\{0,1\}} P_X(x_{\ell,N})\, e^{\lambda x_{\ell,1} x_{\ell,n-1}(x_{\ell,N}-p)}$$

$$\vdots$$

$$\cdot \underbrace{\sum_{x_{\ell,n}\in\{0,1\}} P_X(x_{\ell,n})\, e^{\lambda x_{\ell,n+1} x_{\ell,n-1}(x_{\ell,n}-p)}}_{= \mathrm{E}\left[e^{\lambda x_{\ell,n+1} x_{\ell,n-1}(X_{\ell,n}-p)}\right] \le e^{\lambda^2/8}} \tag{B.38}$$

$$\le e^{\frac{\lambda^2}{8}(L-1)(N-1)} e^{\frac{\lambda^2}{8}(N-1)} \tag{B.39}$$

$$= e^{\frac{\lambda^2}{8}L(N-1)}, \tag{B.40}$$

which proves (B.21). The step from (B.29) to (B.35) follows from (B.34). In (B.36) we took the common factor $e^{\lambda^2(L-1)/8}$ out of the rightmost product. Then, the rightmost product of (B.36) does not depend on the variables $\{x_{\ell',n-1}\}_{\ell'\in\{1,\ldots,L\}\setminus\{\ell\}}$, and thus we can interchange it with

$$\prod_{\ell'\in\{1,\ldots,L\}\setminus\{\ell\}} \sum_{x_{\ell',n-1}\in\{0,1\}} P_X(x_{\ell',n-1})$$

$$= \sum_{x_{1,n-1}\in\{0,1\}} P_X(x_{1,n-1}) \cdots \sum_{x_{\ell-1,n-1}\in\{0,1\}} P_X(x_{\ell-1,n-1})$$

$$\cdot \sum_{x_{\ell+1,n-1}\in\{0,1\}} P_X(x_{\ell+1,n-1}) \cdots \sum_{x_{L,n-1}\in\{0,1\}} P_X(x_{L,n-1}) \tag{B.41}$$

$$= 1, \tag{B.42}$$

which yields (B.37). Each sum in (B.41) evaluates to 1, because $P_X(0) + P_X(1) = 1$ (cf. (B.30)).

Finally, from (B.37) to (B.38) we rearranged the factors of the rightmost product in (B.37) according to the following dependency analysis. For $n' \in \{1, \ldots, N\} \setminus \{n\}$, let us define the variables

$$y_{\ell,n'} := e^{\lambda x_{\ell,n'} x_{\ell,n-1}(x_{\ell,n'-1}-p)}, \qquad \lambda \in \mathbb{R}. \tag{B.43}$$

Then the mentioned product can be written as

$$\prod_{n'\in\{1,\ldots,N\}\setminus\{n\}} e^{\lambda x_{\ell,n'} x_{\ell,n-1}(x_{\ell,n'-1}-p)}$$

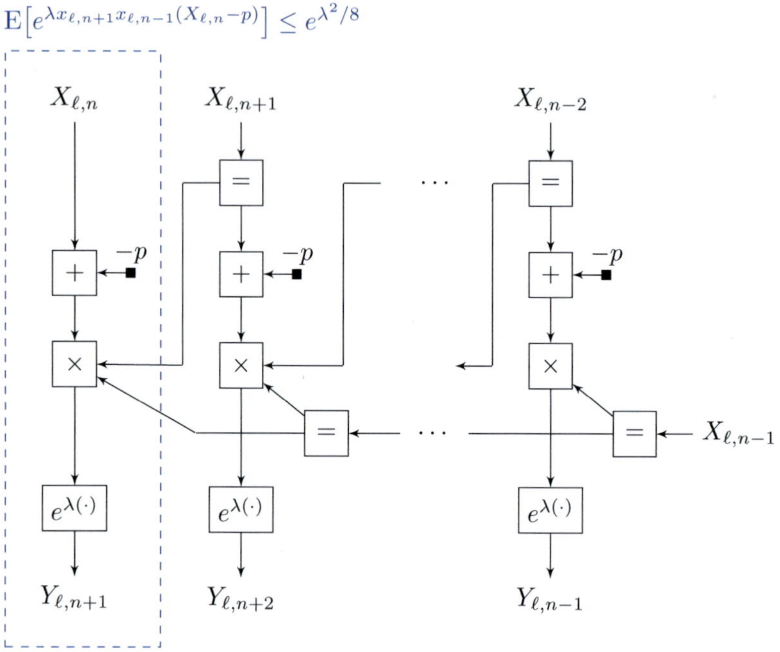

Figure B.2: Factor graph of the variables $\{y_{\ell,n'}\}_{n' \in \{1,\ldots,N\}\setminus\{n\}}$ defined in (B.43) ordered as in the right-hand side of (B.45).

$$= \prod_{n' \in \{1,\ldots,N\}\setminus\{n\}} y_{\ell,n'} \tag{B.44}$$

$$= y_{\ell,n+1} \cdot \ldots \cdot y_{\ell,N} \cdot y_{\ell,1} \cdot \ldots \cdot y_{\ell,n-1} \tag{B.45}$$

$$= e^{\lambda x_{\ell,n+1} x_{\ell,n-1}(x_{\ell,n}-p)} \cdot \ldots \cdot e^{\lambda x_{\ell,N} x_{\ell,n-1}(x_{\ell,N-1}-p)} \cdot e^{\lambda x_{\ell,1} x_{\ell,n-1}(x_{\ell,N}-p)} \cdot \ldots \cdot e^{\lambda x_{\ell,n-1} x_{\ell,n-1}(x_{\ell,n-2}-p)}, \tag{B.46}$$

where (B.44) follows from the definition of $y_{\ell,n'}$ as in (B.43), and from (B.44) to (B.45) we rearranged the product order from $n' = 1, \ldots, n-1, n+1, \ldots, N$ to $n' = n+1, \ldots, N, 1, \ldots, n-1$, respectively.

Since the variable $y_{\ell,n}$ is not a factor of the product in (B.44), the variable $x_{\ell,n}$ appears only in the factor $y_{\ell,n+1}$, which breaks up the dependence chain. This is illustrated with a factor graph (we use the same notion as in [36,38]) of the variables $y_{\ell,n+1}, \ldots, y_{\ell,N}, y_{\ell,1}, \ldots, y_{\ell,n-1}$ shown in Figure B.2. Note that this factor graph contains only constraints, thus all its factors are Dirac delta functions. Using the described arrangement together with the appropriate sums of the left-most product of the right-hand side of (B.37) results in the expression (B.38). Then the innermost sum in (B.38) can be considered as an expectation which we upper bound analogously as in (B.34). Proceeding the same way yields inequality (B.39) at the end. In the factor graph setting, this procedure can be regarded as closing boxes (illustrated by the dashed box in Figure B.2) from left to right, where we close a box by upper bounding the corresponding expectation. ■

Next, we give an upper bound of the lower tail of the random variable $S_{\ell,n}$ considered in Lemma B.2.

Lemma B.3. *Let $S_{\ell,n}$ be defined as in (B.19), then for $0 < \tilde{\eta} < 1$, $\theta > 0$, we have*

$$\Pr\left[S_{\ell,n} \leq -\theta(1-\tilde{\eta})\right] < e^{-\frac{2\theta^2(1-\tilde{\eta})^2}{LN}} \tag{B.47}$$

□

Proof of Lemma B.3. For $\lambda < 0$, we have

$$\begin{aligned}
\Pr\left[S_{\ell,n} \leq -\theta(1-\tilde{\eta})\right] &= \Pr\left[e^{\lambda S_{\ell,n}} \geq e^{-\lambda\theta(1-\tilde{\eta})}\right] && \text{(B.48)}\\
&\leq \min_{\lambda<0} \frac{\mathrm{E}\left[e^{\lambda S_{\ell,n}}\right]}{e^{-\lambda\theta(1-\tilde{\eta})}} && \text{(B.49)}\\
&< \min_{\lambda<0} \frac{e^{\frac{\lambda^2}{8}LN}}{e^{-\lambda\theta(1-\tilde{\eta})}} && \text{(B.50)}\\
&= e^{-\frac{2\theta^2(1-\tilde{\eta})^2}{LN}}. && \text{(B.51)}
\end{aligned}$$

Equality (B.48) holds since the function $x \mapsto e^{\lambda x}$, $\lambda < 0$, is strictly monotonic decreasing. Applying Markov's inequality (Lemma B.5) yields (B.49), and (B.50) follows from Lemma B.2. The bound on the right-hand side of (B.50) is minimized as follows

$$\begin{aligned}
\min_{\lambda<0} \frac{e^{\frac{\lambda^2}{8}LN}}{e^{-\lambda\theta(1-\tilde{\eta})}} &= e^{\min_{\lambda<0}\left(\frac{\lambda^2}{8}LN+\lambda\theta(1-\tilde{\eta})\right)} && \text{(B.52)}\\
&= e^{\left.\frac{\lambda^2}{8}LN+\lambda\theta(1-\tilde{\eta})\right|_{\lambda=\lambda_{\min}}} && \text{(B.53)}
\end{aligned}$$

with the unique minimizer

$$\frac{d}{d\lambda}\left(\frac{\lambda^2}{8}LN + \lambda\theta(1-\tilde{\eta})\right) = 0 \tag{B.54}$$

$$\frac{\lambda}{4}LN + \theta(1-\tilde{\eta}) = 0 \tag{B.55}$$

$$\lambda = \lambda_{\min} := -\frac{4\theta(1-\tilde{\eta})}{LN} < 0. \tag{B.56}$$

Inserting (B.56) into (B.53) yields the bound on the right-hand side of (B.51). ■

B.2 Chernoff Bound on the Tails of the Binomial Distribution

The facts in this section are undoubtedly well known, but for the convenience of the reader, we will give proofs.

Lemma B.4. *For* $0 < p_1, p_2 < 1$, *we have*

$$p_1 \ln\left(\frac{p_1}{p_2}\right) + (1-p_1)\ln\left(\frac{1-p_1}{1-p_2}\right) \geq 0, \tag{B.57}$$

with equality if and only if $p_1 = p_2$. □

Proof of Lemma B.4. We start with the identity

$$\ln(x) = -\ln\left(\frac{1}{x}\right), \qquad x \in \mathbb{R}_{>0}, \tag{B.58}$$

and obtain

$$\begin{aligned} & p_1 \ln\left(\frac{p_1}{p_2}\right) + (1-p_1)\ln\left(\frac{1-p_1}{1-p_2}\right) \\ &= -\left(p_1 \ln\left(\frac{p_2}{p_1}\right) + (1-p_1)\ln\left(\frac{1-p_2}{1-p_1}\right)\right) && \text{(B.59)} \\ &\geq -\left(p_1 \left(\frac{p_2}{p_1} - 1\right) + (1-p_1)\left(\frac{1-p_2}{1-p_1} - 1\right)\right) && \text{(B.60)} \\ &= -\big(p_2 - p_1 + 1 - p_2 - (1-p_1)\big) && \text{(B.61)} \\ &= 0, && \text{(B.62)} \end{aligned}$$

where in (B.60) we used the inequality

$$\ln(x) \leq x - 1, \qquad x \in \mathbb{R}_{>0}, \tag{B.63}$$

with equality if and only if $x = 1$. ■

Lemma B.5 (Markov's Inequality). *If* X *is a nonnegative random variable, i.e.,* $\Pr[X < 0] = 0$, *then*

$$\Pr[X \geq a] \leq \frac{\mathrm{E}[X]}{a}, \tag{B.64}$$

for all $a > 0$. □

We note that (B.64) is only meaningful for $a > \mathrm{E}[X]$.

Proof of Lemma B.5. The assumption $\Pr[X < 0] = 0$ implies that

$$a\,\mathrm{I}[X \geq a] \leq X \tag{B.65}$$

holds almost surely, for $a > 0$. Because the expectation is a monotonic operator we can take the expectation on both sides of (B.65), which yields

$$a\,\mathrm{E}\big[\mathrm{I}[X \geq a]\big] \leq \mathrm{E}[X] \tag{B.66}$$
$$a\Pr[X \geq a] \leq \mathrm{E}[X]. \tag{B.67}$$

■

Next, a tight upper bound on the lower tail of the binomial distribution.

Lemma B.6. *Let $X \sim \mathrm{Bin}(L, p)$, then for $0 < \delta < 1$*

$$\Pr[X \leq (1-\delta)Lp] \leq e^{-D_{KL}((1-\delta)p\|p)L}, \tag{B.68}$$

with Kullback–Leibler divergence (or relative entropy)

$$D_{KL}(p_1\|p_2) := p_1 \ln\left(\frac{p_1}{p_2}\right) + (1-p_1)\ln\left(\frac{1-p_1}{1-p_2}\right), \tag{B.69}$$

for $0 < p_1, p_2 < 1$. □

We note that $D_{KL}(p_1\|p_2) \geq 0$ (cf. Lemma B.4), and thus the upper bound in (B.68) decreases exponentially in L.

Proof of Lemma B.6. First we note that for every $t < 0$, we have by monotonicity

$$\Pr[X \leq (1-\delta)Lp] = \Pr\left[e^{tX} \geq e^{t(1-\delta)Lp}\right]. \tag{B.70}$$

Then, applying Markov's inequality (Lemma B.5) to the right-hand side of (B.70) yields

$$\Pr\left[e^{tX} \geq e^{t(1-\delta)Lp}\right] \leq \frac{\mathrm{E}\left[e^{tX}\right]}{e^{t(1-\delta)Lp}} \tag{B.71}$$
$$= \frac{\left(1-p+pe^{t}\right)^{L}}{e^{t(1-\delta)Lp}} \tag{B.72}$$
$$= f(t)^{L}, \tag{B.73}$$

with

$$f(t) := \frac{1-p+pe^t}{e^{t(1-\delta)p}} \tag{B.74}$$
$$= (1-p)e^{-t(1-\delta)p} + pe^{t(1-(1-\delta)p)}, \tag{B.75}$$

for all $t < 0$.

Now, we minimize $f(t)$ over all $t < 0$ by setting the derivative of f

$$f'(t) = -(1-\delta)p(1-p)e^{-t(1-\delta)p} + (1-(1-\delta)p)pe^{t(1-(1-\delta)p)} \tag{B.76}$$
$$= \big((1-(1-\delta)p)e^t - (1-\delta)(1-p)\big)pe^{-t(1-\delta)p} \tag{B.77}$$

equal to zero, i.e., $f'(t_{\min}) = 0$ yields an unique candidate $t_{\min}$ with

$$e^{t_{\min}} = \frac{(1-\delta)(1-p)}{1-(1-\delta)p} \tag{B.78}$$
$$= \frac{1-\delta-(1-\delta)p}{1-(1-\delta)p}. \tag{B.79}$$

Because $0 < \delta, p < 1$, it follows from (B.79) that $e^{t_{\min}} < 1$ and thus $t_{\min} < 0$, implying that $t_{\min}$ is a valid candidate.

Inserting (B.78) into (B.74) yields

$$f(t_{\min}) = e^{-t_{\min}(1-\delta)p}\left(1-p+pe^{t_{\min}}\right) \tag{B.80}$$
$$= \left(\frac{(1-\delta)(1-p)}{1-(1-\delta)p}\right)^{-(1-\delta)p}\left(1-p+p\frac{(1-\delta)(1-p)}{1-(1-\delta)p}\right) \tag{B.81}$$
$$= (1-\delta)^{-(1-\delta)p}\left(\frac{1-p}{1-(1-\delta)p}\right)^{-(1-\delta)p}\frac{1-p}{1-(1-\delta)p} \tag{B.82}$$
$$= (1-\delta)^{-(1-\delta)p}\left(\frac{1-(1-\delta)p}{1-p}\right)^{-(1-(1-\delta)p)} \tag{B.83}$$
$$= e^{-(1-\delta)p\ln(1-\delta)}\, e^{-(1-(1-\delta)p)\ln\left(\frac{1-(1-\delta)p}{1-p}\right)} \tag{B.84}$$
$$= e^{-D_{KL}((1-\delta)p\|p)}. \tag{B.85}$$

From (B.83) to (B.84) we applied the identity $a^b = e^{\ln(a^b)} = e^{b\ln(a)}$, and (B.85) follows from (B.69).

The right-hand side of (B.85) is indeed the global minimum of f on $]-\infty, 0]$, i.e.,

$$\min_{t<0} f(t) = f(t_{\min}), \tag{B.86}$$

because at the boundaries we have (cf. Lemma B.4)

$$f(t_{\min}) < f(0) = 1, \tag{B.87}$$

and

$$f(t_{\min}) < \lim_{t \to -\infty} f(t) = \infty. \tag{B.88}$$

Finally, from (B.70) and (B.73) it follows that

$$\begin{aligned} \Pr[X \le (1-\delta)Lp] &\le \min_{t<0} f(t)^L && \text{(B.89)} \\ &= f(t_{\min})^L && \text{(B.90)} \\ &= e^{-D_{KL}((1-\delta)p\|p)L}, && \text{(B.91)} \end{aligned}$$

where the step from (B.89) to (B.90) is justified by the discussion of (B.86), and (B.91) follows from (B.85). ■

Finally, we give an upper bound on both tails of the binomial distribution.

Lemma B.7. *Let* $X \sim \text{Bin}(L, p)$, $0 < p < 1$. *Then*

$$\Pr\big[|X - Lp| \ge \delta Lp\big] \le 2e^{-\frac{1}{3}\delta^2 Lp}, \tag{B.92}$$

for $0 < \delta < 1$. □

Proof of Lemma B.7. By the union bound, we have

$$\begin{aligned} &\Pr\big[|X - Lp| \ge \delta Lp\big] \\ &\quad = \Pr[X \le (1-\delta)Lp] + \Pr[X \ge (1+\delta)Lp]. \end{aligned} \tag{B.93}$$

From (B.89) we know

$$\Pr[X \le (1-\delta)Lp] \le f(t)^L, \tag{B.94}$$

with (cf. (B.74))

$$\begin{aligned} \ln\big(f(t)\big) &= \ln\big(1 - p + pe^t\big) - t(1-\delta)p && \text{(B.95)} \\ &\le (e^t - 1)p - t(1-\delta)p, && \text{(B.96)} \end{aligned}$$

for $t < 0$, where in (B.96) we applied (B.63). Setting $t := \ln(1-\delta) < 0$ yields

$$\begin{aligned} \ln\big(f(t)\big) &\le -p\delta - p(1-\delta)\ln(1-\delta) && \text{(B.97)} \\ &\le -\frac{1}{2}\delta^2 p, && \text{(B.98)} \end{aligned}$$

where (B.98) holds since

$$g_1(\delta) := -\delta - (1-\delta)\ln(1-\delta) + \frac{1}{2}\delta^2 \le 0, \qquad 0 < \delta < 1. \tag{B.99}$$

The derivative of g_1 is equal to

$$g_1'(\delta) = \ln(1-\delta) + \delta. \tag{B.100}$$

Thus, we have $g_1'(\delta) \le 0$, for $0 < \delta < 1$, implying that $g_1(\delta)$ is nonincreasing. Since $g_1(0) = 0$, it follows that (B.99) holds for $0 < \delta < 1$. Then, combining (B.94) and (B.98) yields

$$\begin{aligned} \Pr[X \le (1-\delta)Lp] &\le f(t)^L && \text{(B.101)} \\ &\le e^{-\frac{1}{2}\delta^2 Lp}. && \text{(B.102)} \end{aligned}$$

Concerning the upper tail we proceed similary. Applying Markov's inequality (Lemma B.5), we obtain

$$\begin{aligned} \Pr[X \ge (1+\delta)Lp] &= \Pr\big[e^{tX} \ge e^{t(1+\delta)Lp}\big] && \text{(B.103)} \\ &\le \frac{\mathrm{E}\big[e^{tX}\big]}{e^{t(1+\delta)Lp}} && \text{(B.104)} \\ &= \frac{\big(1-p+pe^t\big)^L}{e^{t(1+\delta)Lp}} && \text{(B.105)} \\ &\le \frac{\big(e^{pe^t-p}\big)^L}{e^{t(1+\delta)Lp}} && \text{(B.106)} \\ &= \frac{e^{(e^t-1)Lp}}{e^{t(1+\delta)Lp}}, && \text{(B.107)} \end{aligned}$$

for $t > 0$. The step from (B.105) to (B.106) follows from $1 + x \le e^x$, for all $x \in \mathbb{R}$. Setting $t := \ln(1+\delta) > 0$ yields

$$\Pr[X \geq (1+\delta)Lp] \leq \left(\frac{e^{(e^t-1)}}{e^{t(1+\delta)}}\right)^{Lp} \tag{B.108}$$

$$= \left(\frac{e^{\delta}}{e^{(1+\delta)\ln(1+\delta)}}\right)^{Lp} \tag{B.109}$$

$$\leq \left(e^{-\frac{1}{3}\delta^2}\right)^{Lp}. \tag{B.110}$$

The inequality (B.110) holds since

$$g_2(\delta) := \delta - (1+\delta)\ln(1+\delta) + \frac{1}{3}\delta^2 \leq 0, \qquad 0 < \delta < 1, \tag{B.111}$$

which can be seen by computing the derivatives

$$g_2'(\delta) = 1 - \frac{1+\delta}{1+\delta} - \ln(1+\delta) + \frac{2}{3}\delta \tag{B.112}$$

$$= -\ln(1+\delta) + \frac{2}{3}\delta, \tag{B.113}$$

$$g_2''(\delta) = -\frac{1}{1+\delta} + \frac{2}{3}. \tag{B.114}$$

We observe that $g_2''(\delta) < 0$ for $0 < \delta < 1/2$ and $g_2''(\delta) > 0$ for $\delta > 1/2$. Thus, $g_2'(\delta)$ first decreases and then increases over the interval $[0,1]$. But since $g_2'(0) = 0$ and $g_2'(1) < 0$, we can conclude that $g_2'(\delta) \leq 0$ in $[0,1]$, which implies that $g_2(\delta)$ is nonincreasing. Since $g_2(0) = 0$, it follows that $g_2(\delta) \leq 0$, for $0 < \delta < 1$.

In total, we obtain

$$\Pr\big[|X - Lp| \geq \delta Lp\big]$$

$$= \Pr[X \leq (1-\delta)Lp] + \Pr[X \geq (1+\delta)Lp] \tag{B.115}$$

$$\leq e^{-\frac{1}{2}\delta^2 Lp} + e^{-\frac{1}{3}\delta^2 Lp} \tag{B.116}$$

$$\leq 2e^{-\frac{1}{3}\delta^2 Lp}, \tag{B.117}$$

which concludes the proof. ∎

B.3 Typical Binary Matrices

In this section we consider random binary matrices $\boldsymbol{A} \in \{0,1\}^{L \times N}$ with i.i.d. entries $a_{\ell,n}$, $(\ell, n) \in \{1, \ldots, L\} \times \{1, \ldots, N\}$, parameterized by

$$p := \Pr[a_{\ell,n} = 1], \tag{B.118}$$

where $a_{\ell,n}$ is the entry in row ℓ and column n of $\boldsymbol{A}$. For those random matrices we will use the shorthand notation $\boldsymbol{A} \overset{\text{i.i.d.}}{\sim} \text{Ber}(p)^{L \times N}$.

In order to evaluate the memorization capacity in Chapter 5, we need to study the set of binary matrices that are (strongly) typical to $\boldsymbol{A} \overset{\text{i.i.d.}}{\sim} \text{Ber}(p)^{L \times N}$. To this end, we define

$$\mathcal{A}_\varepsilon^{(L,N)}(p) := \left\{ \boldsymbol{A} \in \{0,1\}^{L \times N} : \left| \frac{1}{LN} \sum_{\ell=1}^{L} \sum_{n=1}^{N} a_{\ell,n} - p \right| \leq \varepsilon \right\}, \tag{B.119}$$

for $0 < p < 1$, $\varepsilon > 0$, i.e., $\mathcal{A}_\varepsilon^{(L,N)}(p)$ contains binary matrices that have approximately LNp nonzero entries. The results of this section state some well-known properties of $\mathcal{A}_\varepsilon^{(L,N)}(p)$, e.g. [11, Chapter 3], but here they are especially tailored to binary matrices. Moreover, our definition (B.119) is also not standard.

The first statement is essentially another formulation of the weak law of large numbers:

Lemma B.8. *If* $\boldsymbol{A} \overset{\text{i.i.d.}}{\sim} \text{Ber}(p)^{L \times N}$, *then*

$$\Pr\big[\boldsymbol{A} \in \mathcal{A}_\varepsilon^{(L,N)}(p)\big] > 1 - \varepsilon, \tag{B.120}$$

for L sufficiently large, and

$$\lim_{L \to \infty} \Pr\big[\boldsymbol{A} \in \mathcal{A}_\varepsilon^{(L,N)}(p)\big] = 1. \tag{B.121}$$

□

Proof of Lemma B.8. For $\ell \in \{1, \ldots, L\}$, we define the random variables

$$X_\ell := \frac{1}{N} \sum_{n=1}^{N} a_{\ell,n}. \tag{B.122}$$

The assumption $\boldsymbol{A} \overset{\text{i.i.d.}}{\sim} \text{Ber}(p)^{L\times N}$ implies that $X_1, \ldots, X_L$ are i.i.d. with

$$\begin{aligned}
\mathrm{E}[X_\ell] &= \frac{1}{N}\sum_{n=1}^{N} \mathrm{E}[a_{\ell,n}] && \text{(B.123)}\\
&= \frac{1}{N}\sum_{n=1}^{N} p && \text{(B.124)}\\
&= p, && \text{(B.125)}
\end{aligned}$$

and

$$\begin{aligned}
\mathrm{Var}[X_\ell] &= \frac{1}{N^2}\mathrm{Var}\left[\sum_{n=1}^{N} a_{\ell,n}\right] && \text{(B.126)}\\
&= \frac{1}{N^2}\sum_{n=1}^{N} \mathrm{Var}[a_{\ell,n}] && \text{(B.127)}\\
&= \frac{1}{N^2}\sum_{n=1}^{N} \left(\mathrm{E}[a_{\ell,n}^2] - \mathrm{E}[a_{\ell,n}]^2\right) && \text{(B.128)}\\
&= \frac{1}{N^2}\sum_{n=1}^{N} (p - p^2) && \text{(B.129)}\\
&= \frac{1}{N} p(1-p). && \text{(B.130)}
\end{aligned}$$

The step from (B.126) to (B.127) holds because $a_{\ell,1}, \ldots, a_{\ell,N}$ are independent. Then, we have

$$\begin{aligned}
\Pr\left[\boldsymbol{A} \in \mathcal{A}_\varepsilon^{(L,N)}(p)\right] &= \Pr\left[\left|\frac{1}{LN}\sum_{\ell=1}^{L}\sum_{n=1}^{N} a_{\ell,n} - p\right| \le \varepsilon\right] && \text{(B.131)}\\
&= 1 - \Pr\left[\left|\frac{1}{L}\sum_{\ell=1}^{L} X_\ell - p\right| > \varepsilon\right] && \text{(B.132)}\\
&= 1 - \Pr\left[\left(\frac{1}{L}\sum_{\ell=1}^{L} X_\ell - p\right)^2 > \varepsilon^2\right] && \text{(B.133)}\\
&\ge 1 - \frac{\mathrm{E}\left[\left(\frac{1}{L}\sum_{\ell=1}^{L} X_\ell - p\right)^2\right]}{\varepsilon^2} && \text{(B.134)}
\end{aligned}$$

$$= 1 - \frac{\operatorname{Var}\left[\frac{1}{L}\sum_{\ell=1}^{L} X_\ell\right]}{\varepsilon^2} \tag{B.135}$$

$$= 1 - \frac{\frac{1}{L^2}\operatorname{Var}\left[\sum_{\ell=1}^{L} X_\ell\right]}{\varepsilon^2} \tag{B.136}$$

$$= 1 - \frac{\frac{1}{L}\operatorname{Var}[X_\ell]}{\varepsilon^2} \tag{B.137}$$

$$= 1 - \frac{p(1-p)}{LN\varepsilon^2}. \tag{B.138}$$

Inequality (B.134) follows from Markov's inequality (cf. Lemma B.5) and (B.135) holds since $\mathrm{E}\big[\frac{1}{L}\sum_{\ell=1}^{L} X_\ell\big] = p$, cf. (B.125). The step from (B.136) to (B.137) holds since $X_1, \ldots, X_L$ are i.i.d. Finally, in (B.138) we used (B.130). Thus, if

$$L > \frac{p(1-p)}{N\varepsilon^3}, \tag{B.139}$$

then (B.138) becomes

$$\Pr\big[\boldsymbol{A} \in \mathcal{A}_\varepsilon^{(L,N)}(p)\big] > 1 - \varepsilon, \tag{B.140}$$

and if $L \to \infty$, the right-hand side of (B.138) approaches 1, which proves (B.121). ■

We could give a more direct proof by applying the weak law of large numbers, which states that for any $\varepsilon > 0$

$$\lim_{L\to\infty} \Pr\left[\left|\frac{1}{L}\sum_{\ell=1}^{L} X_\ell - \mathrm{E}[X_\ell]\right| > \varepsilon\right] = 0, \tag{B.141}$$

to the right-hand side of (B.132).

In the following we will use the binary entropy function

$$H_b(p) := -p\log_2(p) - (1-p)\log_2(1-p), \qquad 0 < p < 1, \tag{B.142}$$

which is the entropy of $X \sim \mathrm{Ber}(p)$, cf. [11]. Note that

$$0 < H_b(p) \le 1, \tag{B.143}$$

for $0 < p < 1$, where the upper bound holds with equality if and only if $p = 1/2$, cf. Figure 5.1 on page 54.

Lemma B.9. *If* $\boldsymbol{A} \overset{\text{i.i.d.}}{\sim} \text{Ber}(p)^{L\times N}$ *and* $\bar{\boldsymbol{A}} \in \mathcal{A}_\varepsilon^{(L,N)}(p)$, *then there exists* $\eta_\varepsilon > 0$ *such that*

$$2^{-LN(H_b(p)+\eta_\varepsilon)} \leq \Pr[\boldsymbol{A} = \bar{\boldsymbol{A}}] \leq 2^{-LN(H_b(p)-\eta_\varepsilon)}, \tag{B.144}$$

with $\lim_{\varepsilon\to 0} \eta_\varepsilon = 0$. □

Proof of Lemma B.9. Since $a_{\ell,n} \overset{\text{i.i.d.}}{\sim} \text{Ber}(p)$, for $(\ell, n) \in \{1,\dots,L\} \times \{1,\dots,N\}$, we have

$$\Pr[\boldsymbol{A} = \bar{\boldsymbol{A}}] = \prod_{\ell=1}^{L}\prod_{n=1}^{N} \Pr[a_{\ell,n} = \bar{a}_{\ell,n}] \tag{B.145}$$

$$= \prod_{\ell=1}^{L}\prod_{n=1}^{N} p^{\bar{a}_{\ell,n}}(1-p)^{1-\bar{a}_{\ell,n}} \tag{B.146}$$

$$= p^{\bar{N}_1}(1-p)^{LN-\bar{N}_1}, \tag{B.147}$$

with

$$\bar{N}_1 := \sum_{\ell=1}^{L}\sum_{n=1}^{N} \bar{a}_{\ell,n}, \tag{B.148}$$

and thus

$$\frac{1}{LN}\log_2\big(\Pr[\boldsymbol{A} = \bar{\boldsymbol{A}}]\big)$$

$$= \frac{\bar{N}_1}{LN}\log_2(p) + \left(1 - \frac{\bar{N}_1}{LN}\right)\log_2(1-p) \tag{B.149}$$

$$= \left(\frac{\bar{N}_1}{LN} - p + p\right)\log_2(p) + \left(1 - \frac{\bar{N}_1}{LN} - p + p\right)\log_2(1-p) \tag{B.150}$$

$$= p\log_2(p) + (1-p)\log_2(1-p) + \left(\frac{\bar{N}_1}{LN} - p\right)\big(\log_2(p) - \log_2(1-p)\big) \tag{B.151}$$

$$= -H_b(p) + \left(\frac{\bar{N}_1}{LN} - p\right)\big(\log_2(p) - \log_2(1-p)\big). \tag{B.152}$$

Equation (B.152) implies

$$\begin{aligned}
&\left|\frac{1}{LN}\log_2\big(\Pr[\boldsymbol{A}=\bar{\boldsymbol{A}}]\big)+H_b(p)\right| \\
&\qquad = \left|\frac{\bar{N}_1}{LN}-p\right|\big|\log_2(p)-\log_2(1-p)\big| && \text{(B.153)}\\
&\qquad \le \varepsilon\,\big|\log_2(p)-\log_2(1-p)\big| && \text{(B.154)}\\
&\qquad =: \eta_\varepsilon, && \text{(B.155)}
\end{aligned}$$

where inequality (B.154) follows from the assumption $\bar{\boldsymbol{A}} \in \mathcal{A}_\varepsilon^{(L,N)}(p)$. ■

Lemma B.10. *If* $\boldsymbol{A} \overset{\text{i.i.d.}}{\sim} \mathrm{Ber}(p)^{L\times N}$, *then there exists* $\eta_\varepsilon > 0$, *with* $\lim_{\varepsilon\to 0}\eta_\varepsilon = 0$, *such that*

$$(1-\varepsilon)\cdot 2^{LN(H_b(p)-\eta_\varepsilon)} < \big|\mathcal{A}_\varepsilon^{(L,N)}(p)\big| \le 2^{LN(H_b(p)+\eta_\varepsilon)}, \qquad \text{(B.156)}$$

for L sufficiently large, and

$$\lim_{L\to\infty}\frac{1}{L}\log_2\big(\big|\mathcal{A}_\varepsilon^{(L,N)}(p)\big|\big) = NH_b(p), \qquad \text{(B.157)}$$

as long as $\varepsilon \to 0$. □

Proof of Lemma B.10. For all $L \ge 1$, we have

$$\begin{aligned}
1 &= \sum_{\bar{\boldsymbol{A}}\in\{0,1\}^{L\times N}} \Pr[\boldsymbol{A}=\bar{\boldsymbol{A}}] && \text{(B.158)}\\
&\ge \sum_{\bar{\boldsymbol{A}}\in\mathcal{A}_\varepsilon^{(L,N)}(p)} \Pr[\boldsymbol{A}=\bar{\boldsymbol{A}}] && \text{(B.159)}\\
&\ge \sum_{\bar{\boldsymbol{A}}\in\mathcal{A}_\varepsilon^{(L,N)}(p)} 2^{-LN(H_b(p)+\eta_\varepsilon)} && \text{(B.160)}\\
&= 2^{-LN(H_b(p)+\eta_\varepsilon)} \sum_{\bar{\boldsymbol{A}}\in\mathcal{A}_\varepsilon^{(L,N)}(p)} 1 && \text{(B.161)}\\
&= 2^{-LN(H_b(p)+\eta_\varepsilon)}\big|\mathcal{A}_\varepsilon^{(L,N)}(p)\big|, && \text{(B.162)}
\end{aligned}$$

which proves the upper bound in (B.156). Inequality (B.159) holds because $\mathcal{A}_\varepsilon^{(L,N)}(p) \subseteq \{0,1\}^{L\times N}$ and (B.160) follows from the lower bound of Lemma B.9.

The lower bound of (B.156) can be derived as follows. For L sufficiently large, we obtain

$$
\begin{aligned}
1-\varepsilon &< \Pr\big[\boldsymbol{A} \in \mathcal{A}_{\varepsilon}^{(L,N)}(p)\big] && \text{(B.163)}\\
&= \sum_{\bar{\boldsymbol{A}} \in \mathcal{A}_{\varepsilon}^{(L,N)}(p)} \Pr[\boldsymbol{A} = \bar{\boldsymbol{A}}] && \text{(B.164)}\\
&\leq \sum_{\bar{\boldsymbol{A}} \in \mathcal{A}_{\varepsilon}^{(L,N)}(p)} 2^{-LN(H_b(p)-\eta_\varepsilon)} && \text{(B.165)}\\
&= \big|\mathcal{A}_{\varepsilon}^{(L,N)}(p)\big| \cdot 2^{-LN(H_b(p)-\eta_\varepsilon)}, && \text{(B.166)}
\end{aligned}
$$

where (B.163) follows from Lemma B.8 and (B.165) follows from the upper bound of Lemma B.9.

To show (B.157), we take the logarithm of (B.156) and divide by L to obtain

$$
\begin{aligned}
&\frac{1}{L}\log_2(1-\varepsilon) + N(H_b(p)-\eta_\varepsilon)\\
&\qquad < \frac{1}{L}\log_2\big(\big|\mathcal{A}_{\varepsilon}^{(L,N)}(p)\big|\big) \leq N(H_b(p)+\eta_\varepsilon) && \text{(B.167)}\\
&\frac{1}{L}\log_2(1-\varepsilon) - N\eta_\varepsilon\\
&\qquad < \frac{1}{L}\log_2\big(\big|\mathcal{A}_{\varepsilon}^{(L,N)}(p)\big|\big) - NH_b(p) \leq \underbrace{N\eta_\varepsilon - \frac{1}{L}\log_2(1-\varepsilon)}_{>0}, && \text{(B.168)}
\end{aligned}
$$

which implies

$$
\left|\frac{1}{L}\log_2\big(\big|\mathcal{A}_{\varepsilon}^{(L,N)}(p)\big|\big) - NH_b(p)\right| \leq N\eta_\varepsilon - \frac{1}{L}\log_2(1-\varepsilon), \tag{B.169}
$$

where the right-hand side of (B.169) vanishes as $L \to \infty$ and $\varepsilon \to 0$, because $\lim_{\varepsilon\to 0}\eta_\varepsilon = 0$ (cf. (B.155)). ■

Note that in (B.156), the upper bound holds for all $L \geq 1$, whereas the lower bound holds only if L is sufficiently large, more precisely, only if (B.139).

B.4 Proof of Proposition 4.2

Here, we prove the statement on page 25. Let $i \in \{1, \dots, L\}$ and let $n \in \{0, \dots, N-1\}$ be fixed but arbitrary. First, we consider the case $y_i[n] = 0$, i.e., $n \notin J_i$ and $n \in J_i^{\mathrm{c}}$. Then, we have

$$\begin{aligned}
&\big\langle \boldsymbol{y}[n-1], \boldsymbol{w}_i \big\rangle + \eta_i \\
&\quad = \sum_{\tilde{n} \in J_i} \big\langle \boldsymbol{y}[n-1], \boldsymbol{y}[\tilde{n}-1] \big\rangle - \sum_{\tilde{n} \in J_i^{\mathrm{c}}} \big\langle \boldsymbol{y}[n-1], \boldsymbol{y}[\tilde{n}-1] \big\rangle + \eta_i && \text{(B.170)} \\
&\quad < |J_i|(1+\delta_2)Lp^2 - \sum_{\tilde{n} \in J_i^{\mathrm{c}} \setminus \{n\}} \big\langle \boldsymbol{y}[n-1], \boldsymbol{y}[\tilde{n}-1] \big\rangle \\
&\qquad\quad - \big\langle \boldsymbol{y}[n-1], \boldsymbol{y}[n-1] \big\rangle + \eta_i && \text{(B.171)} \\
&\quad < |J_i|(1+\delta_2)Lp^2 - \big(|J_i^{\mathrm{c}}| - 1\big)(1-\delta_2)Lp^2 - (1-\delta_2)Lp + \eta && \text{(B.172)} \\
&\quad = (1+\delta_2)|J_i|Lp^2 - (1-\delta_2)|J_i^{\mathrm{c}}| \left(\frac{|J_i^{\mathrm{c}}| - 1}{|J_i^{\mathrm{c}}|} p + \frac{1}{|J_i^{\mathrm{c}}|} \right) Lp + \eta && \text{(B.173)} \\
&\quad \leq (1+\delta_2)|J_i|Lp^2 - (1-\delta_2)|J_i^{\mathrm{c}}| \widetilde{N}_p(N) Lp + \eta && \text{(B.174)} \\
&\quad = \theta_i, && \text{(B.175)}
\end{aligned}$$

where in (B.170) we inserted (4.47). From (B.170) to (B.171) we applied the assumption (4.45) to the sum on the left-hand side, and we also took out the summand for $\tilde{n} = n$ of the sum on the right-hand side since by assumption $n \in J_i^{\mathrm{c}}$. Inequality (B.172) follows from (4.45) and (2.2). In (B.173) we factored out $(1-\delta_2)|J_i^{\mathrm{c}}|Lp$, and (B.174) holds since

$$\frac{|J_i^{\mathrm{c}}| - 1}{|J_i^{\mathrm{c}}|} p + \frac{1}{|J_i^{\mathrm{c}}|} \geq \widetilde{N}_p(N), \qquad \text{(B.176)}$$

for $|J_i^{\mathrm{c}}| \leq N$, with function $\widetilde{N}_p(\cdot)$ as defined in (4.30). Finally, (B.175) holds by definition of θ_i, cf. (4.48). Thus (B.175) implies $\xi_i(\boldsymbol{y}[n-1]) = 0 = y_i[n]$, i.e., there is no false firing.

In the case of $y_i[n] = 1$, i.e., $n \in J_i$ and $n \notin J_i^{\mathrm{c}}$, we have

$$\begin{aligned}
&\big\langle \boldsymbol{y}[n-1], \boldsymbol{w}_i \big\rangle + \eta_i \\
&\quad = \sum_{\tilde{n} \in J_i} \big\langle \boldsymbol{y}[n-1], \boldsymbol{y}[\tilde{n}-1] \big\rangle - \sum_{\tilde{n} \in J_i^{\mathrm{c}}} \big\langle \boldsymbol{y}[n-1], \boldsymbol{y}[\tilde{n}-1] \big\rangle + \eta_i && \text{(B.177)} \\
&\quad > \sum_{\tilde{n} \in J_i \setminus \{n\}} \big\langle \boldsymbol{y}[n-1], \boldsymbol{y}[\tilde{n}-1] \big\rangle + \big\langle \boldsymbol{y}[n-1], \boldsymbol{y}[n-1] \big\rangle \\
&\qquad\quad - |J_i^{\mathrm{c}}|(1+\delta_2)Lp^2 + \eta_i && \text{(B.178)}
\end{aligned}$$

$$> \big(|J_i|-1\big)(1-\delta_2)Lp^2 + (1-\delta_2)Lp - |J_i^{\mathrm{c}}|(1+\delta_2)Lp^2 - \eta \tag{B.179}$$

$$= (1-\delta_2)|J_i|\left(\frac{|J_i|-1}{|J_i|}p + \frac{1}{|J_i|}\right)Lp - (1+\delta_2)|J_i^{\mathrm{c}}|Lp^2 - \eta \tag{B.180}$$

$$\geq (1-\delta_2)|J_i|\widetilde{N}_p(N)Lp - (1+\delta_2)|J_i^{\mathrm{c}}|Lp^2 - \eta \tag{B.181}$$

$$= \Big((1-\delta_2)|J_i|\widetilde{N}_p - (1+\delta_2)|J_i^{\mathrm{c}}|p - \tilde{\eta}\Big)Lp \tag{B.182}$$

$$= \Big((1+\delta_2)|J_i|p - (1-\delta_2)|J_i^{\mathrm{c}}|\widetilde{N}_p + \tilde{\eta}\Big)Lp \tag{B.183}$$

$$= \theta_i, \tag{B.184}$$

where in (B.177) we inserted (4.47). From (B.177) to (B.178) we applied the assumption (4.45) to the sum on the right-hand side, and we also took out the summand for $\tilde{n} = n$ of the sum on the left-hand side since by assumption $n \in J_i$. Inequality (B.179) follows from (4.45) and (2.2). In (B.180) we factored out $(1-\delta_2)|J_i|Lp$, and (B.181) holds since

$$\frac{|J_i|-1}{|J_i|}p + \frac{1}{|J_i|} \geq \widetilde{N}_p(N), \tag{B.185}$$

for $|J_i| \leq N$, with function $\widetilde{N}_p(\cdot)$ as defined in (4.30). In (B.182) we factored out the term Lp and used $\eta = \tilde{\eta}Lp$, cf. (4.46). To show the step from (B.182) to (B.183) we first rewrite δ_2 as

$$\delta_2 = \frac{1-p-2\tilde{\eta}}{1-p+2pN} \tag{B.186}$$

$$= \frac{\frac{1-p}{N} - 2\frac{\tilde{\eta}}{N}}{\frac{1-p+2pN}{N}} \tag{B.187}$$

$$= \frac{\widetilde{N}_p - p - 2\frac{\tilde{\eta}}{N}}{\widetilde{N}_p + p} \tag{B.188}$$

with $\widetilde{N}_p = \widetilde{N}_p(N)$, and thus

$$1-\delta_2 = \frac{2p + 2\frac{\tilde{\eta}}{N}}{\widetilde{N}_p + p}, \tag{B.189}$$

$$1+\delta_2 = \frac{2\widetilde{N}_p - 2\frac{\tilde{\eta}}{N}}{\widetilde{N}_p + p}, \tag{B.190}$$

which we now insert into (cf. (B.182))

$$
\begin{aligned}
&(1-\delta_2)|J_i|\widetilde{N}_p - (1+\delta_2)|J_i^{\mathrm{c}}|p - \tilde{\eta} \\
&= \frac{2p|J_i|\widetilde{N}_p + 2\frac{\tilde{\eta}}{N}|J_i|\widetilde{N}_p - 2\widetilde{N}_p|J_i^{\mathrm{c}}|p + 2\frac{\tilde{\eta}}{N}|J_i^{\mathrm{c}}|p - \tilde{\eta}\widetilde{N}_p - \tilde{\eta}p}{\widetilde{N}_p + p} && \text{(B.191)}\\
&= \frac{2p|J_i|\widetilde{N}_p - 2\widetilde{N}_p|J_i^{\mathrm{c}}|p + \big(2\frac{|J_i|}{N} - 1\big)\tilde{\eta}\widetilde{N}_p + \big(2\frac{|J_i^{\mathrm{c}}|}{N} - 1\big)\tilde{\eta}p}{\widetilde{N}_p + p} && \text{(B.192)}\\
&= \frac{2p|J_i|\widetilde{N}_p - 2\widetilde{N}_p|J_i^{\mathrm{c}}|p + \big(1 - 2\frac{|J_i^{\mathrm{c}}|}{N}\big)\tilde{\eta}\widetilde{N}_p + \big(1 - 2\frac{|J_i|}{N}\big)\tilde{\eta}p}{\widetilde{N}_p + p} && \text{(B.193)}\\
&= \frac{2p|J_i|\widetilde{N}_p - 2\frac{\tilde{\eta}}{N}|J_i|p - 2\widetilde{N}_p|J_i^{\mathrm{c}}|p - 2\frac{\tilde{\eta}}{N}|J_i^{\mathrm{c}}|\widetilde{N}_p + \tilde{\eta}\widetilde{N}_p + \tilde{\eta}p}{\widetilde{N}_p + p} && \text{(B.194)}\\
&= (1+\delta_2)|J_i|p - (1-\delta_2)|J_i^{\mathrm{c}}|\widetilde{N}_p + \tilde{\eta}, && \text{(B.195)}
\end{aligned}
$$

where from (B.192) to (B.193) we used the identity $|J_i| + |J_i^{\mathrm{c}}| = N$. Finally, (B.184) follows from (4.48). Thus (B.184) implies $\xi_i(\boldsymbol{y}[n-1]) = 1 = y_i[n]$, i.e., there is no missing firing.

In total, we have $\xi_i(\boldsymbol{y}[n-1]) = y_i[n]$ which concludes the proof. ∎

B.5 Expectation of the Weights

For $\boldsymbol{Y} \overset{\text{i.i.d.}}{\sim} \mathrm{Ber}(p)^{L\times N}$, $0 < p < 1$, let

$$\boldsymbol{w}_i := \sum_{n\in J_i} \big(\boldsymbol{y}[n-1] - \boldsymbol{s}\big) \tag{B.196}$$

$$= \sum_{n=0}^{N-1} y_i[n]\big(\boldsymbol{y}[n-1] - \boldsymbol{s}\big), \qquad i \in \{1,\dots,L\}, \tag{B.197}$$

for some fixed vector $\boldsymbol{s} \in \mathbb{R}^L$. Then, we have

$$\mathrm{E}[\boldsymbol{w}_i] = \mathrm{E}\left[\sum_{n=0}^{N-1} y_i[n]\big(\boldsymbol{y}[n-1] - \boldsymbol{s}\big)\right] \tag{B.198}$$

$$= \sum_{n=0}^{N-1} \mathrm{E}\big[y_i[n]\big(\boldsymbol{y}[n-1] - \boldsymbol{s}\big)\big] \tag{B.199}$$

$$= \sum_{n=0}^{N-1} \mathrm{E}\big[y_i[n]\big]\,\mathrm{E}\big[\boldsymbol{y}[n-1] - \boldsymbol{s}\big] \tag{B.200}$$

$$= \sum_{n=0}^{N-1} p\left(\mathrm{E}\big[\boldsymbol{y}[n-1]\big] - \boldsymbol{s}\right) \tag{B.201}$$

$$= \sum_{n=0}^{N-1} p\big(p\mathbf{1}_L - \boldsymbol{s}\big) \tag{B.202}$$

$$= Np\big(p\mathbf{1}_L - \boldsymbol{s}\big). \tag{B.203}$$

The step from (B.196) to (B.197) follows from the definition of the set $J_i \subseteq \{0,1,\dots,N-1\}$ as in (4.92). Equality (B.199) follows from the linearity of expectation. The step from (B.199) to (B.200) holds because the random variable $y_i[n]$ and the random vector $\boldsymbol{y}[n-1]$ are independent. Equality (B.201) holds because $y_i[n] \sim \mathrm{Ber}(p)$ and by linearity of expectation, and (B.202) holds because

$$\mathrm{E}\big[\boldsymbol{y}[n-1]\big] = \mathrm{E}\Big[\big(y_1[n-1],\dots,y_L[n-1]\big)^{\mathsf{T}}\Big] \tag{B.204}$$

$$= \Big(\mathrm{E}\big[y_1[n-1]\big],\dots,\mathrm{E}\big[y_L[n-1]\big]\Big)^{\mathsf{T}} \tag{B.205}$$

$$= (p,\dots,p)^{\mathsf{T}} \tag{B.206}$$

$$= p\mathbf{1}_L. \tag{B.207}$$

B.6 Least-Squares Solution via Gaussian Message Passing

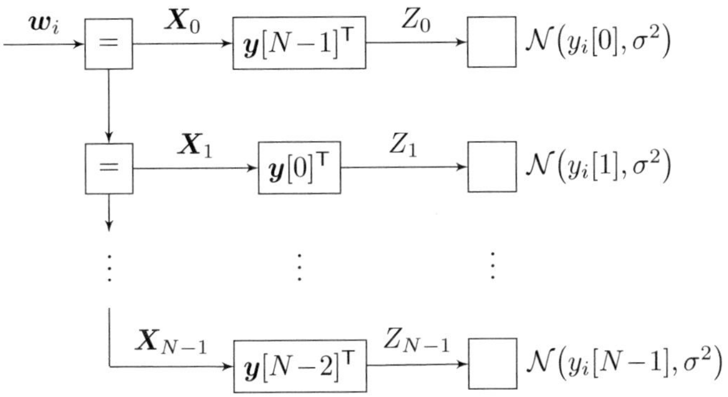

Figure B.3: Factor graph of (B.212).

We can also minimize

$$\left\|\tilde{\boldsymbol{Y}}\boldsymbol{w}_i - \tilde{\boldsymbol{y}}_i\right\|^2 \tag{B.208}$$

by Gaussian message passing as in [36, 38]. To this end, we rewrite (B.208) as

$$\begin{aligned}
&\underset{\boldsymbol{w}_i \in \mathbb{R}^L}{\operatorname{argmin}} \left\|\tilde{\boldsymbol{Y}}\boldsymbol{w}_i - \tilde{\boldsymbol{y}}_i\right\|^2 \\
&\quad = \underset{\boldsymbol{w}_i \in \mathbb{R}^L}{\operatorname{argmax}}\; e^{-\left\|\tilde{\boldsymbol{Y}}\boldsymbol{w}_i - \tilde{\boldsymbol{y}}_i\right\|^2} && \text{(B.209)} \\
&\quad = \underset{\boldsymbol{w}_i \in \mathbb{R}^L}{\operatorname{argmax}}\; e^{-\sum_{n=0}^{N-1}\left(\boldsymbol{y}[n-1]^{\mathsf{T}}\boldsymbol{w}_i - y_i[n]\right)^2} && \text{(B.210)} \\
&\quad = \underset{\boldsymbol{w}_i \in \mathbb{R}^L}{\operatorname{argmax}} \prod_{n=0}^{N-1} e^{-\left(\boldsymbol{y}[n-1]^{\mathsf{T}}\boldsymbol{w}_i - y_i[n]\right)^2} && \text{(B.211)} \\
&\quad = \underset{\boldsymbol{w}_i \in \mathbb{R}^L}{\operatorname{argmax}} \prod_{n=0}^{N-1} \frac{1}{\sqrt{2\pi\sigma}} e^{-\left(\boldsymbol{y}[n-1]^{\mathsf{T}}\boldsymbol{w}_i - y_i[n]\right)^2/(2\sigma^2)}, && \text{(B.212)}
\end{aligned}$$

for $\sigma > 0$. A factor graph of (B.212) is given in Figure B.3 using the same conventions as in [36, 38].

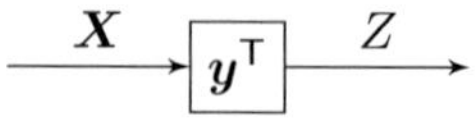

Figure B.4: Factor graph of $\delta(z - \boldsymbol{y}^{\mathsf{T}}\boldsymbol{x})$, for $\boldsymbol{x}, \boldsymbol{y} \in \mathbb{R}^L$, and $z \in \mathbb{R}$.

From [37] we know that the sum-product backward message for a Gaussian variable $Z \sim \mathcal{N}\big(\overleftarrow{W}_Z^{-1}\overleftarrow{\xi}_Z, \overleftarrow{W}_Z^{-1}\big)$ in Figure B.4 is given by

$$\overleftarrow{\boldsymbol{W}}_{\boldsymbol{X}} = \boldsymbol{y}\,\overleftarrow{W}_Z\,\boldsymbol{y}^{\mathsf{T}}, \tag{B.213}$$
$$\overleftarrow{\boldsymbol{\xi}}_{\boldsymbol{X}} = \boldsymbol{y}\,\overleftarrow{\xi}_Z. \tag{B.214}$$

Applying (B.213) and (B.214) to the factor graph in Figure B.3 yields

$$\overleftarrow{\boldsymbol{W}}_{\boldsymbol{w}_i} = \sum_{n=0}^{N-1} \overleftarrow{\boldsymbol{W}}_{\boldsymbol{X}_n} \tag{B.215}$$
$$= \sum_{n=0}^{N-1} \boldsymbol{y}[n-1]\frac{1}{\sigma^2}\boldsymbol{y}[n-1]^{\mathsf{T}} \tag{B.216}$$
$$= \frac{1}{\sigma^2}\sum_{n=0}^{N-1} \boldsymbol{y}[n]\boldsymbol{y}[n]^{\mathsf{T}}, \tag{B.217}$$

and

$$\overleftarrow{\boldsymbol{\xi}}_{\boldsymbol{w}_i} = \sum_{n=0}^{N-1} \overleftarrow{\boldsymbol{\xi}}_{\boldsymbol{X}_n} \tag{B.218}$$
$$= \sum_{n=0}^{N-1} \boldsymbol{y}[n-1]\,\overleftarrow{\xi}_{Z_n} \tag{B.219}$$
$$= \frac{1}{\sigma^2}\sum_{n=0}^{N-1} y_i[n]\boldsymbol{y}[n-1]. \tag{B.220}$$

Equality (B.215) holds since the Gaussian message through the equality node is equal to the sum of its incoming messages, cf. [36,38]. The same rule is applied in (B.218). In (B.216) we applied (B.213), and (B.217) holds since all indices of $\boldsymbol{y}[\cdot]$ are taken modulo N. In (B.219) we applied (B.214), and (B.220) follows from $Z_n \sim \mathcal{N}\big(y_i[n], \sigma^2\big)$.

Finally, the minimizing weight vector of (B.212) is the mean of its message and thus we obtain

$$\begin{aligned}
\boldsymbol{w}_i &= \overleftarrow{\boldsymbol{m}}_{\boldsymbol{w}_i} && \text{(B.221)}\\
&= \overleftarrow{\boldsymbol{W}}_{\boldsymbol{w}_i}^{-1} \overleftarrow{\boldsymbol{\xi}}_{\boldsymbol{w}_i} && \text{(B.222)}\\
&= \left(\frac{1}{\sigma^2} \sum_{n=0}^{N-1} \boldsymbol{y}[n]\boldsymbol{y}[n]^\mathsf{T} \right)^{-1} \frac{1}{\sigma^2} \sum_{n=0}^{N-1} y_i[n]\boldsymbol{y}[n-1] && \text{(B.223)}\\
&= \left(\sum_{n=0}^{N-1} \boldsymbol{y}[n]\boldsymbol{y}[n]^\mathsf{T} \right)^{-1} \sum_{n=0}^{N-1} y_i[n]\boldsymbol{y}[n-1], && \text{(B.224)}
\end{aligned}$$

which is equal to (4.191). In (B.222) we assumed that the precision matrix $\overleftarrow{\boldsymbol{W}}_{\boldsymbol{w}_i} \in \mathbb{R}^{L \times L}$ is invertible.

B.7 The Cardinality of $\mathcal{Y}_N^{(K)}$

For $K \geq 2$, let

$$\mathcal{Y}_N^{(K)} := \left\{ \big(y[0], \ldots, y[NK]\big)^\mathsf{T} \in \{0,1\}^{NK+1} : \right.$$
$$\left. \sum_{k=0}^{K-1} y\big[n + k \bmod (NK+1)\big] \in \{0,1\},\ n \in \{0, \ldots, NK\} \right\} \tag{B.225}$$

be the set of all binary vectors (of dimension $NK + 1$) which have in every circular window of length K at most one firing, or equivalently, after a firing at least $K - 1$ zeros have to follow.

For $k \in \{1, \ldots, K\}$, $K \in \mathbb{N}$, let $\boldsymbol{e}_k \in \{0,1\}^K$ be the unit column-vector (of dimension K) with a single one at index k and zeros elsewhere, i.e., $\boldsymbol{e}_1 = (1, 0, \ldots, 0)^\mathsf{T}$, $\boldsymbol{e}_2 = (0, 1, 0, \ldots, 0)^\mathsf{T}$, etc.

Lemma B.11. *The cardinality of* $\mathcal{Y}_N^{(K)}$ *is given by*

$$\big|\mathcal{Y}_N^{(K)}\big| = \big(\boldsymbol{e}_1^\mathsf{T} + K\boldsymbol{e}_K^\mathsf{T}\big) \boldsymbol{A}_\mathrm{f}^{NK} \boldsymbol{e}_1 \tag{B.226}$$

with

$$\boldsymbol{A}_\mathrm{f} := \left(\boldsymbol{e}_1 + \boldsymbol{e}_2 \,\middle|\, \boldsymbol{e}_3 \,\middle|\, \cdots \,\middle|\, \boldsymbol{e}_K \,\middle|\, \boldsymbol{e}_1 \right) \in \{0,1\}^{K \times K}. \tag{B.227}$$

□

Proof of Lemma B.11. Let

$$\mathcal{A} := \{a_1, \ldots, a_K\} \tag{B.228}$$

be the set of K states, and let

$$\kappa \colon \mathcal{A}^2 \to \{0,1\},\ \ (s_\ell, s_\mathrm{r}) \mapsto \begin{cases} 1, & \text{if } (s_\ell, s_\mathrm{r}) \in \mathcal{A}_\mathrm{valid}^2 \\ 0, & \text{otherwise} \end{cases} \tag{B.229}$$

with allowed state transitions

$$\mathcal{A}_\mathrm{valid}^2 := \big\{(a_{k-1}, a_k) : k \in \{2, \ldots, K\}\big\} \cup \big\{(a_1, a_1), (a_K, a_1)\big\}. \tag{B.230}$$

The state transitions $\mathcal{A}_\mathrm{valid}^2 \subset \mathcal{A}^2$ essentially encode the constraint that

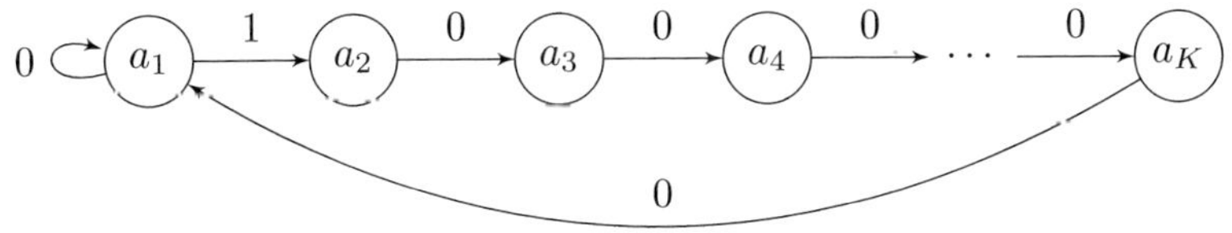

Figure B.5: State transition diagram of $\mathcal{A}^2_{\text{valid}}$ defined as in (B.230).

$K-1$ zeros have to follow after each 1 as illustrated in Figure B.5.

Next, we define the function $f_{\text{ind}}\colon \mathcal{A}^{NK+1} \to \{0,1\}$ as

$$f_{\text{ind}}(s_0,\ldots,s_{NK}) := \kappa(s_{NK},s_0)\prod_{n=0}^{NK-1}\kappa(s_n,s_{n+1}). \tag{B.231}$$

Then, the edge labels in Figure B.5 indicate a bijective mapping between $\mathcal{Y}_N^{(K)}$ and the set

$$\big\{(s_0,\ldots,s_{NK}) \in \mathcal{A}^{NK+1} : f_{\text{ind}}(s_0,\ldots,s_{NK}) = 1\big\}, \tag{B.232}$$

and thus we have

$$\big|\mathcal{Y}_N^{(K)}\big| = \big|\big\{(s_0,\ldots,s_{NK}) \in \mathcal{A}^{NK+1} : f_{\text{ind}}(s_0,\ldots,s_{NK}) = 1\big\}\big| \tag{B.233}$$

$$= \sum_{(s_0,\ldots,s_{NK})\in\mathcal{A}^{NK+1}} f_{\text{ind}}(s_0,\ldots,s_{NK}), \tag{B.234}$$

i.e., $\big|\mathcal{Y}_N^{(K)}\big|$ is equal to the partition sum of f_{ind}, which we determine by means of sum-product message passing [36,38]. Since the factor graph of f_{ind} given in Figure B.6, cf. (B.231), is not cycle-free, we first compute

$$Z_{NK}(a_k) := \sum_{(s_1,\ldots,s_{NK})\in\mathcal{A}^{NK}} f_{\text{ind}}(a_k,s_1,\ldots,s_{NK}), \tag{B.235}$$

for $k \in \{1,\ldots,K\}$, the partition sum (for the case $s_0 = a_k$) of the cycle-free factor graph shown in Figure B.7, and then

$$\big|\mathcal{Y}_N^{(K)}\big| = \sum_{k=1}^{K} Z_{NK}(a_k). \tag{B.236}$$

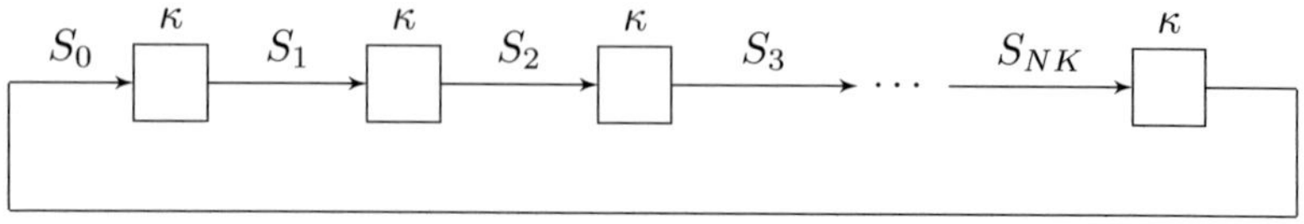

Figure B.6: Factor graph of (B.231).

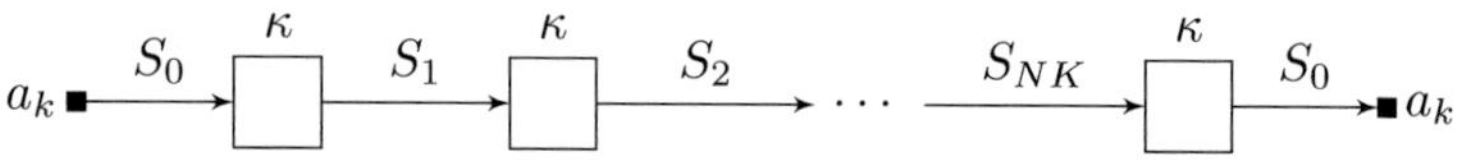

Figure B.7: Factor graph of (B.231), for $S_0 = a_k$.

The partition sum $Z_{NK}(a_k)$ can now be computed by (forward) message passing

$$Z_{NK}(a_k) = \sum_{s \in \mathcal{A}} \kappa(s, a_k) \overrightarrow{\mu}_{S_{NK}}(s) \tag{B.237}$$

$$= \begin{cases} \overrightarrow{\mu}_{S_{NK}}(a_1) + \overrightarrow{\mu}_{S_{NK}}(a_K), & \text{if } k = 1 \\ \overrightarrow{\mu}_{S_{NK}}(a_{k-1}), & \text{if } k \in \{2, \ldots, K\}, \end{cases} \tag{B.238}$$

where the message $\overrightarrow{\mu}_{S_{NK}}(\cdot)$ can be computed recursively by

$$\overrightarrow{\mu}_{S_n}(s) = \sum_{\tilde{s} \in \mathcal{A}} \kappa(\tilde{s}, s) \overrightarrow{\mu}_{S_{n-1}}(\tilde{s}), \qquad s \in \mathcal{A}, \tag{B.239}$$

for $n \in \{1, \ldots, NK\}$, and initial message $\overrightarrow{\mu}_{S_0}(s) = \mathrm{I}[s = a_k]$, $s \in \mathcal{A}$. The recursion (B.239) can be written in vector/matrix form as

$$\overrightarrow{\boldsymbol{\mu}}_{S_n} = \boldsymbol{A}_{\mathrm{f}} \overrightarrow{\boldsymbol{\mu}}_{S_{n-1}}, \qquad n \in \{1, \ldots, NK\}, \tag{B.240}$$

and $\overrightarrow{\boldsymbol{\mu}}_{S_0} = \boldsymbol{e}_k$ with

$$\overrightarrow{\boldsymbol{\mu}}_{S_n} := \left(\overrightarrow{\mu}_{S_n}(a_1), \ldots, \overrightarrow{\mu}_{S_n}(a_K)\right)^{\mathsf{T}} \in \mathbb{R}^K, \tag{B.241}$$

$$\boldsymbol{A}_{\mathrm{f}} := \begin{pmatrix} 1 & 0 & \cdots & 0 & 1 \\ & & & & 0 \\ & & \boldsymbol{I}_{K-1} & & \vdots \\ & & & & 0 \end{pmatrix} \in \{0,1\}^{K \times K}. \tag{B.242}$$

Thus, we can rewrite (B.238) as

$$Z_{NK}(a_k) = \begin{cases} \boldsymbol{e}_1^\mathsf{T} \vec{\boldsymbol{\mu}}_{S_{NK}} + \boldsymbol{e}_K^\mathsf{T} \vec{\boldsymbol{\mu}}_{S_{NK}}, & \text{if } k = 1 \\ \boldsymbol{e}_{k-1}^\mathsf{T} \vec{\boldsymbol{\mu}}_{S_{NK}}, & \text{if } k \in \{2, \ldots, K\} \end{cases} \tag{B.243}$$

$$= \begin{cases} \boldsymbol{e}_1^\mathsf{T} \boldsymbol{A}_\mathrm{f}^{NK} \boldsymbol{e}_1 + \boldsymbol{e}_K^\mathsf{T} \boldsymbol{A}_\mathrm{f}^{NK} \boldsymbol{e}_1, & \text{if } k = 1 \\ \boldsymbol{e}_{k-1}^\mathsf{T} \boldsymbol{A}_\mathrm{f}^{NK} \boldsymbol{e}_k, & \text{if } k \in \{2, \ldots, K\}, \end{cases} \tag{B.244}$$

where we repeatedly applied (B.240), and from (B.236) we obtain

$$|\mathcal{Y}_N^{(K)}| = \sum_{k=1}^{K} Z_{NK}(a_k) \tag{B.245}$$

$$= \boldsymbol{e}_1^\mathsf{T} \boldsymbol{A}_\mathrm{f}^{NK} \boldsymbol{e}_1 + \boldsymbol{e}_K^\mathsf{T} \boldsymbol{A}_\mathrm{f}^{NK} \boldsymbol{e}_1 + \sum_{k=2}^{K} \boldsymbol{e}_{k-1}^\mathsf{T} \boldsymbol{A}_\mathrm{f}^{NK} \boldsymbol{e}_k. \tag{B.246}$$

It turns out (without proof) that

$$\boldsymbol{e}_{k-1}^\mathsf{T} \boldsymbol{A}_\mathrm{f}^{NK} \boldsymbol{e}_k = \boldsymbol{e}_K^\mathsf{T} \boldsymbol{A}_\mathrm{f}^{NK} \boldsymbol{e}_1, \qquad k \in \{2, \ldots, K\}, \tag{B.247}$$

and thus (B.246) becomes

$$|\mathcal{Y}_N^{(K)}| = \boldsymbol{e}_1^\mathsf{T} \boldsymbol{A}_\mathrm{f}^{NK} \boldsymbol{e}_1 + K \boldsymbol{e}_K^\mathsf{T} \boldsymbol{A}_\mathrm{f}^{NK} \boldsymbol{e}_1, \tag{B.248}$$

which concludes the proof. ■

B.7.1 Analytical Expression of $|\mathcal{Y}_N^{(K)}|$ for N Fixed

For $n \in \mathbb{N}$, let

$$\vec{\boldsymbol{\mu}}_{S_{nK}} := \left(\beta_1^{(n)}, \ldots, \beta_K^{(n)}\right)^\mathsf{T} \in \mathbb{R}^K \tag{B.249}$$

and $\boldsymbol{A}_\mathrm{f} \in \{0,1\}^{K \times K}$ as in (B.227). Then, we have

Lemma B.12. *The vector* $\vec{\boldsymbol{\mu}}_{S_{(n+1)K}} \in \mathbb{R}^K$ *defined by*

$$\vec{\boldsymbol{\mu}}_{S_{(n+1)K}} := \boldsymbol{A}_\mathrm{f}^K \vec{\boldsymbol{\mu}}_{S_{nK}} \tag{B.250}$$

has components

$$\beta_k^{(n+1)} = \beta_1^{(n)} + \sum_{k'=k}^{K} \beta_{k'}^{(n)}, \qquad k \in \{1, \ldots, K\}. \tag{B.251}$$

□

Proof of Lemma B.12. From the definition (B.227) of $\boldsymbol{A}_{\mathrm{f}} \in \{0,1\}^{K\times K}$, we have

$$\boldsymbol{A}_{\mathrm{f}}\,\boldsymbol{e}_k = \begin{cases} \boldsymbol{e}_1 + \boldsymbol{e}_2, & \text{if } k = 1 \\ \boldsymbol{e}_{k+1}, & \text{if } k \in \{2,\ldots,K-1\} \\ \boldsymbol{e}_1, & \text{if } k = K, \end{cases} \tag{B.252}$$

and thus

$$\boldsymbol{A}_{\mathrm{f}}^2 = \boldsymbol{A}_{\mathrm{f}} \left(\boldsymbol{e}_1 + \boldsymbol{e}_2 \,\middle|\, \boldsymbol{e}_3 \,\middle|\, \cdots \,\middle|\, \boldsymbol{e}_K \,\middle|\, \boldsymbol{e}_1 \right) \tag{B.253}$$

$$= \left(\boldsymbol{A}_{\mathrm{f}}\,\boldsymbol{e}_1 + \boldsymbol{A}_{\mathrm{f}}\,\boldsymbol{e}_2 \,\middle|\, \boldsymbol{A}_{\mathrm{f}}\,\boldsymbol{e}_3 \,\middle|\, \cdots \,\middle|\, \boldsymbol{A}_{\mathrm{f}}\,\boldsymbol{e}_K \,\middle|\, \boldsymbol{A}_{\mathrm{f}}\,\boldsymbol{e}_1 \right) \tag{B.254}$$

$$= \left(\boldsymbol{e}_1 + \boldsymbol{e}_2 + \boldsymbol{e}_3 \,\middle|\, \boldsymbol{e}_4 \,\middle|\, \cdots \,\middle|\, \boldsymbol{e}_K \,\middle|\, \boldsymbol{e}_1 \,\middle|\, \boldsymbol{e}_1 + \boldsymbol{e}_2 \right). \tag{B.255}$$

Proceeding in this way eventually yields

$$\boldsymbol{A}_{\mathrm{f}}^K = \left(2\boldsymbol{e}_1 + \boldsymbol{e}_2 + \ldots + \boldsymbol{e}_K \,\middle|\, \boldsymbol{e}_1 + \boldsymbol{e}_2 \,\middle|\, \cdots \,\middle|\, \boldsymbol{e}_1 + \ldots + \boldsymbol{e}_K \right). \tag{B.256}$$

By definition we can write

$$\vec{\boldsymbol{\mu}}_{S_{nK}} = \sum_{k=1}^{K} \beta_k^{(n)} \boldsymbol{e}_k \tag{B.257}$$

which we insert into (B.250)

$$\vec{\boldsymbol{\mu}}_{S_{(n+1)K}} = \boldsymbol{A}_{\mathrm{f}}^K \vec{\boldsymbol{\mu}}_{S_{nK}} \tag{B.258}$$

$$= \sum_{k=1}^{K} \beta_k^{(n)} \boldsymbol{A}_{\mathrm{f}}^K \boldsymbol{e}_k \tag{B.259}$$

$$= \beta_1^{(n)} \left(\boldsymbol{e}_1 + \sum_{k=1}^{K} \boldsymbol{e}_k \right) + \sum_{k=2}^{K} \beta_k^{(n)} \sum_{k'=1}^{k} \boldsymbol{e}_{k'}, \tag{B.260}$$

where we used the characterization (B.256). Then, rearranging the terms in (B.260), i.e., summarizing the coefficients for each $\boldsymbol{e}_\ell$ yields

$$\vec{\boldsymbol{\mu}}_{S_{(n+1)K}} = \sum_{\ell=1}^{K} \beta_\ell^{(n+1)} \boldsymbol{e}_\ell \tag{B.261}$$

with

$$\beta_\ell^{(n+1)} = \begin{cases} 2\beta_1^{(n)} + \sum_{k=2}^{K} \beta_k^{(n)}, & \text{if } \ell = 1 \\ \beta_1^{(n)} + \sum_{k=\ell}^{K} \beta_k^{(n)}, & \text{if } \ell \in \{2, \ldots, K\}. \end{cases} \tag{B.262}$$

which is equivalent to (B.251). ■

Now, we apply the recursion (B.251) (or (B.262)) for $\vec{\boldsymbol{\mu}}_{S_0} := \boldsymbol{e}_1 \in \mathbb{R}^K$:

$$\vec{\boldsymbol{\mu}}_{S_0} = \boldsymbol{e}_1 \tag{B.263}$$

$$\downarrow \text{(B.251)}$$

$$\vec{\boldsymbol{\mu}}_{S_K} = 2\boldsymbol{e}_1 + \boldsymbol{e}_2 + \boldsymbol{e}_3 + \ldots + \boldsymbol{e}_K \tag{B.264}$$

$$\downarrow \text{(B.251)}$$

$$\begin{aligned} \vec{\boldsymbol{\mu}}_{S_{2K}} &= (4 + K - 1)\boldsymbol{e}_1 + (2 + K - 1)\boldsymbol{e}_2 \\ &\quad + (2 + K - 2)\boldsymbol{e}_3 + \ldots + 3\boldsymbol{e}_K \end{aligned} \tag{B.265}$$

$$\downarrow \text{(B.251)}$$

$$\begin{aligned} \vec{\boldsymbol{\mu}}_{S_{3K}} &= \left(2(K+3) + \sum_{k=3}^{K+1} k\right)\boldsymbol{e}_1 + \left(K + 3 + \sum_{k=3}^{K+1} k\right)\boldsymbol{e}_2 \\ &\quad + \left(K + 3 + \sum_{k=3}^{K} k\right)\boldsymbol{e}_3 + \ldots + (K + 3 + 3)\boldsymbol{e}_K \end{aligned} \tag{B.266}$$

$$\downarrow \text{(B.251)}$$

$$\begin{aligned} \vec{\boldsymbol{\mu}}_{S_{4K}} &= \underbrace{\left(4(K+3) + 2\sum_{k=3}^{K+1} k + (K-1)(K+3) + \sum_{\ell=3}^{K+1}\sum_{k=3}^{\ell} k\right)}_{=:\, \beta_1^{(4)}}\boldsymbol{e}_1 \\ &\quad + \left(2(K+3) + \sum_{k=3}^{K+1} k + (K-1)(K+3) + \sum_{\ell=3}^{K+1}\sum_{k=3}^{\ell} k\right)\boldsymbol{e}_2 \\ &\quad + \left(2(K+3) + \sum_{k=3}^{K+1} k + (K-2)(K+3) + \sum_{\ell=3}^{K}\sum_{k=3}^{\ell} k\right)\boldsymbol{e}_3 \end{aligned}$$

$$+\ldots+\left(2(K+3)+\sum_{k=3}^{K+1} k+1\cdot(K+3)+3\right)\boldsymbol{e}_K \tag{B.267}$$

$\downarrow$ (B.251)

$$\begin{aligned}\vec{\boldsymbol{\mu}}_{S_{5K}} = &\left(2\beta_1^{(4)}+(K-1)\left(2(K+3)+\sum_{k=3}^{K+1} k\right)+(K+3)\sum_{k=1}^{K-1} k\right.\\ &\left.\qquad +\sum_{i=3}^{K+1}\sum_{\ell=3}^{i}\sum_{k=3}^{\ell} k\right)\boldsymbol{e}_1\\ &+\left(\beta_1^{(4)}+(K-1)\left(2(K+3)+\sum_{k=3}^{K+1} k\right)+(K+3)\sum_{k=1}^{K-1} k\right.\\ &\left.\qquad +\sum_{i=3}^{K+1}\sum_{\ell=3}^{i}\sum_{k=3}^{\ell} k\right)\boldsymbol{e}_2\\ &+\left(\beta_1^{(4)}+(K-2)\left(2(K+3)+\sum_{k=3}^{K+1} k\right)+(K+3)\sum_{k=1}^{K-2} k\right.\\ &\left.\qquad +\sum_{i=3}^{K}\sum_{\ell=3}^{i}\sum_{k=3}^{\ell} k\right)\boldsymbol{e}_3\\ &+\\ &\vdots\\ &+\left(\beta_1^{(4)}+1\cdot\left(2(K+3)+\sum_{k=3}^{K+1} k\right)+(K+3)\sum_{k=1}^{1} k+3\right)\boldsymbol{e}_K\end{aligned} \tag{B.268}$$

For $N \in \{1,2,\ldots\}$ fixed, we obtain $\left|\mathcal{Y}_N^{(K)}\right|$ from the messages $\vec{\boldsymbol{\mu}}_{S_{NK}}$ as follows

$$\left|\mathcal{Y}_N^{(K)}\right| = \left(\boldsymbol{e}_1^{\mathsf{T}}+K\boldsymbol{e}_K^{\mathsf{T}}\right)\boldsymbol{A}_{\mathrm{f}}^{NK}\boldsymbol{e}_1 \tag{B.269}$$

$$= \left(\boldsymbol{e}_1^{\mathsf{T}}+K\boldsymbol{e}_K^{\mathsf{T}}\right)\vec{\boldsymbol{\mu}}_{S_{NK}} \tag{B.270}$$

$$= \beta_1^{(N)}+K\beta_K^{(N)}, \tag{B.271}$$

where (B.269) follows from Lemma B.11, and (B.270) from the definition (B.240) with $\vec{\boldsymbol{\mu}}_{S_0}=\boldsymbol{e}_1$. The step from (B.270) to (B.271) follows from Lemma B.12.

N	$\lvert\mathcal{Y}_N^{(K)}\rvert = \beta_1^{(N)} + K\beta_K^{(N)}$
1	$K+2$
2	$4K+3$
3	$\frac{3}{2}K^2 + \frac{19}{2}K + 4$
4	$\frac{2}{3}K^3 + \frac{15}{2}K^2 + \frac{107}{6}K + 5$
5	$\frac{5}{24}K^4 + \frac{21}{4}K^3 + \frac{535}{24}K^2 + \frac{117}{4}K + 6$

Table B.1: The cardinality of $\mathcal{Y}_N^{(K)}$ for N fixed and K general.

# Firings	$\boldsymbol{y} \in \mathcal{Y}_2^{(3)}$
0	$\mathbf{0}_7$
1	$\boldsymbol{e}_1$
	$\vdots$
	$\boldsymbol{e}_7$
2	$\boldsymbol{e}_1 + \boldsymbol{e}_4$
	$\boldsymbol{e}_1 + \boldsymbol{e}_5$
	$\boldsymbol{e}_2 + \boldsymbol{e}_5$
	$\boldsymbol{e}_2 + \boldsymbol{e}_6$
	$\boldsymbol{e}_3 + \boldsymbol{e}_6$
	$\boldsymbol{e}_3 + \boldsymbol{e}_7$
	$\boldsymbol{e}_4 + \boldsymbol{e}_7$

Table B.2: All 15 elements of the set $\mathcal{Y}_2^{(3)} \subset \{0,1\}^7$.

# Firings	$\boldsymbol{y} \in \mathcal{Y}_2^{(4)}$
0	$\mathbf{0}_9$
1	$\boldsymbol{e}_1$
	$\vdots$
	$\boldsymbol{e}_9$
2	$\boldsymbol{e}_1 + \boldsymbol{e}_5$
	$\boldsymbol{e}_1 + \boldsymbol{e}_6$
	$\boldsymbol{e}_2 + \boldsymbol{e}_6$
	$\boldsymbol{e}_2 + \boldsymbol{e}_7$
	$\boldsymbol{e}_3 + \boldsymbol{e}_7$
	$\boldsymbol{e}_3 + \boldsymbol{e}_8$
	$\boldsymbol{e}_4 + \boldsymbol{e}_8$
	$\boldsymbol{e}_4 + \boldsymbol{e}_9$
	$\boldsymbol{e}_5 + \boldsymbol{e}_9$

Table B.3: All 19 elements of the set $\mathcal{Y}_2^{(4)} \subset \{0,1\}^9$.

In Table B.1 the expression (B.271) is evaluated for $N \in \{1,2,3,4,5\}$ by means of the messages (B.264) – (B.268).

Examples

For $N = 1$, the set $\mathcal{Y}_1^{(K)}$ contains the all-zeros vector $\mathbf{0}_{K+1}$ and the $K+1$ vectors with a single one/firing, i.e., the vectors $\boldsymbol{e}_1, \ldots, \boldsymbol{e}_{K+1}$. Thus, we have $\left|\mathcal{Y}_1^{(K)}\right| = K + 2$ which coincides with the first row of Table B.1.

For $N = 2$, all elements of the two sets $\mathcal{Y}_2^{(3)}$ and $\mathcal{Y}_2^{(4)}$ are given in Table B.2 and Table B.3, respectively.

Asymptotic Behaviour

Let $K \in \{2, 3, \ldots\}$ be fixed. Then from the recursions (B.264) – (B.268) it becomes clear that

$$\left|\mathcal{Y}_N^{(K)}\right| \propto \sum_{k_{N-2}=3}^{K+1} \cdots \sum_{k_2=3}^{k_3} \sum_{k_1=3}^{k_2} k_1 \tag{B.272}$$

$$\propto \sum_{k_{N-2}=0}^{K+1} \cdots \sum_{k_2=0}^{k_3} \sum_{k_1=0}^{k_2} k_1 \tag{B.273}$$

$$= \binom{K+1+N-2}{N-1} \tag{B.274}$$

$$= \frac{(K+N-1)!}{(N-1)!\,K!} \tag{B.275}$$

$$= \frac{1}{(N-1)!} \prod_{n=1}^{N-1} (K+n) \tag{B.276}$$

$$\propto K^{N-1}, \tag{B.277}$$

for $N \geq 3$, where the step from (B.273) to (B.274) follows from Lemma B.13 below. Thus, $|\mathcal{Y}_N^{(K)}|$ grows as a polynomial (in K) of degree $N-1$, cf. Table B.1.

Lemma B.13. *For $p \in \mathbb{N}$, $p \geq 2$, and $k_p \in \mathbb{N}$, $k_p \geq 1$*

$$\sum_{k_{p-1}=0}^{k_p} \cdots \sum_{k_1=0}^{k_2} k_1 = \binom{k_p+p-1}{p}. \tag{B.278}$$

□

Proof of Lemma B.13. We prove (B.278) by induction over $p \geq 2$. For $p = 2$, the left-hand side of (B.278) becomes

$$\sum_{k_1=0}^{k_2} k_1 = \frac{1}{2} k_2(k_2+1), \tag{B.279}$$

which is the famous Gauss summation formula (can be proved by induction over k_2), and the right-hand side of (B.278) evaluates to

$$\binom{k_2+1}{2} = \frac{(k_2+1)!}{2!(k_2-1)!} = \frac{1}{2}(k_2+1)k_2. \tag{B.280}$$

For $p \in \mathbb{N}$, $p \geq 2$, we assume that (B.278) holds. Then, we have

$$\sum_{k_p=0}^{k_{p+1}} \sum_{k_{p-1}=0}^{k_p} \cdots \sum_{k_1=0}^{k_2} k_1 = \sum_{k_p=0}^{k_{p+1}} \binom{k_p+p-1}{p} \tag{B.281}$$

$$= \sum_{i=0}^{k_{p+1}-1} \binom{p+i}{p} \tag{B.282}$$

$$= \binom{p+k_{p+1}}{p+1}. \tag{B.283}$$

Equality (B.281) holds by induction hypothesis. In (B.282) we did the variable substitution $i := k_p - 1$ and $\binom{p+i}{p} = 0$, for $i < 0$. The step from (B.282) to (B.283) follows from the identity

$$\sum_{i=0}^{m-1} \binom{n+i}{d} = \binom{n+m}{d+1}, \tag{B.284}$$

which can be proved by induction over $m \in \mathbb{N}$ (with $\binom{n+i}{d} = 0$, for $n + i < d$) and Pascal's rule. ■

B.8 The Logarithm Grows Slower than any Polynomial

For the sake of completeness, we give a proof of the basic limit:

Lemma B.14. *For any fixed* $\varepsilon > 0$,

$$\lim_{x\to\infty} \frac{\ln(x)}{x^{\varepsilon}} = 0. \tag{B.285}$$

□

Proof of Lemma B.14. We give two different proofs. First, we have

$$\begin{aligned}
\lim_{x\to\infty} \frac{\ln(x)}{x^{\varepsilon}} &= \lim_{x\to\infty} \frac{\ln(x)}{e^{\varepsilon \ln(x)}} && \text{(B.286)}\\
&= \lim_{y\to\infty} \frac{y}{e^{\varepsilon y}} && \text{(B.287)}\\
&= \frac{1}{\varepsilon} \lim_{t\to\infty} \frac{t}{e^{t}} && \text{(B.288)}\\
&= 0, && \text{(B.289)}
\end{aligned}$$

where (B.286) follows from $a^b = e^{\ln(a^b)}$. In (B.287) we did the variable substitution $y := \ln(x)$, and in (B.288) we did another substitution $t := \varepsilon y$. The step from (B.288) to (B.289) holds because

$$\begin{aligned}
e^t &= \sum_{k=0}^{\infty} \frac{t^k}{k!} && \text{(B.290)}\\
&> 1 + t + \frac{t^2}{2!} && \text{(B.291)}
\end{aligned}$$

for $t > 0$, and thus

$$\frac{t}{e^t} < \frac{t}{1 + t + \frac{t^2}{2!}} \xrightarrow{t\to\infty} 0. \tag{B.292}$$

Second and more direct, we obtain

$$\begin{aligned}
\lim_{x\to\infty} \frac{\ln(x)}{x^{\varepsilon}} &= \lim_{x\to\infty} \frac{\frac{1}{x}}{\varepsilon x^{\varepsilon-1}} && \text{(B.293)}\\
&= \lim_{x\to\infty} \frac{1}{\varepsilon x^{\varepsilon}} && \text{(B.294)}\\
&= 0. && \text{(B.295)}
\end{aligned}$$

The first equality (B.293) follows from L'Hôpital's rule which states

$$\lim_{x \to \infty} \frac{f(x)}{g(x)} = \lim_{x \to \infty} \frac{f'(x)}{g'(x)} \tag{B.296}$$

if $\lim_{x \to \infty} f(x) = \lim_{x \to \infty} g(x) = \infty$. ■

B.9 Two Inequalities: $(1+1/x)^x$ vs. $1+x$

The two inequalities in the following proposition seem to be standard, nonetheless we could not find them (or any related form) in the literature. It has to be mentioned that the literature on inequalities and bounds is vast.

Proposition B.1. *For all $x \in \mathbb{R}$, $x \geq 0$,*

$$\left(1+\frac{1}{x}\right)^x \geq 1+x, \qquad 0 \leq x \leq 1, \tag{B.297}$$

and

$$\left(1+\frac{1}{x}\right)^x \leq 1+x, \qquad x \geq 1. \tag{B.298}$$

□

An illustration is given in Figure B.8.

Proof of Proposition B.1. For $0 \leq x \leq 1$, inequality (B.297) can directly be obtained by starting with the trivial inequality

$$xz\ln(xz) \leq z\ln(z), \qquad z > 0. \tag{B.299}$$

Then, inserting $z := 1/(1+x)$ into (B.299) yields

$$\frac{x}{1+x}\ln\left(\frac{x}{1+x}\right) \leq \frac{1}{1+x}\ln\left(\frac{1}{1+x}\right) \tag{B.300}$$

$$x\ln\left(\frac{x}{1+x}\right) \leq \ln\left(\frac{1}{1+x}\right) \tag{B.301}$$

$$-x\ln\left(\frac{x}{1+x}\right) \geq -\ln\left(\frac{1}{1+x}\right) \tag{B.302}$$

$$x\ln\left(1+\frac{1}{x}\right) \geq \ln(1+x) \tag{B.303}$$

$$\ln\left(\left(1+\frac{1}{x}\right)^x\right) \geq \ln(1+x), \tag{B.304}$$

which is equivalent to (B.297), because $\ln(\cdot)$ is strictly monotonic increasing. The step from (B.302) to (B.303) follows from the identity

$$a\ln(x) = \ln(x^a), \qquad x \in \mathbb{R}_{>0}, \tag{B.305}$$

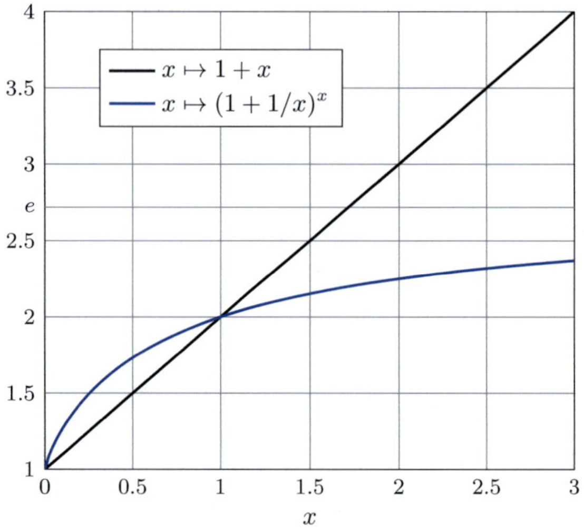

Figure B.8: Graphs of $x \mapsto (1 + 1/x)^x$ and $x \mapsto 1 + x$.

for $a \in \mathbb{R}$, which is again applied from (B.303) to (B.304).

In order to prove (B.298), we define the functions

$$f(x) := \left(1 + \frac{1}{x}\right)^x, \tag{B.306}$$

$$g_1(x) := x(x+1), \tag{B.307}$$

$$g_0(x) := x + 1, \tag{B.308}$$

for $x \geq 1$. Then, we compute the derivative of f

$$f'(x) = \frac{d}{dx} e^{x \ln\left(1 + \frac{1}{x}\right)} \tag{B.309}$$

$$= e^{x \ln\left(1 + \frac{1}{x}\right)} \frac{d}{dx}\left(x \ln\left(1 + \frac{1}{x}\right)\right) \tag{B.310}$$

$$= f(x)\left(\ln\left(1 + \frac{1}{x}\right) + x \frac{1}{1 + \frac{1}{x}}\left(-\frac{1}{x^2}\right)\right) \tag{B.311}$$

$$= f(x)\left(\ln\left(1 + \frac{1}{x}\right) - \frac{1}{x+1}\right). \tag{B.312}$$

From Lemma B.15 below it follows that $f'(x) \geq 0$, for $x > 0$, and

$$\lim_{x \to \infty} f(x) = \lim_{x \to \infty} e^{x \ln\left(1 + \frac{1}{x}\right)} \tag{B.313}$$

$$= e. \tag{B.314}$$

Thus, f is strictly monotonic increasing and

$$f(x) \leq e, \tag{B.315}$$

cf. Figure B.8.

Lemma B.15 also implies that

$$f'(x) \leq f(x)\left(\frac{1}{x} - \frac{1}{x+1}\right) \tag{B.316}$$

$$= \frac{f(x)}{x(x+1)} \tag{B.317}$$

$$\leq \frac{e}{x(x+1)} \tag{B.318}$$

$$\leq \frac{e}{2} \tag{B.319}$$

$$\leq 2x+1 \tag{B.320}$$

$$= g_1'(x), \tag{B.321}$$

for $x \geq 1$. Thus, g_1 grows faster than f and because $f(1) = g_1(1) = 2$, we have

$$f(x) \leq g_1(x), \qquad x \geq 1. \tag{B.322}$$

Finally, from (B.317) and (B.322) we obtain

$$f'(x) \leq 1 \tag{B.323}$$

$$= g_0'(x), \tag{B.324}$$

for $x \geq 1$. Thus, g_0 grows faster than f and because $f(1) = g_0(1) = 2$, we have

$$f(x) \leq g_0(x), \qquad x \geq 1, \tag{B.325}$$

which proves (B.298). ■

Lemma B.15. *For any $x \in \mathbb{R}$, $x > 0$,*

$$\frac{1}{x+1} \leq \ln\left(1 + \frac{1}{x}\right) \leq \frac{1}{x}, \tag{B.326}$$

and

$$\lim_{x\to\infty} x \ln\left(1 + \frac{1}{x}\right) = 1. \tag{B.327}$$

□

Proof of Lemma B.15. Let $t \in \left[1, 1+\frac{1}{x}\right]$. Then, clearly

$$\frac{1}{1+\frac{1}{x}} \leq \frac{1}{t} \leq 1. \tag{B.328}$$

Thus, we have

$$\int_1^{1+\frac{1}{x}} \frac{1}{1+\frac{1}{x}}\,dt \leq \int_1^{1+\frac{1}{x}} \frac{1}{t}\,dt \leq \int_1^{1+\frac{1}{x}} 1\,dt, \tag{B.329}$$

which is equivalent to (B.326).

Then, by multiplying (B.326) with $x > 0$, we obtain

$$\frac{x}{x+1} \leq x \ln\left(1+\frac{1}{x}\right) \leq 1, \tag{B.330}$$

and thus

$$1 \leq \lim_{x\to\infty} x \ln\left(1+\frac{1}{x}\right) \leq 1, \tag{B.331}$$

which proves (B.327). ■

Abbreviations

EPSP	Excitatory Postsynaptic Potential
GD	Gradient Descent
i.i.d.	independent and identically distributed
IR	Impulse Response
LSTM	Long Short-term Memory
LTD	Long-term Depression
LTP	Long-term Potentiation
MGF	Moment Generating Function
RNN	Recurrent Neural Network
SGD	Stochastic Gradient Descent
STDP	Spike-timing-dependent Plasticity
w.r.t.	with respect to

List of Symbols

General

$\sum$	Summation.
$\prod$	Product.
$\int_{\mathcal{D}}$	Integration over the set $\mathcal{D}$.
$a := b$	a is equal to b by definition.
$a \propto b$	a is proportional to b.
$\square$	End of statement.
$\blacksquare$	End of proof.

Sets

$\{\mathcal{A} : -\}$	The set of all elements in $\mathcal{A}$ that satisfy the condition after the colon.
$\lvert\mathcal{A}\rvert$	Cardinality, i.e., number of elements of the set $\mathcal{A}$.
$a \in \mathcal{A}$	Set membership, i.e., a is an element of $\mathcal{A}$.
$\mathcal{A} \subseteq \mathcal{B}$	Subset, i.e., $a \in \mathcal{A} \implies a \in \mathcal{B}$.
$\mathcal{A} \setminus \mathcal{B}$	Setminus, i.e., $\{a \in \mathcal{A} : a \notin \mathcal{B}\}$.
$\mathcal{A} \times \mathcal{B}$	Cartesian product, i.e., $\{(a, b) : a \in \mathcal{A}, b \in \mathcal{B}\}$.
$\mathcal{A}^n$	n-fold Cartesian product, i.e., $\mathcal{A} \times \cdots \times \mathcal{A}$ (n times).
$\mathbb{N}$	Natural numbers, i.e., $\{0, 1, 2, \ldots\}$.
$\mathbb{R}$	Real numbers.
$\mathbb{R}_{>0}$	Positive real numbers, i.e., $\{x \in \mathbb{R} : x > 0\}$.
$[a, b]$	Closed interval, i.e., $\{x \in \mathbb{R} : a \leq x \leq b\}$.
$]a, b[$	Open interval, i.e., $\{x \in \mathbb{R} : a < x < b\}$.

Special Functions

I[*statement*]	Indicator fuction: Equal to 1 if *statement* is true and 0 otherwise.
$\sigma_\theta(\cdot)$	Thresholding function, i.e., $\sigma_\theta \colon x \mapsto \mathrm{I}[x \geq \theta]$.
$\log_2(\cdot)$	Binary logarithm (base 2).
$\ln(\cdot)$	Natural logarithm (base e).
$\exp(\cdot)$	Exponential function and $e^a := \exp(a)$.
$\delta(\cdot)$	Dirac delta.
$\delta_\tau(\cdot)$	Shifted Dirac delta, i.e., $\delta_\tau \colon t \mapsto \delta(t-\tau)$.
$(f * g)(\cdot)$	Convolution of the functions $f(\cdot)$ and $g(\cdot)$.
$f'(\cdot)$	Derivative of the function $f(\cdot)$.
$a \bmod b$	Modulo, i.e., $a \bmod b := a - \lfloor \frac{a}{b} \rfloor \cdot b$, where $\lfloor x \rfloor$ denotes the largest integer not larger than x.
lim	Limit.

Vector and Matrix Operations

$\mathbf{0}_L$	All-zeros vector of dimension L.
$\mathbf{1}_L$	All-ones vector of dimension L.
$\boldsymbol{e}_i$	Unit vector: all-zeros vector except the i-th component equals to 1.
$\boldsymbol{I}_L$	Identity matrix of dimension $L \times L$.
$\boldsymbol{a} \odot \boldsymbol{b}$	Component-wise product of the vectors $\boldsymbol{a}$ and $\boldsymbol{b}$.
$\langle \boldsymbol{a}, \boldsymbol{b} \rangle$	Standard inner product between the vectors $\boldsymbol{a}$ and $\boldsymbol{b}$.
$\Vert\boldsymbol{a}\Vert$	L_2-norm of vector $\boldsymbol{a}$.
$\Vert\boldsymbol{a}\Vert_1$	L_1-norm of vector $\boldsymbol{a}$.
$\boldsymbol{a}^\mathsf{T}$ or $\boldsymbol{A}^\mathsf{T}$	Transpose of a vector $\boldsymbol{a}$ or a matrix $\boldsymbol{A}$.
$(\boldsymbol{a})_\ell$ or a_ℓ	The ℓ-th component of vector $\boldsymbol{a}$.
$(\boldsymbol{A})_{\ell,n}$ or $a_{\ell,n}$	The component in row ℓ and column n of matrix $\boldsymbol{A}$.
$\operatorname{rank}(\boldsymbol{A})$	Rank of matrix $\boldsymbol{A}$, i.e., the dimension of the vector space spanned by the columns of $\boldsymbol{A}$.
$\operatorname{tr}(\boldsymbol{A})$	Trace of matrix $\boldsymbol{A}$, i.e., $\operatorname{tr}(\boldsymbol{A}) := \sum_\ell a_{\ell,\ell}$.
$\operatorname{diag}(\boldsymbol{a})$	Diagonal matrix whose entries are the elements of the vector $\boldsymbol{a}$.
$\operatorname{diag}(\boldsymbol{A})$	Column vector containing the diagonal elements of the matrix $\boldsymbol{A}$.

Probability

$\Pr[\cdot]$	Probability of an event.
$\Pr[\cdot\|\cdot]$	Conditional probability of an event.
$\mathrm{E}[\cdot]$	Expectation (or mean) of a random variable.
$\mathrm{Var}[\cdot]$	Variance of a random variable.
$a \sim \mathcal{D}$	Random variable a is distributed according to $\mathcal{D}$.
$\mathrm{Ber}(p)$	Bernoulli distribution with parameter p.
$\mathrm{Bin}(N, p)$	Binomial distribution with parameters N and p.
$\mathcal{N}(\mu, \sigma^2)$	Gaussian distribution with mean μ and variance σ^2.
$\mathcal{U}(\mathcal{A})$	Uniform distribution over the set $\mathcal{A}$.
$H_b(\cdot)$	Binary entropy function.
$D_{KL}(\cdot \\| \cdot)$	Kullback–Leibler divergence (or relative entropy).

Bibliography

[1] N. Alon and J. Spencer, *The Probabilistic Method*, 3rd ed. Wiley & Sons, 2008.

[2] J. Anumula, D. Neil, T. Delbruck, and S.-C. Liu, "Feature representations for neuromorphic audio spike streams," *Frontiers in Neuroscience*, vol. 12, pp. 1–12, February 2018.

[3] R. C. Atkinson and R. M. Shiffrin, "Human memory: a proposed system and its control processes," *Psychology of Learning and Motivation*, vol. 2, pp. 89–195, 1968.

[4] A. D. Baddeley and G. Hitch, "Working memory," *Psychology of Learning and Motivation*, vol. 8, pp. 47–89, 1974.

[5] A. Balaji, A. Das, Y. Wu, K. Huynh, F. G. Dell'Anna, G. Indiveri, J. L. Krichmar, N. D. Dutt, S. Schaafsma, and F. Catthoor, "Mapping spiking neural networks to neuromorphic hardware," *IEEE Transactions on Very Large Scale Integration (VLSI) Systems*, vol. 28, no. 1, pp. 76–86, January 2020.

[6] G. Bellec, F. Scherr, A. Subramoney, E. Hajek, D. Salaj, R. Legenstein, and W. Maass, "A solution to the learning dilemma for recurrent networks of spiking neurons," *Nature Communications*, vol. 11, no. 3625, pp. 1–15, July 2020.

[7] A. N. Burkitt, "A review of the integrate-and-fire neuron model: I. homogeneous synaptic input," *Biological Cybernetics*, vol. 95, no. 1, pp. 1–19, July 2006.

[8] R. Chaudhuri and I. Fiete, "Bipartite expander hopfield networks as self-decoding high-capacity error correcting codes," in *Advances*

in Neural Information Processing Systems (NeurIPS), vol. 32, Vancouver, Canada, December 2019.

[9] H. Chernoff, "A measure of asymptotic efficiency for tests of a hypothesis based on the sum of observations," *Annals of Mathematical Statistics*, vol. 23, no. 4, pp. 493–507, 1952.

[10] T.-D. Chiueh and R. M. Goodman, "Recurrent correlation associative memories," *IEEE Transactions on Neural Networks*, vol. 2, no. 2, pp. 275–284, March 1991.

[11] T. M. Cover and J. A. Thomas, *Elements of Information Theory*, 2nd ed. Wiley & Sons, 2006.

[12] N. Cowan, "What are the differences between long-term, short-term, and working memory?" *Progress in Brain Research*, vol. 169, pp. 323–338, 2008.

[13] M. Demircigil, J. Heusel, M. Löwe, S. Upgang, and F. Vermet, "On a model of associative memory with huge storage capacity," *Journal of Statistical Physics*, vol. 168, no. 2, pp. 288–299, May 2017.

[14] P. U. Diehl and M. Cook, "Unsupervised learning of digit recognition using spike-timing-dependent plasticity," *Frontiers in Computational Neuroscience*, vol. 9, no. 99, pp. 1–9, August 2015.

[15] P. Ferré, F. Mamalet, and S. J. Thorpe, "Unsupervised feature learning with winner-takes-all based stdp," *Frontiers in Computational Neuroscience*, vol. 12, no. 24, pp. 1–12, April 2018.

[16] R. V. Florian, "Reinforcement learning through modulation of spike-timing-dependent synaptic plasticity," *Neural Computation*, vol. 19, no. 6, pp. 1468–1502, June 2007.

[17] E. Gardner, "The space of interactions in neural network models," *Journal of Physics A: Mathematical and General*, vol. 21, no. 1, pp. 257–270, July 1988.

[18] W. Gerstner, "Time structure of the activity in neural network models," *Physical Review E*, vol. 51, no. 1, pp. 738–758, January 1995.

[19] W. Gerstner and W. M. Kistler, *Spiking Neuron Models – Single Neurons, Populations, Plasticity*. Cambridge University Press, 2002.

[20] W. Gerstner, W. M. Kistler, R. Naud, and L. Paninski, *Neuronal Dynamics – From single neurons to networks and models of cognition.* Cambridge University Press, 2014.

[21] W. Gerstner, R. Ritz, and J. L. van Hemmen, "Why spikes? hebbian learning and retrieval of time-resolved excitation patterns," *Biological Cybernetics*, vol. 69, no. 5, pp. 503–515, October 1993.

[22] W. Gerstner and J. L. van Hemmen, "Associative memory in a network of 'spiking' neurons," *Network: Computation in Neural Systems*, vol. 3, no. 2, pp. 139–164, 1992.

[23] T. Hayakawa, T. Kaneko, and T. Aoyagi, "A biologically plausible learning rule for the infomax on recurrent neural networks," *Frontiers in Computational Neuroscience*, vol. 8, pp. 1–19, November 2014.

[24] S. Haykin, *Neural Networks: A Comprehensive Foundation*, 2nd ed. Prentice-Hall, 1999.

[25] D. O. Hebb, *The Organization of Behavior.* Wiley & Sons, 1949.

[26] A. Herz, B. Sulzer, R. Kühn, and J. L. van Hemmen, "The hebb rule: Storing static and dynamic objects in an associative neural network," *Europhysics Letters*, vol. 7, no. 7, pp. 663–669, December 1988.

[27] ——, "Hebbian learning reconsidered: Representation of static and dynamic objects in associative neural nets," *Biological Cybernetics*, vol. 60, no. 6, pp. 457–467, April 1989.

[28] S. Hochreiter and J. Schmidhuber, "Long short-term memory," *Neural Computation*, vol. 9, no. 8, pp. 1735–1780, November 1997.

[29] J. J. Hopfield, "Neural networks and physical systems with emergent collective computational abilities," *Proceedings of the National Academy of Sciences of the USA*, vol. 79, no. 8, pp. 2554–2558, April 1982.

[30] E. Izhikevich, "Which model to use for cortical spiking neurons?" *IEEE Transactions on Neural Networks*, vol. 15, no. 5, pp. 1063–1070, September 2004.

[31] ——, "Polychronization: computation with spikes," *Neural Computation*, vol. 18, no. 2, pp. 245–282, February 2006.

[32] S. Jankowski, A. Lozowski, and J. M. Zurada, "Complex-valued multistate neural associative memory," *IEEE Transactions on Neural Networks*, vol. 7, no. 6, pp. 1491–1496, November 1996.

[33] R. Keusch and H.-A. Loeliger, "Half-space and box constraints as nuv priors: First results," in *arXiv:2109.00036*, August 2021.

[34] D. Krotov and J. J. Hopfield, "Large associative memory problem in neurobiology and machine learning," in *arXiv:2008.06996*, August 2020.

[35] Z. C. Lipton, J. Berkowitz, and C. Elkan, "A critical review of recurrent neural networks for sequence learning," in *arXiv:1506.00019*, May 2015.

[36] H.-A. Loeliger, "An introduction to factor graphs," *IEEE Signal Processing Magazine*, vol. 21, no. 1, pp. 28–41, January 2004.

[37] H.-A. Loeliger, L. Bruderer, H. Malmberg, F. Wadehn, and N. Zalmai, "On sparsity by nuv-em, gaussian message passing, and kalman smoothing," in *Proceedings of the 2016 Information Theory and Applications Workshop (ITA)*, La Jolla, CA, USA, February 2016.

[38] H.-A. Loeliger, J. Dauwels, J. Hu, S. Korl, L. Ping, and F. R. Kschischang, "The factor graph approach to model-based signal processing," *Proceedings of the IEEE*, vol. 95, no. 6, pp. 1295–1322, June 2007.

[39] H.-A. Loeliger and S. Neff, "Pulse-domain signal parsing and neural computation," in *Proceedings of the 2015 IEEE International Symposium on Information Theory (ISIT)*, Hong Kong, China, June 2015, pp. 1322–1326.

[40] D. MacKay, *Information Theory, Inference, and Learning Algorithms.* Cambridge University Press, 2003.

[41] J. C. Magee, "Dendritic integration of excitatory synaptic input," *Nature Reviews Neuroscience*, vol. 1, no. 3, pp. 181–190, December 2000.

[42] Z. Marzi, J. Hespanha, and U. Madhow, "On the information in spike timing: Neural codes derived from polychronous groups," in *Proceedings of the 2018 Information Theory and Applications Workshop (ITA)*, San Diego, CA, USA, February 2018.

[43] T. Masquelier and S. J. Thorpe, "Unsupervised learning of visual features through spike timing dependent plasticity," *PLoS Computational Biology*, vol. 3, no. 2, February 2007.

[44] W. McCulloch and W. Pitts, "A logical calculus of the ideas immanent in nervous activity," *The bulletin of mathematical biophysics*, vol. 5, pp. 115–133, December 1943.

[45] R. McEliece, E. Posner, E. Rodemich, and S. Venkatesh, "The capacity of the hopfield associative memory," *IEEE Transactions on Information Theory*, vol. 33, no. 4, pp. 461–482, July 1987.

[46] P. A. Merolla, J. V. Arthur, R. Alvarez-Icaza, A. S. Cassidy, J. Sawada, F. Akopyan, B. L. Jackson, N. Imam, C. Guo, Y. Nakamura, B. Brezzo, I. Vo, S. K. Esser, R. Appuswamy, B. Taba, A. Amir, M. D. Flickner, W. P. Risk, R. Manohar, and D. S. Modha, "A million spiking-neuron integrated circuit with a scalable communication network and interface," *Science*, vol. 345, no. 6197, pp. 668–673, August 2014.

[47] G. A. Miller, "The magical number seven, plus or minus two: some limits on our capacity for processing information," *Psychological Review*, vol. 63, no. 2, pp. 81–97, 1956.

[48] S. Miyoshi, H.-F. Yanai, and M. Okada, "Associative memory by recurrent neural networks with delay elements," *Neural Networks*, vol. 17, no. 1, pp. 55–63, January 2004.

[49] P. Muratore, C. Capone, and P. S. Paolucci, "Target spike patterns enable efficient and biologically plausible learning for complex temporal tasks," *PLoS One*, vol. 16, no. 2, February 2021.

[50] P. Murer and H.-A. Loeliger, "Online memorization of random firing sequences by a recurrent neural network," in *Proceedings of the 2020 IEEE International Symposium on Information Theory (ISIT)*, Los Angeles, USA, June 2020, pp. 2504–2509.

[51] S. Neff, "A new approach to information processing with filters and pulses," Ph.D. dissertation, No. 23672, ETH Zurich, 2016.

[52] J.-P. Pfister, T. Toyoizumi, D. Barber, and W. Gerstner, "Optimal spike-timing-dependent plasticity for precise action potential firing in supervised learning," *Neural Computation*, vol. 18, no. 6, pp. 1318–1348, June 2006.

[53] L. Pillaud-Vivien, A. Rudi, and F. Bach, "Statistical optimality of stochastic gradient descent on hard learning problems through multiple passes," in *Advances in Neural Information Processing Systems (NeurIPS)*, vol. 31, Montréal, Canada, December 2018.

[54] I. Pozzi, S. Bohté, and P. R. Roelfsema, "A biologically plausible learning rule for deep learning in the brain," in *arXiv:1811.01768*, July 2019.

[55] N. Qiao, H. Mostafa, F. Corradi, M. Osswald, F. Stefanini, D. Sumislawska, and G. Indiveri, "A reconfigurable on-line learning spiking neuromorphic processor comprising 256 neurons and 128k synapses," *Frontiers in Neuroscience*, vol. 9, no. 141, pp. 1–17, April 2015.

[56] Z. Quan, W. Zeng, X. Li, Y. Liu, Y. Yu, and W. Yang, "Recurrent neural networks with external addressable long-term and working memory for learning long-term dependences," *IEEE Transactions on Neural Networks and Learning Systems*, vol. 31, no. 3, pp. 813–826, March 2020.

[57] D. J. Rezende and W. Gerstner, "Stochastic variational learning in recurrent spiking networks," *Frontiers in Computational Neuroscience*, vol. 8, no. 38, pp. 1–14, April 2014.

[58] P. R. Roelfsema and A. van Ooyen, "Attention-gated reinforcement learning of internal representations for classification," *Neural Computation*, vol. 17, no. 10, pp. 2176–2214, October 2005.

[59] A. H. Salavati, "Coding theory and neural associative memories with exponential pattern retrieval capacity," Ph.D. dissertation, No. 6089, EPFL, 2014.

[60] S. Sampath and V. Srivastava, "On stability and associative recall of memories in attractor neural networks," *PLoS One*, vol. 15, no. 9, September 2020.

[61] H. Sompolinsky and I. Kanter, "Temporal association in asymmetric neural networks," *Physical Review Letters*, vol. 57, no. 22, pp. 2861–2864, December 1986.

[62] R. B. Stein, "Some models of neuronal variability," *Biophysical Journal*, vol. 7, no. 1, pp. 37–68, January 1967.

[63] A. J. Storkey and R. Valabregue, "The basins of attraction of a new hopfield learning rule," *Neural Networks*, vol. 12, no. 6, pp. 869–876, July 1999.

[64] T. Strohmer and R. Vershnin, "A randomized kaczmarz algorithm with exponential convergence," *Journal of Fourier Analysis and Applications*, vol. 15, no. 2, pp. 262–278, 2009.

[65] C. Tan, S. Ma, Y.-H. Dai, and Y. Qian, "Barzilai-borwein step size for stochastic gradient descent," in *Advances in Neural Information Processing Systems (NeurIPS)*, vol. 29, Barcelona, Spain, December 2016.

[66] J. C. Tapson, G. K. Cohen, S. Afshar, K. M. Stiefel, Y. Buskila, R. M. Wang, T. J. Hamilton, and A. van Schaik, "Synthesis of neural networks for spatio-temporal spike pattern recognition and processing," *Frontiers in Neuroscience*, vol. 7, pp. 1–13, August 2013.

[67] K. Tikhomirov, "Singularity of random bernoulli matrices," *Annals of Mathematical Statistics*, vol. 191, no. 2, pp. 593–634, 2020.

[68] R. VanRullen, R. Guyonneau, and S. J. Thorpe, "Spike times make sense," *Trends in Neurosciences*, vol. 28, no. 1, pp. 1–4, January 2005.

[69] R. M. Wang, T. J. Hamilton, J. C. Tapson, and A. van Schaik, "A neuromorphic implementation of multiple spike-timing synaptic plasticity rules for large-scale neural networks," *Frontiers in Neuroscience*, vol. 9, no. 180, pp. 1–17, May 2015.

[70] N. Zalmai, "A state space world for detecting and estimating events and learning sparse signal decompositions," Ph.D. dissertation, No. 24360, ETH Zurich, 2017.

[71] N. Zalmai, R. Keusch, H. Malmberg, and H.-A. Loeliger, "Unsupervised feature extraction, signal labeling, and blind signal separation in a state space world," in *Proceedings of the 2017 25th European Signal Processing Conference (EUSIPCO)*, Kos, Greece, August 2017, pp. 838–842.

About the Author

Patrick Murer was born in Stans, Switzerland, on October 25, 1989. He did a four-year apprenticeship as an electronic technician which he finished with honour in 2009. During this period he also completed the Professional Maturity Certificate.

In 2010, after the one-year compulsory military service at the Swiss army, he passed the entrance examination to study Electrical Engineering and Information Technology at ETH Zurich. There he received his Bachelor's degree in 2013 and his Master's degree with a focus on communication in 2015.

Since 2016, he has been a Ph.D. candidate and a full research and teaching assistant at the Signal and Information Processing Laboratory (ISI) at ETH Zurich under the supervision of Prof. Dr. H.-A. Loeliger.

His research interests lie in the areas of signal processing, machine learning, and neural computation/modeling.

Series in Signal and Information Processing

edited by Hans-Andrea Loeliger

Vol. 1: Hanspeter Schmid, **Single-Amplifier Biquadratic MOSFET-C Filters.** ISBN 3-89649-616-6

Vol. 2: Felix Lustenberger, **On the Design of Analog VLSI Iterative Decoders**. ISBN 3-89649-622-0

Vol. 3: Peter Theodor Wellig, **Zerlegung von Langzeit-Elektromyogrammen zur Prävention von arbeitsbedingten Muskelschäden**. ISBN 3-89649-623-9

Vol. 4: Thomas P. von Hoff, **On the Convergence of Blind Source Separation and Deconvolution.** ISBN 3-89649-624-7

Vol. 5: Markus Erne, **Signal Adaptive Audio Coding using Wavelets and Rate Optimization.** ISBN 3-89649-625-5

Vol. 6: Marcel Joho, **A Systematic Approach to Adaptive Algorithms for Multichannel System Identification, Inverse Modeling, and Blind Identification.** ISBN 3-89649-632-8

Vol. 7: Heinz Mathis, **Nonlinear Functions for Blind Separation and Equalization.** ISBN 3-89649-728-6

Vol. 8: Daniel Lippuner, **Model-Based Step-Size Control for Adaptive Filters.** ISBN 3-89649-755-3

Vol. 9: Ralf Kretzschmar, **A Survey of Neural Network Classifiers for Local Wind Prediction.** ISBN 3-89649-798-7

Vol. 10: Dieter M. Arnold, **Computing Information Rates of Finite State Models with Application to Magnetic Recording.** ISBN 3-89649-852-5

Vol. 11: Pascal O. Vontobel, **Algebraic Coding for Iterative Decoding.** ISBN 3-89649-865-7

Vol. 12: Qun Gao, **Fingerprint Verification using Cellular Neural Networks.** ISBN 3-89649-894-0

Vol. 13: Patrick P. Merkli, **Message-Passing Algorithms and Analog Electronic Circuits.** ISBN 3-89649-987-4

Vol. 14: Markus Hofbauer, **Optimal Linear Separation and Deconvolu-tion of Acoustical Convolutive Mixtures.** ISBN 3-89649-996-3

Vol. 15: Sascha Korl, **A Factor Graph Approach to Signal Modelling, System Identification and Filtering.** ISBN 3-86628-032-7

Vol. 16: Matthias Frey, **On Analog Decoders and Digitally Corrected Converters.** ISBN 3-86628-074-2

Vol: 17: Justin Dauwels, **On Graphical Models for Communications and Machine Learning: Algorithms, Bounds, and Analog Implementation.** ISBN 3-86628-080-7

Vol. 18: Volker Maximillian Koch, **A Factor Graph Approach to Model-Based Signal Separation.** ISBN 3-86628-140-4

Vol. 19: Junli Hu, **On Gaussian Approximations in Message Passing Al-gorithms with Application to Equalization.** ISBN 3-86628-212-5

Vol. 20: Maja Ostojic, **Multitree Search Decoding of Linear Codes.** ISBN 3-86628-363-6

Vol. 21: Murti V.R.S. Devarakonda, **Joint Matched Filtering, Decoding, and Timing Synchronization.** ISBN 3-86628-417-9

Vol. 22: Lukas Bolliger, **Digital Estimation of Continuous-Time Signals Using Factor Graphs.** ISBN 3-86628-432-2

Vol. 23: Christoph Reller, **State-Space Methods in Statistical Signal Processing: New Ideas and Applications.** ISBN 3-86628-447-0

Vol. 24: Jonas Biveroni, **On A/D Converters with Low-Precision Analog Circuits and Digital Post-Correction.** ISBN 3-86628-452-7

Vol. 25: Georg Wilckens, **A New Perspective on Analog-to-Digital Conversion of Continuous-Time Signals.** ISBN 3-86628-469-1

Vol. 26: Jiun-Hung Yu, **A Partial-Inverse Approach to Decoding Reed-Solomon Codes and Polynomial Remainder Codes.** ISBN 3-86628-527-2

Vol. 27: Lukas Bruderer, **Input Estimation and Dynamical System Identification: New Algorithms and Results.** ISBN 3-86628-533-7

Vol. 28: Sarah Neff, **A New Approach to Information Processing with Filters and Pulses.** ISBN 3-86628-575-2

Vol. 29: Christian Schürch, **On Successive Cancellation Decoding of Polar Codes and Related Codes.** ISBN 3-86628-580-9

Vol. 30: Nour Zalmaï, **A State Space World for Detecting and Estimating Events and Learning Sparse Signal Decompositions.** ISBN 978-3-86628-594-1

Vol. 31: Federico Wadehn, **State Space Methods with Applications in Biomedical Signal Processing.** ISBN 978-3-86628-640-5

Vol. 32: Reto A. Wildhaber, **Localized State Space and Polynomial Filters with Applications in Electrocardiography**. ISBN 978-3-86628-652-8

Vol. 33: Hampus Malmberg, **Control-Bounded Converters.** ISBN 978-3-86628-697-9

Vol. 34: Boxiao Ma, **Smoothed-NUV Priors for Imaging and Beyond.** ISBN 978-3-86628-746-4

Hartung-Gorre Verlag, Konstanz – http://www.hartung-gorre.de